HENRY ARMSTRONG
BOXING'S SUPER CHAMP

JOHN JARRETT

Dedication

I wish to dedicate this book to my dear wife Mary in appreciation of her loving encouragement through our years together ... she is part of this book, a book she will never see...Mary lost her big fight a year ago ... she is lovingly missed.

First published by Pitch Publishing, 2023

Pitch Publishing
9 Donnington Park,
85 Birdham Road,
Chichester,
West Sussex,
PO20 7AJ
www.pitchpublishing.co.uk
info@pitchpublishing.co.uk

© 2023, John Jarrett

Every effort has been made to trace the copyright. Any oversight will be rectified in future editions at the earliest opportunity by the publisher.

All rights reserved. No part of this book may be reproduced, sold or utilised in any form or transmitted in any form or by any means, electronic or mechanical, including photocopying, recording or by any information storage and retrieval system, without prior permission in writing from the Publisher.

A CIP catalogue record is available for this book from the British Library.

ISBN 978 1 80150 456 0

Typesetting and origination by Pitch Publishing
Printed and bound in Great Britain by TJ Books, Padstow

Contents

Introduction: Henry Armstrong	4
Chapter One	7
Chapter Two	19
Chapter Three	30
Chapter Four	42
Chapter Five	50
Chapter Six	59
Chapter Seven	68
Chapter Eight	79
Chapter Nine	88
Chapter Ten	97
Chapter Eleven	107
Chapter Twelve	117
Chapter Thirteen	131
Chapter Fourteen	141
Chapter Fifteen	155
Chapter Sixteen	166
Chapter Seventeen	179
Chapter Eighteen	192
Chapter Nineteen	203
Chapter Twenty	214
Chapter Twenty-One	223
Chapter Twenty-Two	237
Chapter Twenty-Three	248
Chapter Twenty-Four	259
Chapter Twenty-Five	273
Chapter Twenty-Six	286
Chapter Twenty-Seven	307
Chapter Twenty-Eight	324
Chapter Twenty-Nine	337
Boxing's Super Champ	344
Bibliography	345
Acknowledgements	346
Index	347

Introduction: Henry Armstrong

ONE MAN in all the recorded history of boxing has held three world titles simultaneously.

A man from Mississippi, there was not much of him (a scant 5ft 5½in) but what he had he threw into action, the like of which had rarely been seen before and seldom will be seen again. If perpetual motion could have human shape this was it. He was known as Henry Armstrong, although his actual name was Henry Jackson.

He won the featherweight, welterweight and lightweight championships of the world in that order in less than ten months during the dying years of peace before the Second World War. Here was the super-champion of boxing. He came from a sharecropper's cabin in the Deep South – the 11th child of 15. He knew hunger, despair and the horrors of Skid Row before his boxing triumphs brought him riches and respect. Armstrong's style, brought to a pitch hitherto unseen, was all-out aggression which smothered opponents in a rain of blows. This stocky guy, with broad chest and shoulders, had phenomenal stamina. He could keep going like this for 15

INTRODUCTION: HENRY ARMSTRONG

rounds, and often did. Two doctors examined Henry and told him that for his body weight (130 pounds/just over 9 stone) he had the heart more fitted to a 190-pound body. Henry figured that was like having a big engine in a small car!

Those astonishing ten months in Armstrong's life began at Madison Square Garden on 29 October 1937, where Mike Jacobs was moving into the Garden to become the man at the top. Jacobs brought featherweight champion Petey Sarron back from South Africa to defend his title against Armstrong. Sarron, a part-Syrian, had never been knocked down, never knocked out. But he was meeting a man they would begin calling 'Homicide Hank', a man whose square features, high cheekbones and near-slanting eyes betrayed the Iroquois blood of his mother.

With Armstrong on the warpath, the veteran from Birmingham, Alabama, was doomed for defeat. Armstrong's whipping right to the jaw, which was his trademark punch, left Sarron sitting in a heap on the canvas.

The new kid on the block was the new featherweight champion and he was hungry for more. Manager Eddie Mead, bankrolled by Al Jolson and George Raft, went after lightweight king Lou Ambers. But Lou's manager, Al Weill, wasn't ready to play at that moment, so Hank's team stepped up two divisions and found welterweight champion Barney Ross looking for a payday. Barney got his payday but it cost him his world championship. He left that in the ring in the Madison Square Garden Bowl on Long Island.

As Homicide Hank hammered Ross into retirement with a 15-round beating, people wondered what this Armstrong guy was going to do next. He won a 15-round thriller to take

Lou's title in a history-making fight, becoming the first, and only, boxer to win and hold three world titles simultaneously. Heading into his rematch with Ambers on 22 August 1939, Armstrong was riding a winning streak of 46 consecutive fights, including seven defences of the welterweight title. Lou Ambers upset Henry's applecart, reclaiming his title in a bloody battle that saw Armstrong bleeding from severe facial injuries.

Hank had relinquished the featherweight title rather than make weight and concentrated on the welterweight crown, which he defended a further eight times. He again reached for the stars, going against Ceferino Garcia for the middleweight title, and many marked him the winner. But the referee gave a controversial draw to the champion. Armstrong's straight ahead, wear-him-down style was very effective but eventually such tactics began to take a toll on the Los Angeles man. After three more welterweight defences he was dethroned by Fritzie Zivic, a vicious puncher who didn't follow the rules too faithfully. Zivic took the decision and prevailed in a rematch, stopping Hank in round 12.

No longer a championship fighter, Armstrong made a comeback, holding his own against top contenders before hanging up the gloves in 1945. Henry won his biggest battle against alcoholism and finally listened to God to become a Baptist minister. Suffering from various ailments, he died in hospital in Los Angeles on 24 October 1988, aged 75.

Henry left a record of 180 fights, won 149, lost 21, 10 draws. He scored 101 knockouts.

Chapter One

HENRY JACKSON SR., a sharecropper and butcher, married America Armstrong, an Iroquois Indian (some sources say Cherokee). They lived on a plantation owned by the senior Jackson's Irish father, who had married one of his slaves. On 12 December 1912, Henry Jackson Jr., the 11th of the couple's 15 children, was born in Columbus, Mississippi. When the oldest Jackson brother, Ollus, first saw Henry he remarked, 'Gee, Mom, he looks like a little rat!' The mother quickly defended her newest child. 'He may look like a rat now, but some day he'll be the big cheese in this family. Call him a rat if you want to, but he'll win, whatever he does. And some day he'll be a fine preacher.'

Although Henry's mother and grandmother wanted him to become a minister, he had a talent for fighting, a drive to become a champion, and a goal of achieving fame and fortune. In 1938 he became the first boxer in history to hold three world titles simultaneously. Later, in 1951, he became an ordained Baptist minister.

'Father Henry Jackson wasn't just Indian, like his mother; he was of Indian, Irish and Negro stock, a sturdy sort of little man with a stern character and a solid reputation. Working the lifelong day so the new baby and the older ones and Mom could eat, he didn't have time to celebrate the fact that he'd become a Senior, with a Junior in the cradle in the cabin; he just went on working to feed and clothe and shelter the family in the log-and-shingle house. He was a sharecropper, one of the millions driven mercilessly by that cruel and jealous despot, King Cotton ... Little Rat grew in the midst of cotton fields and the men and women who worked them – not the men and women who owned them.'[1]

'When Armstrong was a child, to find employment, his father moved the family to a three-room house in St Louis, Missouri, where he worked for the Independent Packing Company. Henry Jackson's hair had come in red and he was known as "Red Jackson." He was small but a fierce brawler in the streets. His fraternal grandmother, Henrietta Chatman, took over the task of disciplining him after his mother's death from consumption in 1918. He was hard to handle, but soon conformed to his grandmother's demands.'[2]

At Toussaint L'Overture Grammar School in St Louis, his small stature attracted teasing from other children and he found it necessary to defend himself. Discovering that he was good at fighting, he determined to become a boxer. He did not neglect his studies, however, and he earned respect when moving on to Vashon High School.

He made good grades and later was elected class president by his fellow students. At his graduation he read a valedictory poem he had written as poet laureate of his class. Outside school he worked to develop his athletic abilities, often running the eight miles distance from home. After school he

---

1 Henry Armstrong, *Gloves, Glory and God*, 1957.
2 Barney Nagler, *Ring*, August 1981.

CHAPTER ONE

set pins in a bowling alley. By the time he had finished high school, his 60-year-old father was suffering from rheumatism and was rarely able to work a full week. His grandmother, now 80 years old and almost blind, shelled pecans for a local nut factory. Henry realised that it was time he started working for real money. Aged 17, he claimed he was 21 and was hired as a section hand for the Missouri Pacific Railroad at $20 a week. As he swung the sledgehammer to drive the spikes in, he recalled that Jack Dempsey had built his strength wielding a pick and shovel.

'One day Henry read in a St Louis newspaper that a favourite fighter of his, Kid Chocolate, had beaten Al Singer at the Polo Grounds in New York City and had earned $75,000 doing it. That was real money! That was fabulous! Why, you could work a year on the railroad at twenty dollars a week and earn just barely more than $1,000. And in seventy-five years … but no, there was just no sensible way of making a comparison. Henry told the man next to him on the handcar that evening about Kid Chocolate's $75,000 purse "and some day I'm going to make that much money in the ring," he concluded.'[3]

Working on the railroad was hard, but it was building muscle in his upper body, although his legs were those of a younger boy. But running everywhere strengthened them as well as his lungs and they never let him down when he started boxing. By the time he was laid off he had learned how to swing a hammer hard and hit the spike head; he also learned that he could hold his own in hard physical labour. Not much

---

3   Henry Armstrong, *Gloves, Glory and God*, 1957.

use, however, when he managed to land a new job, working in the Universal Hat Shop in St Louis. He served a year there, learning how to clean and block hats, making deliveries, doing odd jobs. It was a job and he was paid enough to help at home.

Finishing at five every day, he would spend his time in the coloured YMCA on Pine Street. It was there he met Harry Armstrong, a jovial fighter who would watch him working out and they became friends. Harry was training a young lad named Eddie Foster and he asked Henry if he would go a couple of rounds with Eddie. To his surprise, Henry found the other boy easy to handle, and Harry was impressed. He climbed into the ring and squared up to young Jackson. Henry swung and missed, swung and missed, before Harry held up his hand. A few words of encouragement and they were off again. This time Henry managed to hit Harry and the older man dropped to the canvas.

'Boy, you sure can punch,' he said, getting to his feet and rubbing his jaw. He was already thinking that this boy was worth training. He heard Henry singing in the shower, and as the lad dressed, he said, 'That's it, I'll call him Melody, Melody Jackson.' When they parted that evening, Henry sang all the way home. He had a feeling, with Harry he could get somewhere. The journey had already begun!

In January of 1930, the western boxing championships of the Amateur Athletic Union was to be held at the St Louis Coliseum. When Harry suggested it might be a good idea for Henry to enter, the boy lost no time filling out an application form. He was going to be a real boxer! He figured it wouldn't be a good idea to have anything in his stomach so he didn't eat all that day of the fight. He remembered reading that

CHAPTER ONE

Gene Tunney drank a quart (two pints) of milk during the day before going in the ring. What was good enough for Gene Tunney was good enough for Henry Jackson. He drank a quart of milk!

By seven that evening, with nothing in his stomach but two pints of milk and a sick feeling, he turned up at the Coliseum an hour before they opened the doors. When the doors finally opened, Henry was freezing cold from falling snow and feeling sick and going home seemed a good idea. But he went in to find there was only one black boy entered in the featherweight class, a tough kid named Jimmy Birch. Henry knew of Birch, he was good. He was too good for Henry in the first two rounds – the kid was knocked out standing up but he didn't fall. He even felt better, the sickness leaving him, and he sailed into Birch, throwing his gloves like he didn't want to see them again. Birch was swamped in a sea of leather and when he came to, he was lying on the floor and the referee told him he could go home. Henry Jackson was the featherweight champion of the West!

A local promoter matched the boys again and he got a good crowd at a big hall in Pine Street.

The fight was scheduled for four rounds and the fans loved it. Henry wasn't loving it. By the third he had had enough. His nose was broken, with one eye blackened, lips bleeding, he tore into Birch who was shocked at Jackson's fightback. Birch was due a further shock when Henry knocked him down and out. That was better, son. Harry Armstrong had good news for the winner … they were going on a trip to Pittsburgh.

After winning his fight, Henry was given a slip supposedly worth five dollars in equipment at the local sporting goods shop. First lesson in the fight game! Henry and the other winners discovered the slips were worthless. When the boys looked for the promoter, he had skipped town. And when he got home, the family were shocked when they saw their brother's face.

Emma Lou Jackson, his sister-in-law, was no comforter. 'Why don't you stop all this fighting, Henry?' she urged. 'Get these wild notions out of your head. Settle down, become a preacher.'

'I'm not ready to be a preacher yet, Sis Lou,' he answered slowly. 'Some day, maybe … but just now it looks like it's me for fighting and fighting for me.'[4]

In his third amateur bout in St Louis, Henry knocked out Roy Johnson in two rounds. Next day he went looking for Harry Armstrong. Harry's other young fighter, Eddie Foster, had bought a 1927 model Nash. It needed a new set of tyres among other things but Harry said they would be okay if they took it easy. Next morning they were on the road: Harry, Henry, Eddie and a big police dog, for company and good luck. In Henry's heart was hope, in his pocket, ten dollars. Harry had renamed his troupe of young pugilists: Eddie was 'Mississippi' and Henry was 'Melody' Jackson, with a song in his heart and a sock in his fist. He had won his three fights as an amateur, he was ready for the world!

Unfortunately, the world wasn't quite ready for Mr Jackson. They found a local gym and Henry and Eddie trained hard, trying to impress the local matchmakers and fans, but after five weeks, their dwindling budget almost

---

4   Henry Armstrong, *Gloves, Glory and God*, 1957.

gone, their stomachs beginning to revolt against Harry's daily ration of cabbage, salt pork and whole wheat bread, and no fights!

Just when the boys were thinking of heading back home, Harry got a match for 'Melody' with Jackie Wilson, a good featherweight. Luckily for Jackson, Wilson was injured in training and the matchmaker found a local southpaw, Al Iovino, who had only two bouts but a great amateur record, unfortunately marred by the death of one of his opponents, Leo Mahan. The boys were matched in a four-round bout at Apple Myers Bowl, an open-air arena at North Braddock, about eight miles out of Pittsburgh, on a card topped by Teddy Yarosz and Bucky Lawless.

It was Monday, 27 July 1931, Henry's first pro bout, and he wasn't feeling too good after weeks of Harry's cabbage diet. He didn't feel too good when Iovino's left hooks to the stomach laid him low twice in the second then at two minutes 27 seconds of round three. The kid felt a bit better when they gave him his purse, $35.

The story behind this fight was revealed years later by Harry Keck, sports editor of the *Pittsburgh Sun-Telegraph*. 'I received a letter one day in 1938 from little Jimmy Thomas, a Negro featherweight of Pittsburgh, who was then boxing in California. In it he told me that the great Henry Armstrong was none other than one "Melody Jackson", who had boxed in Pittsburgh seven years before.

'I'm sure of it,' he wrote. 'My manager, Abie Witz, used to pay him a dollar a day to work out with me in the Salvation Army gym in Pittsburgh. You should remember him. Al Iovino knocked him out in the Meyers Bowl.

'With this information, I approached Iovino who no longer was fighting but was working as a carpenter's helper. "I thought there was something about the pictures of Armstrong in the newspapers," said Iovino. "Now that you mention it, I'm sure he's the same fellow. But the man I fought was named Melody Jackson … I had trouble getting bouts because I was a southpaw and could hit. All I ever could do was punch!"'

In recalling the bout with Jackson/Armstrong, Iovino said, 'Melody was deceptive in build. I weighed 123 pounds and he appeared much heavier. He wanted to weigh in in his street clothes, but we made him strip and were surprised when he scaled only 120 pounds. He was all arms and shoulders. He came buzzing after me, boring in from the start, and I let him come, nailing him with lefts to the body and head. He was made to measure for my southpaw counter-punching. He went down twice in the second round from punches to the stomach. The end came in the third from another good one.'

Harry Keck would later recall, 'I caught up with Henry before one of his championship bouts in New York and asked him for an explanation. At first, he denied that he had ever boxed Iovino, but finally admitted it. He said the reason he had kept the bout a hidden chapter in his career was that he would have lost his amateur status had it been known that he fought as a professional. On returning to St Louis he resumed as an amateur under his own name until he went on to Los Angeles, where he got his first real break.'[5]

---

5   Harry Keck, *Pittsburgh Sun-Telegraph*, August 1965, *Boxing Illustrated*.

CHAPTER ONE

Four days later, with a couple of steaks under his belt, Melody Jackson was in action again, facing Sammy Burns over six rounds at Hickey Park in Milville, just outside Pittsburgh. At the bell he sailed into Burns to floor him three times and finish with the decision. Another $35 purse put a smile on his face and he looked around for another bout. Harry was offered several opponents, but the names sounded like Eddie Shea and Benny Bass. Not yet son. The boys decided to go back home and set off for Chicago the next morning where Eddie had a brother.

Staying for a week, they took in Johnny Coulon's gym. Henry was nursing a swollen finger so there was no ring work. They watched fighters like Eddie Shea in another local gym, along with a young fellow named Barney Ross, a guy he would meet one day in his future. Right now they were headed home to St Louis, somewhat downhearted and dejected. But Henry was still filled with a bright future waiting for him out there somewhere. A few days later he called Harry; he had made his mind up. It was California or bust!

He had heard from Harry Armstrong how well the little fellows were doing on the west coast. Speedy Dado, for instance. Why, Dado was drawing super-gates that netted him as much as $5,000 every two weeks! And on the ceiling, over Henry's staring eyes as he lay in bed dreaming, appeared a vision of Speedy Dado, just as he had looked on the cover of a recent issue of *Knockout*, the boxing magazine – smiling, dressed in elegant, expensive clothes. A large diamond ring flashed insistently on one hand ... oranges falling like manna from heaven ... luscious nights under the star-studded sky-blue dome of heaven ... $5,000 purses ... classy clothes and a diamond ring ... these blended alluringly before Henry as he lay there envisioning the California life to come. Then reality barged in for a moment. How to get there? He was broke. Harry was broke. Eddie was broke.[6]

'That trip to California is still one of the nightmares of Henry Armstrong's life,' wrote Nat Fleischer in 1938. 'His face becomes serious and slightly sinister when he speaks of the jungle camps from which they were chased by the other hoboes, the railroad police, the days without food and the many privations of life on the road to which they were subjected. However, he reached California with that indomitable will, more steeled than ever, his spirit burning with that irresistible driving force.'[7]

Finally, as the freight approached Colton, California, they were put off the train at the city limits. They asked other hoboes about getting to Los Angeles and were advised to hitch-hike on the highway rather than try another train.

It was good advice and they were soon perched on a load of sand heading for the city. The driver told them of Central Avenue, the main street of the 'black' area of Los Angeles. He advised them of the best hotel in town, the Dunbar, and dropped them there. But when the boys eyed the men and women inside, visible from the doorway, then looked at themselves, they shrugged and walked away, looking for Central Avenue. As they walked along in the rain, they met an old fighter named Eagle Thomas who gave them each 25 cents and directed them to the Midnight Mission where they could get a bed for the night.

---
6   Henry Armstrong, *Gloves, Glory and God*, 1957.
7   Nat Fleischer, *Black Dynamite Vol. II*, 1938.

CHAPTER ONE

'For the next few days the boys haunted the gyms in Los Angeles – the Main Street, the Manhattan and the Ringside. Unable to get in because of the admission charge, they stood on the kerb and hoped. At this juncture of Henry's career, along came Leroy Haynes, who was to be cast in the role of Good Samaritan. Large Leroy, himself no stranger to the trials and tribulations of the black boxer, lent a sympathetic ear to the little fellow's plea. Not only did Leroy afford the boys entrance to the gym, but he also made an effort to get a manager for Henry. He dug up one Paddy Quaid as a prospective mentor. After watching the stranger work, Quaid declared that he couldn't be bothered with what he called 'just another fighter'.

The boys had better luck with the second prospect, Tom Cox, who promoted 'bootleg boxing' shows. After watching Henry make short work of a spar-mate in two rounds, Cox wasted no time in reaching for his fountain pen and extending Armstrong a long-term contract.[8]

As Harry weighed up the offer to Henry, he made the boy sign his name as Armstrong and not Jackson in case of possible complications that might void the contract. When Cox came up with a $5 advance, the contract was signed and Henry Armstrong was a professional fighter. 'Forget Melody Jackson,' said Harry. 'From now on you're my brother, Henry Armstrong!'

The fighter later claimed that, during his first year as an amateur in Los Angeles, he had between 85 and 90 fights and won all of them. A more plausible accounting is that he won 58 of 62 amateur fights, earning a few dollars on the side for

---

8   Nat Fleischer, *Black Dynamite Vol II*, 1938.

each fight. He shined shoes to make ends meet. In summer 1932, 'Henry Armstrong' competed for a spot on the United States Olympic Team but was eliminated in the trials.[9]

On the journey back to Los Angeles, Harry and Henry made their minds up. No more amateur boxing, the kid was becoming a professional fighter – for the second time.

Cox was around the gyms looking for a buyer for Henry's contract. He found Wirt Ross, the guy they called 'One-Shot'. Ross paid $250 for Henry's contract. 'Report to him at the Main Street gym,' Cox told the boys. 'He's taking over from there on. Good luck.'

---

9   Thomas Hauser, *TopRank.com*, 2011.

Chapter Two

NOVELIST AND screenwriter Budd Schulberg recalled the gym in his book *The Harder They Fall*: 'The Main Street gym looks like a shabbier twin of Stillman's in New York. The street is gaudier than Eighth Avenue. It offers cheap burlesque houses and dime movies for adults only, dim and dingy bars with raucous juke boxes and blousy B-girls, your fortune for a dime, your haircut for a quarter, whisky for fifteen cents, love for a dollar and a five-cent flop. Outside the entrance to the gym was the usual sidewalk gathering: boxers, managers, old fighters, hangers-on.

'Going up the long, grimy stairway that seems to be the standard approach to every fight gym, upstairs were the same dirty grey walls. The same lack of ventilation and sanitation and the same milling activity of consecrated young men with narrow waists and glistening skins, bending, stretching, shadow boxing, sparring, punching the bags or listening earnestly to the instructions of men with fat bellies, boneless noses, dirty sweatshirts, brown hats pushed back on sweaty foreheads, the trainers, the managers, the experts. Only here on Main Street there were even more dark skins, not only black like those that had to come to outnumber the whites in Stillman's, but the yellow and brown skins of the

Filipinos and Mexicans who poured into the gym from the slums of LA.

'In California the Mexicans, fighting their way up out of their brown ghettos, dominate the light divisions: Ortiz, Chavez, Arizmendi and a seemingly endless row of brown sluggers by the name of Garcia. In the centre ring, throwing punches at the air, ducking and weaving as he crowded an imaginary opponent to the ropes, was Arizmendi himself, who seemed to have inherited not only the strong, stoic face of an ancient Aztec, but the courage and endurance as well.'[10]

'At the Main Street gym, Henry looked Ross over. He was a handsome giant of a man with snow white hair, bright blue eyes and an accent that was pure Kentucky despite a lifetime roaming around places like Alaska, the Philippines, Panama and New York City. He was a fight manager who once slugged a referee and when called before the California State Athletic Commission, he turned the tables, placed the poor referee in the role of defendant and finished up defending him!

'They called him "One-Shot" around the gyms and he had a weakness for heavyweights, but he could never find another Dempsey or Joe Louis. He did find Haystack Sloan for whom he invented the "Ice Tong Punch". But Haystack couldn't fight, not even with real ice tongs in his mitt. The best fighter Ross ever had was a little black kid he picked up at the Main Street gym in Los Angeles for two hundred and fifty dollars. The kid's name was Henry Armstrong.'[11]

---

10 Budd Schulberg, *The Harder They Fall*, 1948.
11 John Jarrett, *Dynamite Gloves*, 2001.

CHAPTER TWO

'Undress the little shaver,' said Ross. 'Stick him on the scales and let's see what I've got here.' The scales registered 124½ pounds. Henry had made 118 pounds (8½ stone) for the Olympic trials in San Francisco. Ross listened to the tale of torments and drying out, then said, 'He's still a growing kid. You ought to allow his weight to take care of itself. He don't have to lose weight to fight. And if he has to fight heavier men, we'll build him up. But we aren't going to pull pounds off him – for anybody. That's bad for a growing boy. Joe Gans died on account of cutting weight.'

Henry thought to himself, 'I'm on the right track now. This man knows his business. I'm going to stick with him.'[12]

Henry's first fight as a pro took place a couple of weeks later, 30 August 1932, at the Olympic Auditorium in Los Angeles against Eddie Trujillo, a clever, experienced boxer. The boys went hammer and tongs in the first round and Henry dumped the other kid for a long count. But he got up and back into the fight and did well enough to cop the decision. The crowd gave Henry a good hand and the promoter gave him $50 so everything was fine. It was getting better by the day. Henry was matched back at the Olympic against Al Greenfield four weeks later, another hard one with the decision against Henry, but he knew Ross had overmatched him and it was good experience, and the money was better.

After the Greenfield fight, young Armstrong lost only one fight through the end of 1933, and he was fighting good boys like Perfecto Lopez, a win and two draws, and Kid Moro, two draws over ten rounds. Moro landed more

---

12 Henry Armstrong, *Gloves, Glory and God*, 1957.

blows but Armstrong's aggressiveness gave him an even break. Their first bout ended in a draw at Pismo Beach after a state athletic commissioner reversed the referee's decision in favour of Armstrong. The referee, Freddie Gilmore, was given police protection as protests by the Filipino fans of Moro sparked a near riot.

Moving into 1934, Henry reversed a defeat by Baby Manuel in Los Angeles, taking a ten-rounds decision in Sacramento. Harry had given Henry plenty of advance coaching on how to handle Manuel's southpaw style in the first fight, but that night Henry just couldn't put it into practice. In the rematch, 'Armstrong, 131, walloped and weaved his way to a ten-round decision over Baby Manuel, 126, Florida, here last night. Manuel, crafty on defence, seemed to lack aggressiveness and punch and he was far in arrears at the final bell. It was his first loss in California in more than a dozen fights,' reported the *Reno Evening Gazette* on 27 January.

'With an increased attendance at the Bakersfield Arena, fight fans here last night saw a series of sharply decisive matches featured by a victory of Henry Armstrong over Perfecto Lopez. Armstrong was credited with shading Lopez in a majority of the eight rounds and taking the fight handily, though the boy from Mexico was no slouch as a boxer. During the fifth round Armstrong opened a gash over Lopez's eye and this bothered the Mexican during the following frames.'[13]

Bakersfield, CA, 'With the hope of obtaining a match with world's champion Freddie Miller, Henry Armstrong and Perfecto Lopez are expected to put on a whale of a fight here

---

13 *Bakersfield Californian*, 5 March 1934.

tonight at the Nineteenth Street Arena. One of the neatest feathers in the figurative cap of Armstrong is his knockout victory over Gene Espinosa.' Henry took an eight-rounds decision over Lopez, his second against the feisty Mexican with two draws.

'Henry Armstrong is a real tough boy, according to a statement made recently by his manager, and it is entirely possible that the manager isn't exaggerating things in the least. Henry is due to meet Joe Sanchez next Friday night at the Ventura Athletic Club in the main event and we believe that this will really be a fight. Joe seems to be in pretty good condition and has a lot of friends who will be in his corner. On the other hand there are a few of the gang who think he is not so hot. For instance, Baby Palmore, when he heard about this match, had his first good laugh in six months and promptly reserved himself a ringside seat in order to see his old rival take a beating. Joe isn't so sure he is going to be beaten, however. Armstrong's manager says, "This Armstrong is the greatest club fighter and the most aggressive two-handed fighter in the world." It's a broad statement all right but we are willing to be shown, and it ought to be a good fight.'[14] Well Baby Palmore had his good laugh and Armstrong had his knockout – four rounds.

Kid Moro still held him even in another ten-round bout. Most of the fighters in California were Mexican or Filipinos and they fought three minutes of every round. No wonder the crowds loved them. Young Henry Armstrong was building a good name at the box office and also at a local convenient

---

14 *Oxnard Daily Courier CA*, 6 September 1934.

financial institution, as a barrier against future visits from the wolf!

Henry was also working a busy shoe-shine stand. Harry bought one too, a little further along the same block, so customers who missed one were usually caught by the other. Income was better than ever and they were able to rent a furnished apartment and buy a radio.

The California newspapers were already calling Henry the state featherweight champion.

'CHAMP FIGHTS LOPEZ TONIGHT' – the headline in the *Oxnard Daily Courier* put Henry in the driver's seat even though he was spotting Lopez eight pounds. Perfecto and Henry had met four times, with three fights ending in a draw and the fourth won by the champ on a technical kayo. Lopez claimed he ate something that disagreed with him before the last bout and the fact that he was not forced to make 133 pounds that week would help him tremendously. The record actually stood at two draws, three decisions and the TKO for Henry, and he also won this one with a hard-earned decision over the Mexican.

Armstrong was learning a lot about Mexican fighters and fight fans. The fans, he had learned, were super-enthusiastic but all-fired partial to their boys. Their applause was very one-sided. Just about the only way to convince them was to kayo their favourite. That settled all the arguments.

As 1934 drew to a close, Henry could count on 39 fights with One-Shot Ross. He had won 29 (15 by kayo), drawn six and lost four. One of those defeats was to Baby Arizmendi, a huge favourite with the fans. Alberto 'Baby' Arizmendi, although only 20 years old, had been fighting since he left the

CHAPTER TWO

crib. He was helpless at the age of six, a victim of infantile paralysis. Six years later his amazing career as a prize-fighter was born. Possibly at age 14, the youngest boxer to turn professional, he went on to become Mexico's first fistic star. Newspapers described Arizmendi as 'displaying all the speed and agility of his Aztec ancestry'.

Written in an article on 31 August 1934: 'The first Mexican to claim a world's boxing championship – Alberto "Baby" Arizmendi, who beat Mike Belloise in a 15-round bout last night – was ready to take on all comers in the featherweight class. The stocky little Mexican ripped his way through the New York claimant to the world's featherweight crown to gain recognition of the New York boxing commission as the successor to Kid Chocolate of Cuba. Belloise was able to take only two rounds of the 15, while Albert, son of a Mexican bandit general, spotting the Bronx Irishman nearly two pounds in weight and three inches in height, gave fair-haired Michael the worst beating of his fighting career.'[15]

Arizmendi was the guy Henry Armstrong had to fight if he was going anywhere. 'Henry had been going with a girl who appealed to him. She was Willa Mae Shandy, and her father was the Reverend Walter L. Strauther, pastor of the Morning Star Baptist Church. Henry proposed and won a 'yes'. They were married in August of 1934 by the Reverend A.L. Brewer.

'Henry asked Ross to get him a fight that would bring in some real money. He wanted a comfortable home for his bride and himself. One day, Ross brought good news; he had

---

15 *Moorhead Daily News*, Minnesota, 31 August 1934.

arranged a ten-rounds engagement with Baby Arizmendi in Mexico City on 3 November 1934.

'"He's the fellow who just won what the New York State Athletic Commission calls the championship of the world, isn't he?" Henry asked.

'"Sure – and you're guaranteed $1,500 plus a percentage of the gate for the fight," Ross answered. "The Mexico City fans are crazy to see their boy in action."'[16]

Ross travelled to Mexico City with Henry and when they got off the train a band met them at the station. Headlines in the papers heralded their arrival, planes flew over the city carrying banners welcoming Henry to the city. At the Cosmos Hotel a few days before the fight, Ross said to Henry, 'Don't get too anxious and ambitious, son. You're not supposed to win this fight.' When Henry asked what he meant, Ross tried to calm him. 'Well, Henry,' he said, 'I gave my word that we'd fight the way Arizmendi's manager wanted it. It was the only way I could get you signed ... Just fight to go the full ten rounds.'

Armstrong went out there and fought his fight as the National Stadium became a madhouse, with the Arizmendi fans roaring their support for the Babe. At the final bell, Henry was sure he had done enough to take the decision but he was doomed to disappointment as the referee announced Arizmendi as the winner. The newspaper clippings didn't make very good reading as Henry stuck them in his scrapbook.

'BABY ARIZMENDI IS EASY WINNER IN ARMSTRONG GO,' United Press reported from Mexico

---

16 Henry Armstrong, *Gloves, Glory and God*, 1957.

City on 4 November: 'Baby Arizmendi of Mexico, recognised in New York as world featherweight champion, won an easy ten-round decision over Henry Armstrong, Los Angeles negro boxer, before 25,000 fans in National Stadium here today. Arizmendi's superior boxing and effective body punching enabled him to win almost every round.

'Fighting with a broken left wrist from the second round, Arizmendi gave one of the most courageous exhibitions in Mexican ring history. Armstrong was a rough, tough fighter and mixed willingly but was outgeneralled by the shifty Mexican. Arizmendi came close to knocking out the American in the fifth round but Henry rallied to weather the storm.'[17]

'That's the contest where the promoters ran off with the gate receipts and poor Henry and brother Harry were left stranded for three months. Dame Fortune seemed to be against the brothers there, for, in addition to losing their guarantee, Henry became ill with the Mexican grippe and he had to remain inactive for a month. When over his ailment, Ross got Henry a fight with Joe Conde and he knocked Joe cold in seven rounds. Ventura Arana fancied his chance and was stopped in five rounds. This was better Henry. The promoter decided to put Armstrong back in with Arizmendi, this time over twelve rounds.'[18]

At that time there were two featherweight champions: Freddie Miller was the man according to the National Boxing Association, but it was Baby Arizmendi if you asked the New York State Athletic Association. The young Mexican had

---
17 *Nevada State Journal*, 5 November 1934.
18 Nat Fleischer, *Black Dynamite Vol II*, 1938.

trekked the 3,000 miles to New York and clinched a match with local favourite Mike Belloise. It was August 1934 when the boys got together at the Dyckman Oval in Manhattan, 15 rounds with Arthur Donovan working as referee.

United Press reported: 'The first Mexican to claim a world's boxing championship, Alberto "Baby" Arizmendi, who beat Mike Belloise on a decision last night, was ready to take on all comers in the featherweight class. Arizmendi plowed and ripped his way through the NY claimant to the world's featherweight crown to gain recognition of the NY boxing commission as the successor to Kid Chocolate of Cuba. Belloise was able to take only two rounds of the 15, while Arizmendi gave Belloise the worst beating of his fighting career. The local fighter was decked in the ninth round but fought back to go the route.

'A battle between Miller and Arizmendi seemed a natural. Arizmendi's manager had been trying to arrange such a fight for some time. He figured that his boy, with his stamina, his punching ability and his bull-like neck which measured 17 ½ inches, would emerge undisputed featherweight champion of the world. But he was unable to get this match, and both press and public were after him for a return bout between Arizmendi and Armstrong. He finally agreed, mainly because New Year's Day was drawing near, and most of Mexico's big sporting attractions were held on holidays. It wouldn't do to let the Babe go fightless over the New Year, when a huge crowd could be counted on as a certainty for a return with Armstrong.

'Henry told the good news to Tony Rocha, his Mexican trainer. There was nothing sceptical about Rocha's reaction.

CHAPTER TWO

He jumped for joy! "We train hard for thees baby, Henree – and thees time you beat heem, keed!"

'Henry felt especially good about the fight, because he knew it was being promoted by the Covadonga Sports Association, a reputable Mexican outfit, which put on bull fights and other sports events. At least he figured he would get paid for his exertions this time. During the training period, one of the most intensive he had undergone up to that time, Henry tried to sound out Ross to see whether he had made any arrangement for Henry to take it easy, like the time before. But Ross wouldn't say anything.

'In the dressing room just before they were due to leave for the ring, Ross finally blurted it out. "I guess you wonder about things, Henry … Matter of fact, I agreed that you'd let Arizmendi go the full distance this time like you did the first. But this time we're giving no ground. I want you to go in there and beat him." That was fine with Henry. "I'll beat the Babe's ears off, no matter what kind of deal is cooked up," he said to himself.'

Chapter Three

TUESDAY, 1 January 1935, and in Mexico City all roads led to the bullring El Toreo de Cuatro Caminos, scene of many a bloody battle between man and bull and the guy in the fancy suit didn't always win.

This battle would be between Baby Arizmendi, the idol of his country, and the 25-year-old American boy Henry Armstrong, chasing fame and fortune. There was a crowd of 20,000 jammed into the stadium and the sun, rising in the blue sky, showed a dazzling colourful scene with the citizens dressed in their finery, enjoying the carnival atmosphere, ready to cheer their hero.

Baby didn't let them down. He took everything Henry threw at him and it was plenty. They met in the centre of the ring like two stags, head-to-head, gloves thudding home as the roar from the crowd increased in crescendo. Armstrong powered forward on his spindly legs, bobbing, weaving, forcing the action three minutes every round, and the Mexican knew he had a tiger by the tail.

After the bell there was time for nothing but sock and be socked. It was a two-man preview of blitzkrieg and total war. Armstrong and Arizmendi fought over every square inch of the ring for 12 battering rounds. Cuts were opened and

CHAPTER THREE

blood flowed freely. At the end they were both stained red and dripping.

Again as Henry went to his corner he felt he had won the fight … Again the referee's decision went against him. Next day the Mexican papers gave him some consolation as their fight writers agreed in declaring that Armstrong at least should have been given a draw.

'Baby Arizmendi will get an opportunity against Freddie Miller to further his claims to the world featherweight championship. He earned a match with Miller yesterday by outpointing Henry Armstrong in a 12-round battle. Arizmendi won eight rounds. He counter-punched and boxed his way to the victory.'[19]

'BABY ARIZMENDI IN VICTORY IN MEXICO,' heralded the *Port Arthur News*. 'Alberto (Baby) Arizmendi, New York state featherweight boxing champion, Tuesday night pounded out a 12-round decision over Henry Armstrong before a crowd of 20,000. Arizmendi had a slight margin in six rounds. Four went to Armstrong by a shade and two were judged even. Armstrong finished strong after a slow start and had his Mexican opponent bleeding from a badly damaged right eye, injured in the seventh round.' But Henry had something tangible to show for his second Arizmendi fight – a tidy sum of money.

In February, Henry had another baby on his mind. He received a wire from his wife in Los Angeles with exciting news: she was expecting a baby in a couple of weeks' time. No time to lose, the father-to-be hurried back to LA in good

---

19 *Ogden Standard Examiner*, 2 January 1935.

time to see his baby girl born. The happy parents named her Lanetta.

'Henry felt his sense of family responsibility more than ever, and the determination to make solid advances in his work. He regarded fighting as his profession and had a professional's concern for his career. His family of dependants increased when he brought his father and grandmother from St Louis to live at his home in Los Angeles.'[20]

Six weeks after the Baby Arizmendi fight, Henry was still mixing with the younger ones. He was back in Mexico City to face Baby Rodolfo Casanova in a ten-round bout. He could handle the fighters well enough, it was the referees he had trouble with. He hammered this baby all over the ring and the book says he lost on a foul in round four. It looked a fair punch to the body but Casanova went to the floor and claimed a foul. The referee, naturally, agreed with Baby and the crowd loved it.

Henry was fed up with Mexico, asking One-Shot to get him matched in California where he should have a better chance with the guys who marked the scorecards. After dropping a decision to Davey Abad in Mexico, he took on the sensational Tully Corvo, who had rocketed into the spotlight, racking up four triumphs in ten days. They were matched at the L Street Arena in Sacramento, advertised for the California state featherweight title. Armstrong was a box-office favourite in the state capital and he didn't disappoint his fans, knocking out the Los Angeles high school boxer in round five.

---

20 Henry Armstrong, *Gloves, Glory and God*, 1957.

CHAPTER THREE

Then he was at the Los Angeles Olympic with New York boxer Frankie Covelli to punch out an eight-round decision with 6,500 fans roaring their heads off. New York fighter Davey Abad had outpointed Henry a few months earlier but this night in Los Angeles Abad was given only one round as Armstrong sailed to an easy decision. Henry had warmed up for the fight by taking Mark Diaz at Ventura, the barefoot boy from Manila. Diaz should have put his socks on at least!

'With a western featherweight boxing championship at stake, Alton Black and Henry Armstrong will meet in Reno's Chestnut Arena tonight in the first strictly titular battle to be staged in a local ring since the Johnson–Jeffries fight of 1910. Armstrong will place his California title on the block against the Intermountain and Nevada championships held by Black. A handsome silver belt buckle will be awarded the victor.

'It is typical of both fighters that they never retreat, that they are both hard hitters. There are those who say that Armstrong will stop Black for the first time in his career, and there are enough of them to make the Californian a slight favourite in the betting odds.'

Henry didn't let them down. Black came out slugging, looking for the knockout he had promised, but he met his match as Henry went forward in his weaving, bobbing style and by the eighth round he was forcing Black all over the ring. He didn't come out for round nine and Henry had himself a handsome silver belt buckle to hold his pants up. Three months later Black was back for more and he got it, knockout in eight rounds, and Henry Armstrong was hailed as the king of all the featherweights west of the Mississippi river!

In October 1935, Alan Ward was writing in the *Oakland Tribune*, 'It has been claimed, with sufficient emphasis and repetition to give the assertion a brand of truth, that Mexico City is the Sargasso Sea of pugilism, so far as invading fighters are concerned. Outside scrappers just can't seem to get ahead in Mexico City. This realisation, formulated many moons ago, tends to establish Henry Armstrong, an excellent ringman, despite a record compiled and forwarded by manager "One-Shot" Wirt Ross which lists two defeats in the capital of the land of manana. One of the losses was to Davey Abad, previously licked by Armstrong. The other was to Baby Arizmendi, New York's featherweight champion.

'If Ross's allegations are to be accepted, both Freddie Miller, NBA champion, and Arizmendi are fearful of meeting Armstrong with their titles at stake. Ross's elaborate advertising brochures lead off, with a splash of red ink, with the promise to pay $5,000 to anyone who will deliver either of them into an arena at fight time.'[21]

Armstrong was matched with Lester Marston on promoter Leo Leavitt's fight card the next Monday night. Marston was picked by the State Athletic Commission as the most suitable opponent for Armstrong. Representatives of the State body were unanimous in the opinion the San Francisco boy stood the best chance of winning of any suggested by promoter Leo Leavitt.

In Oakland, California, on 21 October 1935, Henry Armstrong won by kayo after seven rounds with Lester Marston!

---

21 Alan Ward, *Oakland Tribune*, 17 October 1935.

CHAPTER THREE

One of the biggest names to appear in Henry's record was that of Midget Wolgast. The Philadelphian was born Joseph Robert Loscalzo, and when he started fighting at the age of 15 he took the name of popular Philly boxer Bobby Wolgast, and he stood at only 5ft 3½in. In March 1930 he beat Black Bill over 15 rounds to gain recognition from the New York Commission as flyweight champion.

He was a 'boxer's boxer' and Georgie Pace, one-time bantamweight champion, recalled, 'There's nothing Willie Pep couldn't do with a pair of gloves that Midget Wolgast couldn't do. I've never seen any boxer with the speedy execution and the tricky moves that Wolgast had.'[22]

'Sadly he was no puncher, only 17 knockouts listed on his 215-bout record. In 1933, after a trip to Europe where he beat Jackie Brown in London and drew with Valentin Angelmann in Paris, Midget told reporters, "I couldn't stand another day over there. The weather gave me a cold I couldn't kick and the food made me sick. It's great to be back in the good old USA."'[23]

He lost his title in September 1995 and two months later fought Henry Armstrong in Oakland. The former champ lost the decision over ten but drew 40 per cent of the purse against ten per cent for Armstrong, but Henry was taking the match as a stepping stone to gaining recognition in New York. The gamble paid off.

In Oakland on 28 November 1935, Henry Armstrong won a decision over Midget Wolgast. Armstrong dropped Wolgast with a right uppercut for a count of nine in the second round.

---
22 *Ring*, May 1972.
23 *Ring*, October 1990.

Midget came back strong in the next and fought Armstrong on even terms up to the ninth round. Henry's strong rally in the ninth and tenth, combined with the knockdown, gave him the decision.

A nicely typed letter from Ivan Blaettler, manager of Richie Fontaine, landed on the sports desk at the *Oakland Tribune* the last day of October 1935, reading, 'Having heard several stories I was afraid to let Richie box Henry Armstrong. There is no truth in the report. I really feel Fontaine can beat Armstrong but we want to get fairly paid for the bout. To date none of the promoters have offered any real money. When we get the right kind of offer it will go in.'[24]

It took almost four months before Mr Blaettler received the right offer, and the boys stepped into the ring on 26 February 1936 at Oakland's Municipal Auditorium. Richie, Montana-born, was only 20, a pro for five years, against Armstrong, 26, a veteran of 58 fights, installed 2-1 favourite with the betting boys. As expected, Richie came in at 132 pounds, against 125 for Armstrong. He made good use of his seven-pound advantage to bludgeon out a decisive ten-round victory over the favourite in what the fans voted the most thrilling, most entertaining fight since promoter Leo Leavitt set up in Oakland. 'For bruising, toe-to-toe, head-to-head exchanges, the battle of the overgrown featherweights was in a class by itself.'[25]

Los Angeles promoters grabbed the boys for a rematch nearly five weeks later and this time Armstrong prevailed. Two pounds heavier and with his right hand in working order

---
24 *Oakland Tribune*, 31 October 1935.
25 Alen Ward, *Oakland Tribune*, 27 February 1936.

CHAPTER THREE

again, the *Los Angeles Times* felt Armstrong won six rounds, Fontaine four. Fontaine sustained a cut on his forehead from an accidental clash of heads. Armstrong's right eye was puffed at the end of the bout. The *Los Angeles Daily News* reported that Armstrong nearly floored Fontaine with a right to the jaw in the second round and went on to win the next two rounds by wide margins. The *Daily News* favoured Armstrong 6-2-2 in rounds.

'Armstrong has been given consideration by the New York boxing commission as a candidate for the world featherweight championship title from which Baby Arizmendi recently was ousted, and such chances are not running around loose. The game Fontaine weathered two furious rounds in which he took much punishment.'[26]

'There was good news for Henry a few days after he took a ten-round decision from Johnny De Foe in Butte, Montana. "I've got you definitely signed my boy, to meet Arizmendi, 4 August at Wrigley Field in Los Angeles," announced One-Shot Ross. "I want you to go into serious training, my boy, to meet Arizmendi. This is an important fight. Not going to have any others until this is over. If you win you'll be world's champion as far as Mexico and New York State are concerned … and California, too."

'"California?" Henry asked.

'"Sure!" said Ross, smiling broadly. "The Californian athletic commission just recognised Arizmendi as featherweight champion of the world. Far as the money is concerned, that makes the Babe world's champion for fair.

---

26 *Montana Helena Independent*, 1 April 1936.

You know the money fights are mostly in New York. And for this fight with Arizmendi I've got us the largest guarantee we've had yet ... Yes my boy, two thousand dollars. How'd you like that?"

"Just fine," said Henry, surveying a dizzy future. "If I ever wanted a fight, this is it."[27]

Both fighters worked out at the Main Street Gym in Los Angeles and the fans packed the place every day, paying ten cents apiece to watch their favourite. More people of Mexican birth or descent lived in Los Angeles than in any Mexican city, excepting only Mexico City itself. So there was no lack of support for Baby Arizmendi, the national idol. On Central Avenue, heart of the city's coloured community, discussion raged by day and night.

In the dressing room, Harry taped Henry's hands and when he had finished, Henry stepped out and started his shadow boxing to warm up as he usually did, through seven or eight fast rounds. By the time the fighters were in the ring, about 12,000 fans were packed into Wrigley Field. They let out a roar as referee George Blake called them to ring centre for their instructions, and then they were in the corners waiting for the bell.

'While the National Boxing Association may recognise Petey Sarron as the featherweight king, and others class Mike Belloise as the best of the bunch, there is no question of Armstrong's class today in the minds of the 12,000 persons who saw him buzz-saw Arizmendi out of the picture. The Mexican never had a chance. He was four rounds behind

---

27 Henry Armstrong, *Gloves, Glory and God*, 1957.

CHAPTER THREE

before he was able to strike a blow. Armstrong smothered him. At the opening bell, Henry nestled his head against Arizmendi's shoulder and began throwing punches with both hands. The Baby's bushy black hair waved like palm fronds in a windstorm.

'Protecting himself as well as he could, he waited for Armstrong to slow up. But the pace never slackened. Henry was going as hard in the tenth as in the first ten seconds of the first … Arizmendi tried everything. His jabs and hooks were listless for lack of room. He tried to tie up Armstrong and that was like trying to tie up an airplane propeller, and dodging along the ropes was no more effective than trying to run away from his shadow.

'There were no knockdowns, but the Mexican's face was puffy around the eyes and cheekbones from his 30-minute massage. It was a bad night for the experts who had made Arizmendi a 2-1 favourite on the strength of two previous victories over this same Armstrong.'[28]

'Baby Arizmendi of Mexico City today was 126 pounds of human hamburger following a ten-round scrap with Henry Armstrong of St Louis, for the California-New York featherweight boxing championship. Armstrong gave Arizmendi a thorough beating, keeping him plastered against the ropes and flailing with both fists from the first bell to the last … On only two occasions was Arizmendi able to fight his way to the centre of the ring and stage the lightning rallies that have characterised his attack in the past. He came closest to winning a round when he fought his way out from the ropes

---

28 *Reno Evening Gazette*, 5 August 1936.

in the fifth. The Mexican, who is accustomed to taking the lead himself, was unable to escape the bronze shadow and mercilessly was outclassed.'[29]

Among those at Wrigley Field ringside that night was Petey Sarron, National Boxing Association featherweight champion. An enterprising reporter was watching Sarron, and wrote, 'His face an ashen white, an empty ache in the pit of his stomach, he squirmed in his seat and choked as he watched Henry Armstrong hammer Baby Arizmendi into the most brutal, ruthless defeat of his brilliant 11-year stretch of ring warfare last night at Wrigley Field. Paling perceptibly as he blinked with frightened eyes that saw Armstrong, the infernal machine, smoke the idol of Mexico out of the ring with burning, searing leather to take every one of the ten rounds ... Sarron aptly expressed the sentiments of the 16,000 hysterical, stunned spectators when he said, "I'm glad I'm not the one in there with Armstrong tonight."'

Also at ringside was singer Al Jolson and his wife, movie star Ruby Keeler. In his 1988 book *Jolson, The Legend*, Herb Goldman told the story. 'With them was friend Eddie Mead, a fight manager who was a friend of Ruby's from her chorus days in New York. As the fight progressed, Ruby turned to Mead and said, 'That's the kind of fighter you ought to manage, Eddie – that boy Armstrong.'

'"There's just 5,000 reasons why I ain't managing him," replied Mead. "I can buy him for five grand, and all I need is $4,995 more to make the deal."'

---

29 *Washington Evening Star*, 5 August 1936.

CHAPTER THREE

When the fight was over, Al gave Mead his card and told him to call the next day. Al agreed to finance Mead's purchase of the Armstrong contract from Wirt Ross. Mead, anxious for publicity, got Jolie's okay to tell Jack Singer of the *Los Angeles Times* that the sale price was $10,000 instead of $5,000. It proved to be a bad move. Ross raised the price to $10,000 as soon as he saw Singer's story. Al was furious and absolutely refused to give Mead the additional $5,000.

On the same sports pages that carried reports of Henry's title triumph was a cartoonist's image of Kid Chocolate, 'The Cuban beauty, once invincible at 130 pounds, now penniless and battling desperately for a comeback.' Henry's mind flashed back to that day working on the railroad and picking up a newspaper with a report of Chocolate receiving $75,000 for defeating Al Singer in New York. He told a workmate that night, and dreamed of earning that much money, when he was working on the railroad for $20 a week!

For his championship victory over Arizmendi, Henry's purse was $2,000.

Chapter Four

'EDDIE MEAD was still chasing the extra five grand, so he approached George Raft. Before Raft had become a film star, he had done some fighting under Mead's wing, Mead said. Raft readily advanced the money. Henry didn't know till a good while later that Raft had supplied half of Mead's payment in purchase of the contract. But Henry did learn, soon, that George Raft of the films was a warm friend and a helpful one. Raft remained a silent partner in the transaction. Jolson was credited by the papers with having advanced the full amount. Ross got his ten grand, and Eddie Mead got Henry. Things began to happen fast. Within a few days Mead announced he had matched Henry against Mike Belloise, to go ten rounds in Los Angeles on 27 October 1936. This was pretty fast work and Henry felt increased confidence in his new manager.'[30]

'Eddie Mead was a fat man,' wrote Art Cohn, sports editor of the *Oakland Tribune*. 'By fat I mean he weighed 300 pounds. And every ounce of it was happy.'[31]

'Eddie Mead had a memory for a face and a name,' wrote sportswriter Rex Hess. 'He'd have been a great politician,

---
30 Henry Armstrong, *Gloves, Glory and God*, 1957.
31 Art Cohn, *Oakland Tribune*, 27 May 1942.

for it takes more of that "hale fellow, well met" business to get along in the fight racket than most politicians own. And Eddie had it in abundance. A sharp man with the percentage figures when lining up a fight, was Eddie, but as open-hearted as a book otherwise, and that's how he made such friends as George Raft and Al Jolson, who bought Henry Armstrong's contract and practically made a present of the document to Mead.'[32]

Eddie had a good fighter in Joe Lynch who was two-time bantamweight champion in the 1920s and now he had Henry Armstrong on his way to the top.

'By the time we got to know Mead,' wrote boxing writer Barney Nagler, 'Armstrong's purses had put him in the chips. He was hanging out in good saloons, away from his old haunts on the West Side, and had more than one suit of clothes to his name. He was a blubbery bon vivant with a round, soft face that had the mild look of a kid surprised with his hand in the cookie jar. He went to his pocket easily and lived at a pace only hustlers can set and only millionaires can afford.'[33]

'Los Angeles 28 October – Al Jolson's fighter, Henry Armstrong, celebrated today while matchmaker Joe Waterman of the Olympic Auditorium started negotiations for a bout with Peter Sarron for the undisputed featherweight championship of the world. Armstrong won a promised fight with the National Boxing Association champion last night when he took a slim ten-round decision over Mike Belloise of New York. The Armstrong–Belloise bout was recognised by the Boxing Commissions of New York and California as a

---
32 Rex Hess, *Mansfield News Journal*, Ohio.
33 Barney Nagler, *Ring*, November 1982.

world titular affair, but Waterman wants to sign Sarron with Armstrong to clear up the muddled 126-pound class.

'While Jolson howled with delight, Armstrong won Referee Abe Roth's nod after a gruelling but none too exciting fight. The principals spent most of the evening chopping blows in close. Armstrong's aggressiveness earned Roth's approval, but the packed house of 10,400 appeared sharply divided. Apart from a slit eyelid, the New Yorker emerged unmarked. Armstrong was cut about both eyes. He bled freely from the nose and mouth throughout most of the bout.

'The Associated Press carded the bout a draw, with an edge, if any, to Belloise for the most effective blows. Twice, notably in the eighth, he straightened Armstrong up and connected with a short right to the chin that made him wobble unsteadily.'[34]

A few days later, Henry received a disappointment – the New York Boxing Commission hadn't recognised him as champion, because his fight with Belloise had been a ten-rounder. Recognition would be given only if he defeated Belloise in a second fight, over the 15-rounds route. And New York would want that fight!

12 March 1937 – Eddie Mead just couldn't stop smiling. He was back in New York with a hot fighter, a kid called Henry Armstrong, having his first fight on the east coast, main event in the Garden, fighting Mike Belloise, the featherweight champ according to the New York Commission – beat this guy and you have a ticket to the title.

---

34 *Washington Evening Star*, 28 October 1936.

CHAPTER FOUR

John Lardner wrote in his syndicated column: 'Next to his mammy and his sonny boy, Al Jolson's favourite person is a coffee-coloured little negro named Henry Armstrong. Mr Jolson owns a generous piece of the Armstrong torso, and believes that young Henry will sooner or later be the featherweight or lightweight champion of the world or something ... Terrific, colossal, a thunderbolt, a new Gans, a new Dixon, a new Walcott, a black McGovern – those are the things the critics call Armstrong on the coast. His friends call him Henry.

'The thunderbolt will make his eastern debut this week against Mike Belloise, a substitute for the injured Aldo Spoldi, and the heaviest weight on his shoulders will be his coast reputation. Armstrong looks all right in training. Armstrong is a hooker, who wades in on a straight line with his arms cocked low. His speed protects him from punishment. He can see a punch coming, slip it, and bury his hands in your midriff with considerable effect.

'Though he is only 24 years old, the kid has compiled a very fair record for freestyle savagery in the ring. He has beaten Belloise and Baby Arizmendi, both of whom were recognised, at one time or another and also simultaneously, as the featherweight champions of the world. Of course, Mike and the Baby were courtesy champions with no legal claim to the title whatsoever. But that does not alter the fact that Armstrong beat both of them and is now recognised in certain counties, one-arm restaurants, and private estates, including Mr Al Jolson's, as the one and only champion of the world.' [35]

---

35 John Lardner, *Salt Lake Tribune*, 11 March 1937.

Henry McLemore covered the fight for United Press, writing, 'Los Angeles said he was terrific, stupendous, colossal, and a sure-fire killer. But Los Angeles is always saying that about something, so nobody believed it – until Henry Armstrong, coming out of a crouch, threw a left hook flush against the jaw of Mike Belloise, featherweight champion of the world. It was a short, left hook. Didn't travel more than a foot at the most but a bomb couldn't have been more effective. Belloise was paralysed for a moment and then gave way all over, all at once, and pitched forward on his face in the Madison Square Garden's ring. He was out of his head for half an hour.

'Armstrong, sitting in his dressing room, talked of the fight in a quiet voice. "I knew I had him almost ready for the kill in the third round. I let him have a right, a full right, under the heart. He sagged, and I guess he would have gone down if it hadn't been for the ropes. I knew then the finish would come in the fourth."

'Henry Armstrong is the most relentless fighter this observer has ever seen – big man or little man. From bell to bell, he is never more than six inches away from his prey. Always moving in, always punching, he never lets up. His punches come from anywhere. High and low, hooks and jabs, he rains leather. He feints with everything from his feet to the wild wavy brush that serves him for hair ... New York hasn't seen anything at 128 pounds to compare with him and when he fights Aldo Spoldi next Friday night he will be paid the best of all fighting tributes – a sell-out house.'[36]

---

36 Henry McLemore, *Port Arthur News*, Texas, 13 March 1937.

CHAPTER FOUR

'New Yorkers were convinced of California featherweight champion Henry Armstrong's vaunted punching power today after watching him score a four-round knockout over Mike Belloise of New York, recognised feather title holder in this state. In his first eastern appearance Armstrong completely captured the spectators with a smashing attack that had the home-town boy completely bewildered. It was a hard left hook just before the bell ending the fourth round that dropped Belloise. Referee Arthur Donovan had counted seven when the bell rang, but Belloise's seconds could not revive him when the fifth-round bell sounded.

'Even if New York State Athletic Commission still refuses to see the light, clouting Henry Armstrong appeared capable today of bossing the featherweight division with or without recognition. The walloper from California whipped the New York commission's 126-pound champion, Mike Belloise, last fall over the ten-round route, but was refused recognition here. By way of removing all doubts, he flattened Belloise in four rounds at Madison Square Garden.

'Henry knew he had to win spectacularly. It bothered him. When he walked down the aisle of the Garden it was half empty and so cold he shivered; lacking the fancy robes usual in the Garden, he entered the ring with his old amateur boxing shoes and a ragged robe, looking like a tramp and just about the loneliest and most nervous man in the world. His legs were thin as pipe-stems and he was very small – 127 pounds. For the first time in his life he knew real fear.

'Then something happened that Henry will never forget if he lives to be a hundred. A man got up out of a ringside seat near his corner and reached up for his hand. It was George

Raft. Said George as he held Henry's hand, "Hank, old boy, we've got to win for California tonight." New courage flowed into Henry; he actually laughed, and he said, "We'll win!"'[37]

Henry Armstrong arrived in the big time that March night in 1937. When the year ended, he had scored 25 knockouts in 26 fights and was the official featherweight champion of the world, thanks to a victory over Petey Sarron. It was in that year that he landed what he recalled were the two hardest punches he ever threw.

One was in February at Los Angeles against a guy named Moon Mullins. 'I hit Mullins so hard he actually skidded before going down. Pow! He was out, just like a steer you hit with a hammer in the stockyards.' The other punch Henry best remembers occurred later that same year in New York. It was his first fight after knocking out Sarron to become world champion. 'I was fighting a highly advertised knockout artist named Billy Beauhuld. In the fifth round I hit him with an overhand right, just back of the ear, so hard he flipped in mid-air on the way down! It was a shame, because Billy was a very promising fighter. I threw many good punches over the years, of course, but I remember those two best of all.'

It had been a newspaper headline that inspired young Henry Jackson to become a boxer. The headline told of the Cuban flash, Kid Chocolate, making $75,000 for beating Al Singer in New York City. That was in August 1929. In March 1937, this clipping appeared in the sports pages: CHOCOLATE REJECTS GO WITH HENRY ARMSTRONG. From New York, the item read: 'Kid

---

[37] Henry Armstrong, *Gloves, Glory and God*, 1957.

CHAPTER FOUR

Chocolate rejected a featherweight championship match with Henry Armstrong in Los Angeles. Manager Luis Guiterrez says the Cuban will not be ready for bouts with Armstrong or Mike Belloise for another year, no matter how much he is offered.

'No longer the champ, they called the Cuban BonBon, manager Guiterrez was still looking after his Kid.'[38]

On 23 September 1937, in Yankee Stadium, Mike Jacobs staged what was called the Carnival of Champions. It was a fistic gala, but a financial failure. But Mike was not too greatly surprised. This show was pointed straight at Madison Square Garden. Not that the Garden situation bothered Mike too much by that time. But he wanted the whole show for himself. There were 50,000 spectators in the stadium and they had paid $300,000. But the guarantees to the fighters and the cost of production were too great to overcome and Mike lost a fortune. But that spectacular show, four world championship fights, stressed the fact that Mike Jacobs controlled the only worthwhile fistic talent available.

'The few millionaires left in the Garden control,' read the sports pages with chagrin but high interest. There was nothing to do but get Mike into the Garden. Michael's dream finally had come true. He sat in Rickard's old office at last. The Garden did not hire Jacobs. Mike and the Garden became partners. They shared in the profits.

---

38 *The Mobile Times,* Mobile, Alabama, 13 March 1937.

Chapter Five

'MY FIRST contact with Jacobs as a big-time promoter came when he took hold in the Garden in 1937,' recalled Nat Fleischer, editor and publisher of *Ring* magazine. The distance between Nat's office in Madison Square Garden and Mike's desk was less than 100ft. Both men would be at the office by 7.30am and they got into the habit of dropping in on each other and discussing the public reaction to things that were in the making. 'He had an ideal mind for a promoter,' Fleischer would say. 'He could see events in sequences. He could envision a line of developments leading from a loss to the ultimate grand profit, and triumph. In that respect, Mike's career as a promoter was without a match.'[39]

Shortly before moving into the Garden, Jacobs had been putting fights on at the New York Hippodrome. From his office there he called Fleischer and asked him to drop in; he had an idea to put to Nat. He said he was arranging his debut card in the Garden and had decided that a world championship featherweight battle between Petey Sarron and Armstrong would be a fitting attraction. Nat agreed with him.

---

39 *Ring* magazine, March 1950.

CHAPTER FIVE

'Petey Sarron had been doing remarkable things in England and South Africa, as the standout featherweight,' said the *Ring* editor. 'Sarron's rates were regarded as too steep by American promoters. I was told Sarron gets $15,000 every time he starts in South Africa. Why can't you pay him that much?' 'You are asking me to break into the Garden with a loss,' Jacobs replied. 'Eddie Mead, Armstrong's manager, demands 20 per cent with a minimum of seven grand. If I give Sarron 15 grand, I can't make a showing at the gate.' 'I told Mike that he would have to take that risk,' said Fleischer.

'Half an hour later he called me back. "Are you authorised to sign for Sarron?" I assured him that I had that authority, "Here is a contract, for Sarron to fight Armstrong for the world's featherweight championship, for $15,000," Jacobs snorted. "Too much dough. However, sign it."'

Before Nat signed the contract, he read it and queried the clause stating that Sarron would fight only for Jacobs for three years. 'Nat,' Jacobs replied, 'this contract is the type of agreement they all will sign for me or they won't fight for the Twentieth Century S. C. That is how I am going to do business in the Garden. I am THE promoter. I have signed up Armstrong for three years. I have a long-term call on the services of Joe Louis.' 'Jacobs had his way,' Nat said. 'Sarron was signed up for a three-year exclusive.'[40]

'Petey Sarron was a little hairy guy out of Birmingham, Alabama, who liked the fight business because it enabled him to travel all over and he loved to get around. He was tough and strong and although he couldn't part your hair

---

40 Daniel M. Daniel, *The Jacobs Story*, 1949.

with his Sunday punch he could out-game the heaviest of 'em. Petey won his championship from Freddie Miller in 1936. In 15 bouts as champion of the world he won 13 and was in South Africa when he agreed to defend the title against Henry Armstrong in New York on 29 October 1937.

'On paper, Sarron didn't have a chance. Armstrong was going like a house on fire knocking over everyone they threw his way. Hank was a pocket-sized Harry Greb. He never stopped moving in and throwing leather. He would tuck his chin down under his left shoulder, he kept crowding in slamming rights and lefts. If he didn't knock them out they dropped from sheer exhaustion.'[41]

'Three days before the fight, General John J. Phelan of the New York commission, ordered Armstrong to step on the scales. He was 127. Making 126 was easy. At noon on the day of the fight he weighed in at 124½. His nice face seemed bonier than ever, but he was chipper and his barrel-chested torso glistened under the lights over the Garden ring. There was Mead in his fighter's corner, aided and abetted by Harry Armstrong and Frank (Doc) Bagley, a bespectacled pro who had worked with Gene Tunney and was regarded as a "peerless" cut-man.

'The draggy solemnity of a world championship bout filled the ring. Fighter after fighter was introduced. This, mind you, was before television, before the advent of razor blade makers as radio and TV sponsors, and time was cheap. In the ringside seats, molls and mobsters sat in resplendent array. Jolson was there and so was George Raft, who had a rooting interest in Armstrong. Peggy Hopkins Joyce, all larded over with

---

41 Stanley Weston, *Boxing and Wrestling*, May 1954.

CHAPTER FIVE

aloofness and garbed in the white fur of wild animals, was in her usual front pew. Jacobs, at last the main man in American boxing, on his way to becoming Monopoly Mike, clacked his store-bought bicuspids and beamed upon the customers, many of whom had paid the old scalper excessive tribute to sit in pews priced at a mere $5.75 per seat. The crowd had paid $37,408 to see the event. Jacobs probably made as much as that under his well-varnished table.

'Armstrong's reputation for individual terrorism was known widely. Nobody expected him to let his opponent go the distance. To see him do his deed was enough for the customers, who were thrilled as he came bounding down the aisle, squirming inside his robe, working his arms and moving in a seeming glide. And when the bell rang he moved forward to meet Sarron, his skinny legs spread wide and his neck taut, fighting with a calculated fury, racing the clock, unmindful of pain, inevitably a champion.'[42]

'A crowd of 14,000, of whom 11,847 parted with $34,708 to welcome Mike Jacobs in the Garden and see Armstrong, in many respects a miniature edition of Joe Louis, hang up his 22nd knockout in his last 23 fights. The knockout climaxed five of the fastest, most furiously fought rounds Garden fans have seen in years. Sarron, off to a dazzling lead, blew it in the fifth and sixth when Armstrong finally got organised and began to go to town. A crushing left to the pit of the stomach, quickly followed by a murderous right flush to the button polished off the game and clever Sarron after almost six rounds of sterling milling in the Garden.

---

42 Barney Nagler, *Ring* magazine, November 1982.

"'Those two blows hurt me,' said Sarron after the fight.", "but not so badly that I couldn't have got up. I missed one of the referee's counts, I was looking for nine when he said ten." The little Syrian attributed his lack of fire and pep to the ordeal of weight making. He's at his best at 130 pounds. "I think I will make a lightweight out of Peter," said manager Jim Erwin in the dressing room. "I doubt if he'll ever try to make 126 pounds again. It takes too much out of him."

'Johnny Gilbert, the jockey, had bet $1,000 on Sarron against Armstrong at odds of 5-2. Not only are both Syrians, but Sarron is the godfather of Johnny's boy.'[43]

'It was a powerful left hook to the stomach that started the ball rolling for Armstrong. He caught Sarron with that punch square in the breadbasket. Sarron dropped and as he rested on his knees, hurt, but in complete control of his senses, referee Arthur Donovan raced over to Pete Hartley, the official knockdown timer, to pick up his count. The doleful decimal was tolled off and the fight was over. The din that rocked the arena as Armstrong floored his rival was such as to make it almost impossible for the referee to hear the official count and because of that Donovan approached Hartley. That move of the referee undoubtedly proved costly to Sarron. He had never before been down. He was told to take the full rest period and to watch the official.

'He did that, but for five of the ten seconds Donovan was not at the fallen warrior's side. Had he remained with Sarron and been in a position to follow the timer's count. Petey, in my opinion, would have been able to get to his feet but that would

---

43 Eddie Brietz, *Daily Globe*, Ironwood, Michigan, 30 October 1937.

only have delayed the knockout by a few minutes at most. In Sarron's case, as he explained it to me, he thought that when Donovan finally got to him he was beginning the count, whereas Donovan was tolling off seven. But at most it made little difference because Sarron was through – Armstrong's powerful blows had weakened him so that he couldn't possibly have continued for another round.'[44]

At ringside for the *New York Times*, Joseph C. Nichols wrote, 'Sarron clearly won the first four rounds of the sizzling battle by eagerly inviting Armstrong's attack and clearly beating him in counters. Neither fighter paid heed to the so-called finer points of boxing. They merely rushed at each other time and again, both arms swinging, and the encounter was one long succession of thrilling exchanges to the head and body.

'When the sixth round started, Armstrong sprang at his adversary and drove both hands to the body. One punch, a heavy right, apparently robbed Sarron of all his strength, for he was able to do nothing except cover up while Armstrong belaboured relentlessly with lefts and rights to the midsection. Recovering somewhat, Sarron jumped at Armstrong and traded willingly with him until the latter, releasing his long right, crashed it squarely against Sarron's jaw. Sarron slumped to his knees and elbows and slowly lifted himself. But the beaten champion was in no condition to continue. Referee Arthur Donovan stopped the battle at 2.36 of the sixth round.'[45]

---

44 Nat Fleischer, *Black Dynamite Volume II*, 1938.
45 Joseph C. Nichols, *The New York Times*, 30 October 1937.

The remarkable championship reign of Henry Armstrong had begun. 'In the dressing room he was besieged by reporters and press photographers. There were questions and flash bulbs popping, all mixed in together. Finally they left, and Henry was in a daze. Harry had his innings now. He was wildly enthusiastic. "You're in, kid. You've done it – a real champ. Those are Kid Chocolate's shoes you're wearing now, be sure you take good care of them!"

'Mead remained calm outwardly, but Henry could tell that he was delighted deep down inside. It was the second champ for him: the other had been California's Joe Lynch. "Give Henry an Epsom salts bath before he goes to his Harlem party," Mead told Harry. "And try to get him to bed before it's too far toward tomorrow noon." Harry promised he'd perform according to instructions.

'The celebration was at Club Plantation, a Harlem play spot. Henry duly bathed and, feeling great, found his wife and a crowd of friends waiting for him there. That night he tasted as never before the fruits of victory. This was hero worship for fair, from the moment that a roll of drums in the band announced his arrival, until he left hours later.'[46]

'After knocking out Sarron, Armstrong took an extended rest of 21 whole days before returning to the wars. He complained to Eddie Mead two weeks after the featherweight title bout that he was getting rusty and itching for action. Mead scratched his head and said, "You're a champion now – you can't fight every week, it'll cheapen the title. Why don't you run over to the gym and bang your head on the big bag a

---

46 Henry Armstrong, *Gloves, Glory and God*, 1957.

couple of times? Maybe that'll make you feel better." Henry laughed and apologised for complaining. Then he walked over to Stillman's Gym and boxed ten rounds with four different guys, a lightweight and three welterweights. And just think, he didn't get a nickel for it. I guess it's true what they say – you gotta love your work in order to be a success.'[47]

Henry felt better when Eddie told him he was back in the Garden to box Billy Beauhuld, the lightweight champion of New Jersey. Billy was undefeated in 44 straight fights and had backing to take anything Armstrong handed out, but that was before the first bell. Billy had two pounds on Henry but that was all he had.

From ringside, Gayle Talbot reported, 'There was a feeling in informed circles around here today that Lou Ambers, the lightweight boxing champion, would keep his title only so long as he managed to stay out of the same ring with Henry Armstrong. In scoring a technical five-round knockout over Billy Beauhuld, a useful lightweight, last night at the Garden, Armstrong convinced 14,000 fans he was ripe to exchange his featherweight crown for the 135-pound sceptre. The ebony torpedo gave Beauhuld such a painful hiding that Referee Arthur Donovan stopped it as soon as the bell ended the fifth round. Beauhuld looked like he had been shoved through a concrete mixer head first.

'Before last night the boys hadn't been quite convinced that Armstrong could take it. They knew he could hand it out, but his string of knockouts had been a little too reminiscent of Joe Louis's triumphant surge before he ran into Max

---

47 Stanley Weston, *Boxing and Wrestling*, May 1954.

Schmeling. They know now his jaw is as rock-ribbed as his fists. Beauhuld stood up and smashed him with everything in the book and Armstrong only grinned wider and tore in harder. He didn't take one backward step, and he must have thrown 500 punches in five rounds.'[48]

Veteran scribe Hype Igoe wrote: 'Calling Lou Ambers and Barney Ross and tellin' 'em fair that a dark shadow flitters around their cabin doors. Henry Armstrong still is the terror of the Littlemen of Fistiana and it is up to Lou and Barney to do something about it. Armstrong slaughtered brave Billy Beauhuld in Madison Square Garden last night when he got him going and he had him going from the first round on. Arthur Donovan stopped the bout after Beauhuld, a crimson smear, had plopped, beaten, into his chair at the end of the fifth round. The bell saved Beauhuld at seven with Billy on his knees, fish-eyed and horribly groggy. Billy couldn't fathom the little tarantula in front of him. Indeed there seems no way of whipping him.'[49]

---

[48] Gayle Talbot, *The Sheboygan Press,* Wisconsin, 20 November 1937.
[49] Hype Igoe, *Lowell Sun* Mass, 20 November 1937.

Chapter Six

ARMSTRONG'S 1938 campaign started with a knockout of Enrico Venturi in round six of their bout in Madison Square Garden. The Italian took a heavy barrage of body punishment before going down in the sixth, claiming a foul. First Venturi went to his knees, then sprawled on his back. Told to get up by referee Donovan, he shook his head and was counted out. According to Dr Walker of the New York Commission, a fighter so hurt couldn't fall as did Venturi. He would have to drop in the opposite direction to the position taken by Venturi.

'Having taken the measure of one of the outstanding lightweights in Venturi and another in Beauhuld, Armstrong was convinced that he could whip Lou Ambers to win the lightweight championship. He started a hot campaign to get that match but found Herkimer Lou less than enthusiastic for such a bout.

'Al Weill was Lou's manager and he wanted to wait for an outdoor match that would guarantee plenty of money and, while dodging the issue, Barney Ross sneaked in and got the assignment with Armstrong for a world welterweight championship match – the feather king vs. the welterweight king, a handicap match that set a record in that it was the first of its kind in the history of American pugilism.'[50]

Although Weill was acting as matchmaker for Uncle Mike at the time, offers for an indoor match were being made; he turned down the propositions. Jacobs got busy and in no time at all had booked the fight into the Madison Square Garden Bowl in Long Island City for 26 May. On receiving the news, Al Weill resigned his position with Mike at the 20th Century Sporting Club.

'Powerful influences, probably inspired by Weill, began shouting that Ambers' rights to a *lightweight* title bout with Armstrong be protected. So it was agreed that Henry was to weigh in over the lightweight limit in his fight with Ross to protect Ambers and Ross was to weigh no more than 142 at fight time. For the first time in the history of organised boxing, a featherweight champion was being permitted to take on the welterweight champion of the world. Henry stood to take Ross's title, but Ross could only gain a large purse if he won.

'One thing did worry Henry about the fight: he was a featherweight, fighting at 126 pounds, and here he was being thrown in against Ross for the 147-pound title. The law said Henry had to weigh within nine pounds of that weight at the weigh-in, or 138 pounds. That meant he had to put on a lot of weight, somehow!'[51]

'I'll never forget the Ross fight,' Henry was talking to Ted Carroll at the *Ring* office. 'General Phelan of the Commission didn't want to okay the Ross match at first because he thought I was too small, but they finally convinced him I'd come in

---
50 Nat Fleischer, *Black Dynamite Vol II*, 1938.
51 Henry Armstrong, *Gloves, Glory and God*, 1957.

at 138 pounds. Mead had a gimmick for everything so when we hit camp he told me, "Look, kid, you're from St Louis where everybody goes for that Budweiser, and you're going to have to drink plenty of beer for this fight." When Henry protested that he didn't even like beer, Mead said "Well, it's the only way in the world we can put enough weight on you to save this Ross fight."'

But even with all that beer, the best Henry could do the morning of the fight on the scale was 135 pounds. Eddie told him to drink water till weigh-in time.

'A funny thing about Eddie,' said Henry, 'he had a trick of standing behind me at weigh-in time, and just when everybody would be straining for a peep at the scale, he'd take two fingers and push me up in the back if I had to make weight, or he'd push me down on the shoulder with the same two fingers if I had to come in heavy. I don't know yet just how he did it, but he was a wizard at it. Well, at noon that day, I was the most water-logged fighter who ever lived, it's a good thing Ross wasn't a body puncher, because one punch in the belly and the ring would have been flooded! When I got on the scales, Eddie pulled his old magic finger act and I hopped right off as the marker hit 139.'[52]

Then the guys got a break. The heavens opened and the fight was postponed for five days. There was to be no more weighing in, the special arrangements were cancelled. The odds were against Barney Ross because no champion had ever retained his title in the Garden Bowl, yet he remained a steadfast favourite at 7-5.

---

52 Ted Carroll, *Ring*, May 1959.

Henry McLemore was a sportswriter for United Press and on a cold May evening in 1938 he sat ringside in the Madison Square Garden Bowl in Long Island City, New York, and wrote this about his friend Barney Ross, welterweight champion of the world:

'Ross will fight no more. He's through. He told me in his training camp that he would never take but one beating. "Let a guy give it to me – really give me my bumps – and I'll hang up the gloves," Ross said. Well, a guy gave it to him last night. The guy is named Henry Armstrong and he is 133 pounds of almost inhuman properties. I say "inhuman" because a man is not supposed to behave the way Armstrong did last night. He went at a blistering top speed for 15 rounds – and he didn't even sweat. He threw 10,000 punches, and yet when he stood in his corner, ready to come out for the final round, he wasn't even breathing heavily.

'I know this to be true, because the night was cold and I could see his breath in the frosty air. It was as regular as that of a man who had walked only a block or two at a brisk pace. He gave you the impression of being more a machine than a man. "Cut his veins," I heard one spectator say, "and he'll run lubricating oil not blood."

'Yes, cut him open and I am sure you'd find springs and coils and armatures and bits of metal. In the early rounds Ross hit him plenty. But he never changed expression. A right to the chin and he only snorted a bit louder and moved in a bit faster.

'Punches to the body only seemed to set off a hidden power that drove him onto the attack at a faster pace. He fought every round the same from the first to the 15th. He

CHAPTER SIX

was perpetual motion in purple trunks, a buzz saw with gloves on.'[53]

Joe Williams, sportswriter for Scripps-Howard, was there to see Barney Ross helped down from the ring where Henry Armstrong had used him as a punching bag for 15 rounds. 'There was the usual noisy clamour at the ringside as the blue coats cleared the runways for the fighters and their handlers who were headed for the stuffy, smelly dressing rooms. Some of the reporters had passes for the dressing rooms. They joined in the march with the blue coats, elbowing the curious out of the way. From somewhere out of the squirming line a sweaty bandaged hand reached out and touched me on the arm … "I told you they'd have to carry me out of there, didn't I, fellow?" The words came in short takes through puffed, discoloured lips set in the distorted mask of a man whose right eye had the dimensions and angry hues of an eggplant. It was Ross.

'The dethroned champion had come home on his shield and he was proud of it. If he couldn't win, and he must have realised the futility of his task as early as the sixth round, he wanted to be sure to lose like a champion … "They wanted to stop it in the 12th," continued the gasping, fuzzy voice. "But I wouldn't let 'em. I'd have stayed in there until he killed me." There was a strong, high pride in the words. They reflected the resolute spirit of a man who had lost all save honour and had fought to the last barrier to protect it … But nothing remained of the Ross that once traded savage punches with the McLarnins, the Petrolles, the Canzoneris and the Garcias. Only his magnificent heart ticked in the old manner, as he

---

53 Henry McLemore, *Abilene Reporter News*, Texas, 1 June 1938.

floundered around the ring trying to last while blood trickled gently from his nose and mouth.'[54]

Barney Ross was a skinny Jewish kid running wild in the Chicago ghetto. He ran messages for crime boss Al Capone until Capone gave him 20 dollars and chased him away from the rackets. He fought his way through the Golden Gloves to become a champion and started fighting as a professional on the West Coast in 1929. Beating such men as Tony Canzoneri, Billy Petrolle, Battling Battalino, Ray Miller and Jimmy McLarnin, Barney won lightweight, junior welterweight, and welterweight championships of the world. He was still champion of the welterweights for the first three rounds of the Armstrong fight that May night in 1938.

'As the contest began,' recorded Fleischer, 'Henry came out of his corner with a rush but Barney met him with left jabs that reached into his opponent's face. Then they leaned against each other and the real fighting began. It was nip and tuck, with Ross having the round by a safe margin. Barney also took the second through the medium of an attack that reminded the fans of the Ross who faced Jimmy McLarnin in that same Bowl. Those two sessions were Ross's best. Thereafter he was too busy saving himself to think of tossing punches.

'From the ninth on, gameness alone kept Barney on his feet. The fans were expecting, moment after moment, for Barney to drop in his tracks, but he gave an amazing exhibition of courage and ringcraft as he took an unmerciful beating yet stood on his feet for the duration of the contest.

---

54 Joe Williams, *El Paso Herald Post*, Texas, 1 June 1938.

CHAPTER SIX

When the final gong clanged, Barney knew that he had lost his laurels.

'It took Barney Ross to bring out Hurricane Henry's real status in the fight game. Though Ross was a veteran of ten years standing, it must be conceded that he still rated one of the best. Hence the shellacking he received from a youngster who spotted his considerable weight proves that Armstrong is the first super-fighter the game has had since the days of Joe Gans, George Dixon and Joe Walcott.

'The sight of the defending king gained the sympathy of the crowd and, in the last two rounds, it even gained that of Armstrong, who told me after the battle that he purposely let up until the last minute … Henry's admiration for a game champion was such that he was satisfied to win the decision instead of continuing to strive for a knockout.'[55]

'I was leaving the ring now,' Barney recalled. 'Three men grabbed me and hugged me. It was my sportswriter friends, Joe Williams, Grantland Rice and Henry McLemore. "Why didn't you quit, Barney?" they demanded. "Did you want to get killed?" "Champ's privilege," I mumbled through my cracked lips. "A champ's got the right to choose the way he goes out."

'I kept walking. Funny, I thought. I don't hear any shouting. How come they are not raising the roof for the hero of the night, the new champ? In the whole arena, 35,000 people were sitting in silence. And then I suddenly realised that this unbelievable, fantastic silence was the most wonderful tribute I had ever received. It spoke louder, a thousand times louder

---

55 Nat Fleischer, *Black Dynamite Vol. II*, 1938.

than all the cheers I had heard since the day I put on a pair of boxing gloves and won my first fight.'[56]

Harlem went wild when Henry won the welterweight title. He went up to Harlem later that night. The crowds in the streets were something, but the big celebration was at Small's Paradise, so jammed with people Henry never thought he would get in.

'The manager of the club welcomed him with open arms – but as he walked through the club door, he felt a strange touch on his shoulder. He looked quickly around. No man or woman had touched him. It was something from out of this world – something that rocked him. Out of nowhere, out of the past, out of the little cabin in Columbus, Mississippi, came the words he had heard as a child: "You must go over yonder and do great things … Don't forget that I am your God and maker. *Remember?*"

'He still hears those words; he thinks of them not as dreamwords from out of a dim lost boyhood, but as words actually spoken. They came back to him, word for word, the night he whipped Barney Ross for the welterweight title, in 1937 – a haunting reminder that he was to be God's champion.

'Henry stood spellbound and speechless. The crowd was suddenly silent. They stood staring at him, wondering what he was doing. He turned to his host and asked to be excused for a moment – to go alone into a quiet room, somewhere. Alone in the little room, he thanked God for his victory over Barney Ross, and for all the other victories. And for some explanation of why this had happened, in this nightclub.

---

56 Barney Ross, *No Man Stands Alone*, 1959.

'Somehow, the party seemed pretty flat after that. Henry had things on his mind that the crowd could never understand. He was quiet. He went home early. He kept thinking, "Yep, you're champ. But seems like I'm not champ enough, for God. What's He want me to do anyway?" Always, after that, he would steal away from the crowds at victory celebrations and pray a little.'[57]

---

57 Henry Armstrong, *Gloves, Glory and God*, 1957.

Chapter Seven

'LOU AMBERS is billed as the "Herkimer Hurricane" because he comes from Herkimer, New York state, and because his style of boxing is a cross between that of the late Harry Greb and an indignant Chinese laundry man. Son of a day labourer Tony D'Ambrosio, he is a product of the curious "bootleg" boxing circuit that flourished a few years ago in upstate New York, where promoters were too poor or too dishonest to pay taxes. He learned boxing in a church basement, encouraged by his parish priest, Reverend Gustave Purificato, who still comes to all his fights. Lou Ambers has lost only one of his 46 professional bouts. Merciless in the ring, he dislikes watching fights because their brutality gives him insomnia, makes him sick. His ambition is to organise his nine brothers and sisters, all musically inclined, into a jazz band in which he can play banjo and clarinet.'[58]

'A rugged citizen, that Ambers. He couldn't punch and he certainly didn't have a classic boxing style. But he had the heart of a lion and he never tired. Lou had no road of roses to the title. Once a sparring partner to great-name Tony Canzoneri, he got whipped when they first met for the

---

58 *Time* magazine, 11 March 1935.

championship. He got a second chance. This time he upset his old employer. When they had trained together, serious-minded Lou criticised Tony for his habit of smoking a cigar after workouts; the night the title was won by Ambers, Lou went around to Tony's dressing room and poked his head inside, saying, with a grin, "Didn't I tell you to lay off those cigars?"

'Eddie Mead's moon face pouted in a pose of indignation and his gravely West Side voice sounded off: "Twenty years a guy lives off beef stew – and sometimes lucky to get it. The old wrinkles are still in your belly when all of a sudden you got two good things going for you. Now would you give one up?" The fight game's most chronic horseplayer was not talking about the nags. He was referring to the two championships held by his fighter, Henry Armstrong, featherweight and welterweight, both acquired within the past year ... "We'd go after Al Weill's fighter, Lou Ambers, for the lightweight. What's wrong with having three titles going for you?"'[59]

As featherweight champion, the logical move up would have been for Henry to challenge Ambers for the lightweight title. But Mike Jacobs had a score to settle with Al Weill, the manager of Ambers, who had demanded a purse of $82,000 for Ambers to defend his title against Pedro Montanez in one of the four title bouts on the loss-making Carnival of Champions on 23 September 1937. So Jacobs announced that Armstrong would instead challenge Barney Ross for his welterweight title in the Madison Square Garden Bowl on a May evening in 1938.

---

59 Lester Bromberg, *Boxing's Unforgettable Fights*, 1962.

'By his one-sided victory over Ross,' wrote Fleischer, 'Armstrong gained a niche in the Fistic Hall of Fame as one of the greatest fighters of all time. Until that feat was accomplished, there was considerable doubt about his true status, but Henry answered that by giving Barney the worst beating a champion had received in many moons.'[60]

Now Mike Jacobs was ready to talk to Al Weill. For a purse of $32,000, Lou Ambers would defend his lightweight title against Mike's double champion, who would have to be happy with $25,000. Jacobs picked 26 July at Yankee Stadium for Armstrong and Ambers. Soon he realised it was the wrong season for a ball-park attraction. But on the day of the fight, the promoter happily spotted four drops of rain. He promptly rescheduled the fight indoors. The new date was 17 August 1938, the place Madison Square Garden.[61]

'Postponed from last Wednesday when rain doused a sparse gathering at the Polo Grounds, the Henry Armstrong–Lou Ambers fight in Madison Square Garden Wednesday night may yet be a financial as well as an artistic success. Tickets have been selling at a faster clip than before the bout was transplanted to the Eighth Avenue shelter and indications are that the gate will crowd $100,000. That is at least twice the amount that had been taken when the rain came last week. It indicates something fairly important. That it takes a powerful big fight to necessitate a ball park or an outdoor arena these days.

'Joe Louis, himself, is the only man fighting now who is too big for the Garden and its approximate 20,000 capacity.

---
60 Nat Fleischer, *Black Dynamite Vol. II*, 1938.
61 Lester Bromberg, *Boxing's Unforgettable Fights*, 1962.

CHAPTER SEVEN

The days when Benny Leonard and Lew Tendler could pack the big orchards with their lightweight feud appear to be far away. A ball park is an unnatural setting for a pint-size prize fight anyway. From the back rows of the ringside to the grandstand in any direction is a good, spirited walk, and to a customer squatted far up under the sloping roof a couple of little guys like Armstrong and Ambers could easily be mistaken for spots before the eyes. In the Garden now, they will come to life and the spectator will be able to feel a certain intimacy as his favourite is jolted on the chops. The fight itself still looks like a good one. The pair are certain to set a blistering pace and the dusky Armstrong, ruler of the featherweights and the welterweights, remains a 12-5 favourite to knock the lightweight crown right off Ambers' stubborn head.'[62]

Pompton Lakes, New Jersey – Henry Armstrong resumed boxing today for the first time since he began to taper off last Sunday for his postponed lightweight title bout with Lou Ambers, going through seven rounds against two sparring partners. The Los Angeles challenger appeared rather sluggish in his three rounds against Chalky Wright, and in the first half of his four-round go with Lew Feldman of Brooklyn. He warmed to his task, however, and subjected his sparmate to a battering that opened a cut under Feldman's eye in the last minute.

Summit, New Jersey – lightweight champion Lou Ambers went through his first glove drill since the fight was set back a week on Wednesday. Ambers stepped a lively four rounds

---

62 Gayle Talbot, *Kingsport Times*, Tennessee, 15 August 1938.

with Slugger White, the only sparring partner who returned to camp with him. He showed his usual speed afoot and had the Slugger missing badly. Two rounds of shadow boxing and four more of bag punching completed the drill. The Herkimer Hurricane tipped the beam at 135½ after the workout.'[63]

'Last September any fight fan with 40 cents in his pocket could have seen a spindle-shanked little featherweight named Henry Armstrong strutting his stuff in Manhattan's Madison Square Garden. Last week in that same arena, air-conditioned but nonetheless sweltering under floodlights on one of the hottest nights of the year, 20,000 fight fans gladly paid as much as $16.50 a seat to watch the same spindle-shanked little boxer perform. The first pugilist to hold both the featherweight and the welterweight titles at the same time, ambitious Henry Armstrong last week went back to get Lou Ambers' lightweight crown.

'A 3-1 underdog, champion Ambers in the early rounds did nothing to raise his reputation. Under a tattoo of blinding punches he crumpled to the canvas at the end of the fifth round. Saved by the bell, he came out for the sixth only to be knocked down again. But at the count of eight, just as the Garden spectators and millions of radio listeners were mentally collecting their bets, underdog Ambers clambered to his feet. Somehow Ambers kept on his feet through that round and the seventh – and the eighth and the ninth and the tenth. The crowd went crazy.

'By the 13th when he plainly got the better of Armstrong, who by this time was swinging wildly and forfeiting rounds

---

63 *Galveston Daily News*, Texas, 14 August 1938.

CHAPTER SEVEN

because of low blows, the Garden was yelling for a game fighter. After the 15th round, when Referee Billy Cavanaugh held up Armstrong's arm in victory, Henry Armstrong was so exhausted that he probably could not have pronounced his own title: world's featherweight, lightweight and welterweight champion. In his dressing room, the world's first triple ring champion, who had just earned $20,766 in 45 minutes, cracked no smiles. Reason: he had a split lip.'[64]

'Henry Armstrong lay on the leather-covered rubbing table in a stuffy dressing room. He was moaning and spitting blood as Doctor Alexander Schiff bent low over him to begin the messy job of sewing him up. As the doctor set the last of the painful stitches, Armstrong's legs started to thrash about. Quietly the doctor berated him. "Easy Henry, this is the last one."

'As Dr Schiff put away his needle and thread, Henry whispered something in his ear. Hurriedly a pail was held close to the fighter's face and he vomited into it. There was a general exclamation at the amount of blood which cascaded into the pail.'[65]

'Throwing uppercuts inside, Ambers began cutting up Armstrong. The challenger was bleeding from a deep cut inside his mouth. His eyes were cut and his face was flecked with blood. At the end of the tenth round, Billy Cavanaugh, the referee, came to Armstrong's corner. The colloquy has gone down in ring history.

'Cavanaugh: "I'm going to stop it, Henry."

---

64 *Time* magazine, 29 August 1938.
65 Edward Brennan, *New York Journal – American – Boxing Illustrated,* October 1961.

'Armstrong: "Don't stop it, Mr. Cavanaugh. I'm winning on points. I've had him down twice."

'Cavanaugh: "The ring is full of blood. It's your blood."

'Armstrong: "Then I'll stop bleeding. I want this title."

'Cavanaugh: "One more drop of blood on the canvas I'll stop it."

'When the referee left the corner, Armstrong told Mead, "Don't put my mouthpiece in. I got to swallow this blood. If it shows, he'll stop it."'[66]

'Who is going to stop Henry Armstrong?' Nat Fleischer was asking in his *Ring* magazine. 'There is in this scrapper Armstrong, who comes in under 135 pounds, the protein quality of George Dixon. There is in this Homicidal Hank the disdain for giving away weight which was Joe Walcott's. There is in this new sensation, the cleverness and skill which made the glory of Joe Gans. Who is there to quell this deadly combination?

'First, Armstrong whipped Petey Sarron for the featherweight title. Then Henry astonished everybody by giving Barney Ross an unmerciful whaling and taking the welter championship from him. Finally, Armstrong took Ambers into camp, thus becoming the first fighter to gain three world titles. Ring history was written brilliantly when Armstrong carried off his third world championship within a space of ten months by gaining a 15-round decision over Ambers.

'Armstrong was forced to battle as never before. He won despite the handicap of a deep cut in his mouth and the loss

---

66 Barney Nagler, *Ring magazine*, August 1981.

CHAPTER SEVEN

of three rounds for being over-anxious and letting several punches land below the belt.'[67]

'It had been a breathlessly paced battle, leaving spectators excitement-limp. But the press rows were reasonably sure Henry had moved up to his epic third title, in spite of the rounds lost on fouls. As Jim Dawson of the *New York Times* was to write, "Armstrong did everything but knock out the defending champion." Yet the public refused to believe Henry had won. Even as he left the ring, the crowd refused to honour him with cheers … This was irony in its cruellest form, the achievement of a third title at the same time, unparalleled in the ring, had brought Henry Armstrong only a crown of thorns.'[68]

'Now the fighters were stood in their corners, waiting for ring announcer Harry Balogh, "Ladies and gentlemen … Referee Cavanaugh scores seven rounds for Armstrong, six for Ambers, two even. Judge George LeCron scores eight rounds for Armstrong, seven for Ambers. Judge Marty Monroe scores it eight rounds for Ambers, seven for Armstrong. By a majority vote, ladies and gentlemen … It gives me great pleasure indeed, the greatest pleasure of my entire career in pugilism, to have this distinct honour in rendering such a unique decision. One, I venture to say, that will never be duplicated. For the first time in boxing history we have before us tonight the only man in fistiana to win and hold three world championships *at the same time, simultaneously*. I give you the new *lightweight* champion of the world, Henry Armstrong!"

---

67 Nat Fleischer, *Ring magazine*, October 1938.
68 Lester Bromberg, *Boxing's Unforgettable Fights*, 1962.

75

'He called Henry to the centre of the ring and held his right hand high in symbol of the victory. A roar broke from the crowd – and to Henry's amazement, it was a chorus not only of cheers for the new champion, but a chorus of boos, hoots and catcalls. That was hard to take. It hurt Henry more than any blow he had stopped in the ring that night, more than his cut eye and bleeding lip. He had fought his heart out to win that fight – to give the fans what they came to see. Now he had won the decision, the triple crown – and they booed!'[69]

'Lou Ambers, who lost his lightweight crown to Henry Armstrong in Madison Square Garden Wednesday night, was welcomed home yesterday by his neighbours, who shouted lustily: "He's still our champion!" Several thousand persons greeted the fighter when he arrived at Utica last night. He was lifted to the shoulders of several admirers, carried outside the station and placed on top of an automobile for a speech.

'"I tried hard," he said. "I have another match with Armstrong when his lips heal. Next time I'll bring the title back with me. It was the toughest fight I ever had, but I'm confident I can win when we meet again." Ambers was accompanied by the Reverend Gustave Purificator, in whose church basement he learned to fight.'[70]

'A repetition of the 15-round thriller Henry Armstrong and Lou Ambers unveiled in Madison Square Garden was promised New Yorkers today, but they're going to have to wait some time to see it. Both managers, Al Weill and Eddie Mead, agreed to do an encore for Mike Jacobs as soon as Armstrong recovers from the cutting up Ambers gave him.

---

69 Henry Armstrong, *Gloves, Glory and God*, 1957.
70 *Ogdenburg Advance News*, New York, 21 August 1938.

CHAPTER SEVEN

'The holder of the featherweight, lightweight and welterweight titles spent today crating up his collection for shipment to California. Armstrong and Mead go west tomorrow. Later Henry will take a trip to Honolulu with his wife. Mead made it plain Armstrong has no intention of surrendering the featherweight title he won from Petey Sarron last October.

"'We've promised Ed Bang to defend that title on the Christmas Fund show he runs each year for the *Cleveland News*," he said. "Henry's opponent will be Jackie Wilson, Ginger Foran, Mike Belloise or Leo Rodak."

'Ambers, who came out of the hectic battle in much better physical trim than his conqueror, took it easy around town today. He leaves tomorrow on a fishing trip and then will go to Quebec for a visit. "The first thing Lou said to me when he woke up this morning was when to make another Armstrong match for him," said Al Weill. "Mead is willing and we'll fight as soon as his boy is in shape. Ambers will be ready after a month's rest."

'Ambers collected $33,860 for his beating. Armstrong's end was $20,766. Revised figures show the gross gate was $107,280 and the total attendance was 19,216.'[71]

United Press sportswriter Jack Cuddy, a few days after the fight, was already looking to the return fight, and he could only see Ambers regaining his title, writing, 'When Lou Ambers tangles with Henry Armstrong the next time, he'll "moider" him.' Jack goes on to explain: 'I believe the decision was right. I say this although Ambers is my warmest friend

---
71 *Uniontown Morning Herald*, Pennsylvania, 19 August 1938.

among active fighters. I go further by stating that Ambers was lucky to last the full 15 rounds. Because I believe he fought the wrong kind of fight to beat Armstrong.

'Ambers gambled with the "suicide" plan of battle ... Manager Al Weill, trainer Charlie Goldman and Whitey Bimstein, assistant trainer, sold Ambers on the "suicide" plan – on the theory of keeping close to Armstrong and matching punches with him – instead of evading him with Ambers's usual dancing, jumping-jack style. The "suicide" plan worked out all right, in the final analysis. Except for the fact that Ambers lost his title. The "suicide" plan enabled Ambers to make the best showing of his career. Yet it wasn't a winning showing ... I did not argue with Lou because I knew that Lou knew I was right. Lou would have fought his own fight, if he hadn't received orders. And he would have won.'[72]

---

72 Jack Cuddy, *Phoenix Arizona Republic*, 20 August 1938.

Chapter Eight

'HE'S A great little fighter, this Henry Armstrong from Los Angeles.' This was James P Dawson in the *New York Times*, 1 June, expressing his admiration for the man who had just beaten Barney Ross. 'He beat a great fighter in true fighting style to become the first ring warrior in pugilism's long history ever to hold the world featherweight title and the world welterweight crown at the same time … he demonstrated at the opening gong that his style, his strength, his inexhaustible supply of stamina, perseverance, his grim determination, in short, his singular fighting stock in trade, were too much for Ross.'

Two and a half months later, 17 August 1938, Dawson was at ringside to write, 'Henry Armstrong did it last night! The doughty little Californian became the first fighter in all of ring history to hold three titles at the same time when he hammered his way to the decision over stout-hearted, courageous Lou Ambers in 15 rounds.

'It was fast, furious and savage fighting as has ever been seen here before a gathering of 20,000 frenzied fans in Madison Square Garden.

'Armstrong annexed the world lightweight title when he battered his way to a divided, disputed decision over

Ambers after doing everything but knock out the defending champion.'[73]

In his office at *Ring* magazine, situated in Madison Square Garden, editor Nat Fleischer called Ted Carroll to his desk. He had an idea for a feature in his next issue. Compare the fighters of days gone by to this phenomenal fighter Henry Armstrong. 'There are still a few of the old guys hanging around town, Ted; Jacobs Beach, Stillman's Gym,' said Nat. 'Go and talk to them.'

'As Henry Armstrong sweeps across the country leaving a trail of shattered victims in his wake,' Ted Carroll would write in the February 1938 issue of *Ring* magazine, 'the American sporting public is gradually realising that the Human Hurricane must be one of the outstanding pugilists of the century. His remarkable record of 24 knockouts in his last 25 engagements against any and all comers is by all odds the most phenomenal of the past decade. Just how do the savants of sockology rate the modern Terry McGovern with his distinguished predecessors?

'Professor Billy McCarney, whose life has been spent amidst the scent of resin and the thud of leather-encased fists, leads off with the eye-popping announcement that the immortal Terry McGovern might not have done so well with his present-day prototype for the simple reason that the Brooklyn Wonder was a lot easier to hit, while Armstrong possesses an uncanny knack of slipping blows with head and shoulders. "McGovern was a head-on fighter." McCarney believes that Armstrong would have won, because McGovern might have fought himself out in

---

73 James P Dawson, *New York Times*, 18 August 1938.

a terrific early-round drive, and had nothing left if Armstrong had withstood his opening blasts.

'Like a good many others, Uncle Will inclines to the belief that shifty will-o'-the wisp boxers would have proven tough problems for Hammerin' Henry. "Abe Attell, who also went in for conceding plenty of weight, and a great boxer with a co-ordinated attack and defence, would have given Armstrong plenty of trouble," is McCarney's opinion. "The same goes for Jem Driscoll, who was even smarter than Abe, but not as good a puncher."'

A.D. Phillips, who recently celebrated his 86th birthday, is not all for Henry. 'I saw Jack McAuliffe in many of his ring battles. I watched George Dixon come up from a novice into one of the world's greatest bantams and featherweights. I attended most of Terry McGovern's battles when the Brooklyn Terror was at his best. In fact I've seen 'em all – good, bad and just ordinary fighters in every division over more than half a century, and I dare say that Henry Armstrong compares favourably with the best.'

Clarence Gillespie, one of the editors of the old *Police Gazette*, said: 'I think McGovern would have beaten Henry because he was not only a harder puncher but a quicker one and the fellows he hit stayed down after he struck them. My nomination as the toughest possible opponent for Armstrong would have been Ad Wolgast. Ad fought the same kind of a fight and he was a great left hooker.'

At Stillman's Gym, James J Johnston took one eye off his pet heavyweight Bob Pastor to say, 'Why that McGovern knocked out lightweight champs! His opposition was ten times tougher, too. I pick McGovern for my dough. He would have put Armstrong away. Driscoll? Why, Henry wouldn't have laid a glove on Jem. Nor on Abe Attell. Little George Dixon would have blinded him.'

But if the great names of the past fared well with Johnston, it was an entirely different story when Tony Kelly broached his ideas on the matter. 'I like Johnny Dundee, one of the swellest little fellows who ever hit this business, but he couldn't have hurt Armstrong, who, in my opinion, would have chased Johnny all over the ring. You see, this Armstrong takes a terrific punch and sets the most killing pace I have ever seen in the ring,' continued Kelly, a veteran of 40 years of fight following. 'As for Terry McGovern, he would have had to flatten Henry right away to win. That would have been his only chance. I think Armstrong would have taken the Englishmen, Driscoll and Moran, easy. They couldn't break an egg.'

In good voice, roaring Harry Lenny, a good lightweight himself in his day, back at the turn of the century. 'Outside of McGovern, I don't think any of them guys would have beaten Armstrong. McGovern was a very powerful fellow who hurt you with every punch. He didn't weave, but he was a great body puncher. I would favour him over Armstrong.'

Dumb Dan Morgan, the man of a few million words, who steered Jack Britton and Battling Levinsky, among others, to the top, had a few words to say on the subject. 'McGovern was a mass of muscle, much stronger and a better puncher, he would have beaten Armstrong,' said Dan. 'Terry was also just as fast. But Henry would have beaten Owen Moran, and I think he would have caught Driscoll. I think Armstrong would have driven the Englishman before him like St. Paddy drove the snakes out of Ireland.'

CHAPTER EIGHT

When he got back to the office and checked his notes, Ted Carroll found he had nine votes to two in favour of Hurricane Henry Armstrong, boxing's first triple world champion![74]

'Now Henry was on top, and he enjoyed every minute of it. The king of three divisions got the homage he had struggled for, all those years. The adulation was something. "Atta boy, Henry!" It was shouted at him in the streets, whispered by men he had never seen before. Slaps on the back, hero worship from the fans and even from those who knew little or nothing about boxing. Cheers, cheers, cheers! But Henry soon discovered that it was also a case of fight, fight, fight. When you're a champ you have to keep going to stay on top. You have only a few years in which to make your money, and after that you're just another has-been. So he fought. Fought all comers.'[75]

Before he could carry on fighting, however, he had some healing to do. He remembered the words of Dr Alexander Schiff, his personal physician who was also a member of the medical board of the New York State Athletic Commission. In his last fight, Henry had beaten lightweight champion Lou Ambers to complete his triple title collection, the only fighter in boxing history to accomplish this magnificent performance. But it came at a price.

'When Dr Schiff examined Henry after the fight,' recorded noted boxing writer Edward Brennan of the *New York Journal-American*, 'he was moaning and spitting blood. By the time Schiff had finished, there were 37 stitches inside Henry's mouth, three above his left eye and two over his right

---
74 Ted Carroll, *Ring* magazine, February 1938.
75 Henry Armstrong, *Gloves, Glory and God*, 1957.

eye ... The bell ending the 15th round did not end the fight. They kept throwing punches as the timekeeper yanked the cord again and again. The din from the crowd had not been equalled since the Roman Circus ... droplets of blood were recorded six rows back and saved for souvenirs.'[76]

'Dr Alexander Schiff had told Eddie Mead after the Ambers fight: "It would require two and maybe three months for the lip to mend properly and Armstrong will need an additional month to get into condition. Henry has one of the worst cuts in his mouth I've seen in 30 years tending to fighters' wounds."'[77]

While Henry rested and recovered from his traumatic evening with Lou Ambers, Eddie played the horses with his share of the fight purse, plus Henry's share.

'Eddie Mead was a very good manager and I have no complaints,' Henry said one day on a visit to the offices of *Ring* magazine. 'I feel he meant well, but he just wasn't made to handle the kind of money we were getting. I'd been tipped off that property in the San Bernardino Valley was a good thing and I went to Eddie about buying some. "Don't go for that, Henry," he yelled, "I let that Lynch [Eddie's old fighter Joe Lynch] buy himself a 'waterhole' and he went busted. Real estate is too risky, stay away from it. Now excuse me, I'll see you later, I'm going to the racetrack."'[78]

A few days after the Ambers fight, Eddie Mead was telling reporters, 'Henry won't fight until next winter. When he does it probably will be with Ceferino Garcia, the coast

---

76 Edward Brennan, *Boxing Illustrated*, October 1961.
77 *Uniontown Morning Herald*, Pennsylvania, 19 August 1938.
78 Ted Carroll, *Ring* magazine, May 1959.

welterweight, and Henry will put his 147-pound title on the line. Then if Ambers still wants a match, we'll give it to him.'[79]

The Garcia fight was set for Madison Square Garden on Wednesday, 2 November 1938, but with a few days to go, Eddie Mead saw that his boy wasn't ready and pulled him out claiming a wrist injury. Garcia and his manager were furious but they could only go along with it. They wanted the title! The scarred Filipino from Los Angeles had won 12 fights in a row, 11 of them by knockout.

'Sport's oldest cliché, the one about the good little man not being able to lick the good big man, has been dusted off to front for the argument between Armstrong and Garcia on 25 November. Garcia is a good big man for a welterweight. He was big enough and strong enough to give middleweight Glen Lee the worst beating he ever had and he will go into the ring for the 15-round bout around 147 pounds. Armstrong, who is as good a little man as you can find, has fought welterweights but no Garcias. When the fight was made, Garcia was a heavy favourite over the little man. The odds were down to 6-5 and take your choice.'[80]

On the day, Henry weighed in at 134 pounds against 147 for Garcia, a big 13 pounds pull for the Filipino, and he meant to wear Henry down. There was a somewhat disappointing crowd in the Garden, 15,725, paying a gate of $79,931, but they saw a good fight.

Henry was wearing his new dressing gown which sported a skull and crossbones on the back, but Garcia didn't bother to go around him to take a look. He was probably thinking

---
79 Drew Middleton, *Hutchinson News*, Kansas, 19 August 1938.
80 *Brownsville Herald*, Texas, 1 November 1938.

I'll see it when they are leading him out of the ring back to his dressing room, a loser!

'Armstrong was able to swarm all over Garcia for the majority of the bout,' reported the *New York Times*, 'not giving Garcia time to get set on a punch. Garcia was able to keep Armstrong at bay to some extent in the first, third, fourth and sixth rounds. Garcia hurt Armstrong with an overhand right, his vaunted bolo punch, followed by several more right hands. Garcia appeared to be behind in the last couple of rounds, and did catch Armstrong with another right hand in the 15th that stunned him. Garcia finished the bout with cuts over both eyes, a cut on his left cheek, and badly swollen hands that he had hurt in the third and sixth rounds. Armstrong's left eye was completely swollen shut in the 15th round.

'At the final bell, he took the unanimous decision: referee Arthur Donovan 9 to 6 – Judge Billy 'Kid' McPartland 9 to 6 – Judge George LeCron 8 to 7.'[81]

'Garcia was the hardest puncher I ever fought,' recalled Henry. 'He had that bolo punch, a sort of wild sweeping hook or uppercut. His bolo was a very heavy punch, it hurt you all over. He hit me with the hardest shot I ever took. I had a special mouthpiece made to protect that old lip scar. But my seconds were nervous and they forgot to shove it in before the 11th round started. They called to me and when I turned my head to see what they were yelling about, Garcia hit me with a right-hand bolo to the chin that lifted me three feet off the canvas. To this day I say that I was unconscious when I fell. But I landed on my hands, causing my neck to snap, partially

---

81 *New York Times*, 26 November 1938.

CHAPTER EIGHT

reviving me. I looked up and saw *four* Garcias. I jumped right up, and in so doing my head slammed against his chin. That shook him up. I grabbed him, twisted him, punched him hard and kept him busy until I recovered. Had Ceferino known how badly I was hurt, he could have knocked me out easily.'[82]

'There are two fighting essentials which do not show in the box score,' wrote columnist Joe Williams. 'One is heart, the other brain. The suspicion existed that Ceferino Garcia was deficient in both. Last night he proved this to be so. Fighting against a pygmy of a man and with every material advantage on his side, weight, reach and punch, he was beaten. Henry Armstrong, a legitimate lightweight whose industry, ambition and fearlessness have carried him into heavier fields, was clearly the superior in the 15-round test. This was supposed to be a test between a good big man and a good little man, and it was up to the point where the intangibles became important. When this point was reached it was no contest. Practically from the beginning Armstrong made the heavier Garcia fight his kind of fight. At least he was always trying to make him do this.

'I have never thought Armstrong a great fighter, but I'm beginning to fear I underrated him. The fellow always keeps winning. He beats the little fellows, he beats the fellows his own size and when they throw him in there with the big fellows he takes care of them, too. There isn't much else you can ask of him, is there?'[83]

---

82 John Jarrett, *Dynamite Gloves*, 2001.
83 Joe Williams, *Syracuse Herald*, 26 November 1938.

Chapter Nine

TOWARDS THE end of 1938, Henry knew he could no longer make the featherweight limit of 126 pounds – his fights now were with lightweights and welterweights. Manager Eddie Mead knew that Henry's days as featherweight champion of the world were in the past, so, after talking it over with Henry, Eddie informed the New York Commission on 12 September 1938.

Boxing's great triple champion was now just a double champion, lightweight and welterweight. The Commission moved quickly, announcing that they would recognise the winner of a bout between Joey Archibald of Providence, Rhode Island and the pride of New York's Bronx, Mike Belloise.

New York, 17 October 1938 – For the Associated Press Drew Middleton recorded: 'Stocky Joey Archibald pummelled Mike Belloise, dapper idol of New York's neighbourhood fight clubs, into submission and won the featherweight championship of the world as far as New York state is concerned at the St Nicholas Arena tonight. The 6,000 fans who jammed the ancient arena saw one of the best fights between little men New York has had in years. Archibald, less

CHAPTER NINE

polished than Belloise, took command in the second, held it until the seventh, lost it to Belloise's superior boxing ability for three rounds, and then surged back in the last two to gain the unanimous decision of the judges.

'Tired and bloody, the new champion brought the crowd shrieking to its feet in the last two. He bullied Belloise across the ring, hitting him with short vicious chops to the body. Four times in the two rounds the pair tumbled through the ropes. It was Archibald, bleeding from a cut in his forehead and with his left eye almost closed, who was coming on at the finish. Archibald now is featherweight champion as far as the New York State Athletic Commission goes. The National Boxing Association wants him to fight the winner of the Leo Rodak–Freddie Miller bout before it considers him champion.'[84]

'Former champion Henry Armstrong arrived yesterday to preside over the "coronation" of Joey Archibald with a fake crown for the benefit of the papers. It was three weeks before Henry's big fight with Garcia in the Garden and Eddie Mead was worried, apparently more uneasy about the coming battle than any of the past, saying he feared Garcia more than Lou Ambers, the Herkimer boy who had Armstrong groggy before relinquishing his lightweight crown in 15 rounds last summer. "This Garcia can knock you dead with one punch while Ambers is a cream-puff puncher.

"All Ambers does is cut a man up. It took stitches to close Henry's lower lip after that fight, but it has healed completely now. His lower teeth have been fixed and he will be wearing

---

84 Drew Middleton, *Escanaba Daily Press*, Michigan, 18 October 1938.

a new mouthpiece to prevent anything like that happening again." Happily, Mead's fear about the Garcia fight proved groundless. After the fight he announced that Armstrong was not expected to risk either his welter or lightweight titles again before late February or early March. He plans to engage in non-title bouts at Cleveland on 6 December and in Los Angeles early in January. Promoter Mike Jacobs hopes to stage a return Armstrong–Ambers fight for the lightweight title before the indoor season closes here.'[85]

'There was a good crowd of 12,724 in the Cleveland Arena to see an all-star card for the 13th Annual Christmas boxing charity show, staged by the *Cleveland News*. Henry Armstrong began today a holiday vacation from ring warfare after defending the welter title twice in two weeks, beating veteran Ceferino Garcia and last night scored a technical knockout over fellow Californian Al Manfredo in the third round of the scheduled 15-round go. Armstrong declared he was not taking Manfredo lightly, saying "Manfredo is a better boxer than Garcia."

'The 26-year-old challenger brought a 67-19-8 record with 24 knockouts to the ring, and was confident throughout his training here, "I've seen Armstrong fight and I think I know how to beat him," he said. He was wrong. Manfredo was another victim of the tireless, rushing attack of the Los Angeles man. Armstrong, carrying the fighting all the way, wore Manfredo down early in the second round and Al spent his last three minutes in the ring vainly attempting to ward off the champion's rapid-fire punches. Referee Tony LaBranch

---

85 *Syracuse Herald*, 19 October 1938.

CHAPTER NINE

stopped the bout at 1.45 of the round when Manfredo was helpless, his arms dangling at his side.

'A keen observer of Armstrong's performance was former lightweight champion Lou Ambers, who scored a sixth-round knockout over Frankie Wallace, before taking his seat at ringside. He would be matched with Armstrong in a return title bout in the coming months.'[86]

Eddie Mead didn't like winters, especially winters in New York City. Cold and wet! Which is why he was in Los Angeles on 10 January 1939 to put his double champ Henry Armstrong in the ring at the Olympic Auditorium for a ten-rounds go with Baby Arizmendi, the Tampico Kid, a main event that drew more than 10,000 fans in out of the sunshine. The bout was billed as a welterweight title match. Armstrong weighed 134½, Arizmendi 136, just over the lightweight limit.

'Duplicating their last two clashes, it was a gruelling battle for ten rounds that kept the fans in an uproar, with both fighters standing toe to toe, shoulder to shoulder like two tiny bulls.

'The Tampico Kid left the ring a beaten man, one side of his face covered with blood and cheers from his countrymen ringing in his ears, but he could point to a record unequalled by anyone else in the fight game. He had just finished his 52nd round opposite Henry Armstrong with never a knockdown scored against him, nor had he been seriously hurt. In the final counting it was Armstrong's relentless and more powerful punches that brought him referee George Blake's decision. Booed several times for his jerky shoulder movements in the

---

86 Rex Hess, *Lincoln Star*, Nebraska, 6 December 1938.

clinches and his bobbing head, Armstrong lost at least one round for accidentally butting.'[87]

Six months before the fight, the tough Mexican had thrilled the Olympic fans with a ten-round draw with Lou Ambers. Referee Jack Kennedy, apparently, had developed a habit, after eight rounds of a contest, of announcing his scorecard up to that point in the bout, which was 4-3-1 in favour of Ambers. This prompted Arizmendi to finish the last two rounds like a train, thus earning a share of Kennedy's scoring of a draw. As he came out of the ring, Baby wiped the blood from his left eye and said to reporters, 'Henry Armstrong is stronger than Lou and throws too many punches. Ambers is easy to hit. I staggered him, and while I took my best shots at Henry, I couldn't faze him.' Discussing the upcoming Ambers–Armstrong bout, Arizmendi predicted an Armstrong kayo.

Early in March, Eddie was still yearning for the sunshine and booked Henry for a title fight in Havana with Bobby Pacho. The battle-scarred Californian of Mexican descent weighed in on the welterweight limit of 147 pounds, giving him a pull of 13 pounds over the champion, who was making his first fight outside the United States. It was also the first world-title bout in the Cuban capital since Jess Willard knocked out Jack Johnson in 1915. There was a good crowd of more than 10,000 there to see the fight which was refereed by former heavyweight champion Jim Braddock.

'The end came after one minute and ten seconds of the fourth round. Pacho had given the champion a stiff battle

---

87 Robert Meyers, *Ironwood Daily Globe*, Michigan, 11 January 1939.

CHAPTER NINE

in the second and third rounds after having been on the floor twice in the first. He failed to take a count in either instance. The fourth round started fast, with Pacho leaning noggin to noggin with the champion and swapping blows. But Armstrong's stiff clips to the jaw out of his crouching stance weakened Pacho and drove him against the ropes. There his defence fell and Armstrong, grunting with every swing, rocked him with rapid-fire lefts and rights. Finally Pacho started slowly to sag to the canvas with Hammering Hank. Referee Braddock stepped in to part them but Pacho was unable to rise and Braddock dragged him to his corner, where Pacho fell off his stool and had to be assisted from the ring.'[88]

Henry was going home to St Louis for the first time in two years so there was a big family get-together, and a big crowd to greet him at the stadium. In his last fight there, Henry had lost on a foul to Tony Chavez. Now he was meeting Brooklyn's Lew Feldman, a fifth-round victim, just before he started his triple title bid in May 1938.

'Feldman bragged that he had solved his opponent's style, but his number was up from the time Armstrong sailed into him at the opening bell. A right caught Lew on the jaw and he was on the floor for a nine count before the bout was a minute old. Henry never let up as Feldman tried to defend himself against a barrage of lefts and rights. Feldman had said that the way to beat Armstrong was "to keep moving so he won't get a chance to get set," but the only way he ever moved was backward and Henry was on top of him all the time.

---

88 Associated Press, *Portsmouth Times*, Ohio, 5 March 1939.

'When Lew got up from the first knockdown, Henry drove him into a neutral corner. He pounded him unmercifully on the ropes. Feldman grasped the ropes and tried to hold on for a few more seconds and Henry stepped back. Then as Lew left the protection of the ropes, Armstrong charged in again and never stopped throwing punches until a stiff right on the button dropped the Brooklyn boy for the full count. The first round had gone only two minutes and 12 seconds.'[89]

Davey Day travelled from Chicago to New York with two things on his mind. He planned to take the welterweight title from Henry Armstrong and in so doing avenge his good friend and stablemate Barney Ross. Sportswriter Harry Ferguson wasn't impressed as he eased into his press seat at ringside in Madison Square Garden. In his report for United Press, Harry wrote: 'Davey doesn't look like a fighter because he is skinny and stoop shouldered, yet it was Davey's crowd. There were 11,028 people in the house and it seemed all of them were there for Davey. They booed Armstrong when he hit low and they cheered every blow Day struck.

'Armstrong ran into a tartar last night and although he won on a technical knockout in the 12th round, he got some souvenirs from Davey he is likely to carry for a couple of months. He got a gash over his left eye that required four stitches to close and, more important, he injured his left hand in the fifth round and it may turn out to be a fracture. If so, Armstrong will have to pass up a projected bout with Ernie Roderick in London, a fight he figured would earn him $40,000.

---

89 Paul Dix, *Dunkirk Evening Observer*, New York, 17 March 1939.

CHAPTER NINE

'Henry threw 'em from all points of the compass last night and some of 'em were so far south of the belt line that he lost two rounds because of foul blows. Except for those two rounds, he led all the way, finally dropping Day with a right to the ribs that moved only about 14 inches. Davey went to his knees on the canvas, his head rolled crazily and referee Billy Cavanaugh looked up into Armstrong's blood-smeared face and said, "That's all." It happened after two minutes and 49 seconds of the 12th round and it marked the sixth time in a little more than four months that Henry had successfully defended his welterweight championship.

'This is the first time Davey has been stopped. He can really take it, and his only mistake last night was that he thought flesh and blood had a chance against a buzzsaw. And when he comes all the way back to consciousness today (he still was mumbling like a stumblebum a half hour after the fight was over) his biggest regret will be that he failed to avenge his stablemate and friend, Barney Ross.'[90]

'Homicide Hank suffered many an anxious moment in that contest and he was a mighty pleased gladiator when Day finally collapsed in the 12th round. But what troubled Henry more, perhaps, than Day's amazing strong stand, even more than the cut he suffered over his left eye in the eighth round, was the attitude of the audience, which clamoured for Hank's disqualification every time Armstrong landed a body blow. The fans kept up a continuous booing because the referee, Billy Cavanaugh, refused to warn Henry or penalise him for his alleged infractions of the rules.

---

90 Harry Ferguson, *Ogden Standard Examiner*, Utah, 1 April 1939.

'We use the word alleged advisedly. For the fans were, in the opinion of this writer, grossly unfair. Of the many of hundreds of punches which Armstrong tossed at Day, this observer (sitting in the second row of the working press) saw only two which landed just below the belt line. And on each of these occasions, Referee Cavanaugh took the round away from Armstrong. But Cavanaugh correctly refused to be stampeded by the two-bit gamblers who booed every time Armstrong drove a wallop to the midsection. Cavanaugh did an expert job all round and is especially to be praised for the manner in which he ignored the howling galleryites and called his shots as he saw them.

'Still, it is absurd to worry about Henry Armstrong. He has a way of taking care of himself quite adequately. And he may turn in a surprise in England by vanquishing Roderick just as he has done to the last 45 opponents to face him. He is a most resourceful young man as he proved in brilliant fashion against Day.'[91]

---

91 Harry Markson, *Ring* magazine, June 1939.

Armstrong defending his title against Ernie Roderick, 1939

Armstrong hitting the bag

Receiving trophy after defeating Roderick in London

Happy pose, 1938

The winning pose, 1938

With Muhammad Ali

In the gym

'On the Ropes' Vintage Boxing Cards from the Jefferson R. Burdidyck Collection at the Metropolitan Museum of Art, NYC

Armstrong (centre, front row) with former champions at Harringey finale, London.

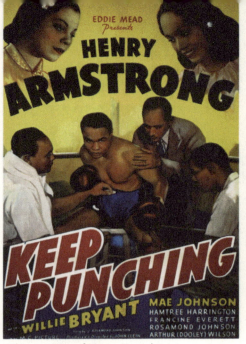
Film poster of Keep Punching

Action shot from Armstrong's fight with Lou Ambers, where he won the lightweight title in 1938

London 1966

In London to be honoured by the Anglo American Sporting Club, January 1966

1937

Lou Ambers regains lightweight title from Armstrong, 1939

Posing on the ropes with Billy Conn and Jean Parker on the set of the film The Pittsburgh Kid, 1941

Al Jolson when he bought Armstrong's contract for manager Eddie Mead

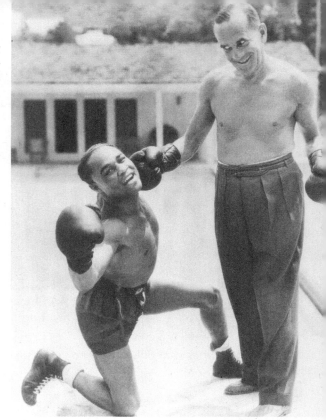

With Mae Johnson and Francine Everett in the film Keep Punching

Chapter Ten

EDDIE MEAD was a happy fella! He was taking his double champ abroad, to London no less, to fight the British welterweight champion Ernie Roderick. 'They had been on a "personal appearance" tour, with Joe Louis as an added attraction before the Arizmendi fight, and Eddie liked the thrill of going places and seeing things. His enthusiasm was contagious; he didn't have much trouble selling Henry on the idea of a trip to England.'[92]

It was revealed after the contest with Davey Day that Armstrong had suffered a fractured bone in his left hand. He still wore the hand in a cast when he boarded the *Queen Mary* for his trip to England. With him went his wife and his four-year-old daughter, Lanetta; his trainer Harry Armstrong, and the latter's wife; Mr and Mrs Eddie Mead; Chalky Wright, a featherweight from California; and Eddie Walker.

'If Armstrong should retain his crown, it will be a demonstration by him that he has been unjustly dealt with on this side of the Big Pond, where the fight fans, urged on by the small fry gamblers, have hooted, booed and hissed him every time he has entered the ring in New York. They

---

92 Henry Armstrong, *Gloves, Glory and God*, 1957.

apparently don't appreciate a good fighter. Instead of making a hero out of the three-time champion, they try to belittle him. Let's see what our English brethren, who know a good fighter when they see one, will have to say about Homicide Hank.'[93]

Ten days before the fight, Drew Middleton was writing from London, 'The British boxing public has gone completely nuts over Henry Armstrong. Four weeks after landing to start work for his welterweight title defence against Ernie Roderick on 25 May, Henry is the talk of the pubs and the pride of the publicists. They didn't know what to make of him at first but they like him fine now. The sportswriters who journeyed down to meet the *Queen Mary* expected a cross between the late Bert Williams and Battling Siki.

'What they found of course was a mild-mannered little guy travelling with his wife and daughter. He did not brag. He used good English. His clothes were seemly. His manners perfect. He did everything right. He spoke proudly of his race. He knocked them off their feet by showing them samples of the poetry he had written. "Tell me," asked a bedazzled journalist, "is this really Armstrong?" But he and his fellow word painters went away enchanted. The next day there were pictures of the sad-eyed little Negro and lengthy stories in every London paper. But what really got them was Henry's intelligence and courtesy. "Armstrong is the finest character I have ever met in boxing," wrote one critic. "He is a credit to his race and to his country."'[94]

'The lords of British boxing gave him a dinner,' wrote J.C. Derks. 'There was Henry in a tuxedo, talking about the long

---

93 Harry Markson, *Ring* magazine, June 1939.
94 Drew Middleton, *Lincoln Star,* Nebraska, 15 May 1929.

way up, about his fights, about the technique and history of boxing. When he left, the titled gentlemen, whose ancestors fought at Agincourt, stood up and elected "Henry Armstrong of St Louis, lightweight and welterweight champion of the world, and honourable member of the National Sporting Club." Thereby they broke an old rule forbidding the election of Negroes to England's swankiest boxing body.

'When his training periods are over, Henry talks about his poetry, and submits it to fellow writers, and he discusses the book he is writing with his fellow craftsmen. All of this is so contrary to preconceived notions of what a prize-fighter is generally supposed to be that England is virtually at Henry Armstrong's feet.'[95]

The man responsible for Henry Armstrong travelling to England was the famous Liverpool Stadium promoter Johnny Best, who had just recently been appointed matchmaker for the Harringay Arena in London. Johnny figured a world title scrap was just the thing to get off to a swinging start. Liverpool's Ernie Roderick had just won the British welter championship with a seven-round knockout over Jake Kilrain before 12,000 cheering fans at Anfield football ground. Ernie would jump at a world-title shot.

Johnny Best knew all about Ernie Roderick for he had given the lad his start. Roderick was a fine boxer with a kayo punch in his gloves and nine years' professional experience behind him. Ernie was engaged to Edna Tarleton, sister of his manager and tutor, Merseyside legend Nel Tarleton. Ernie promised Edna the world title and he meant to keep his

---

95 J.C. Derks, *Salt Lake Tribune*, Utah, 25 May 1939.

promise. A natural welterweight, he would have a 12 pounds advantage over the world champion as well as the upper hand in height and reach.

Armstrong was impressing everyone who watched his workouts at Clacton-by-the-Sea. He had weighed 142 pounds when he started training but his weight was coming down to 135 a few days before the fight. 'I naturally hope I will win,' he told visitors, 'but the fight game is too full of chances to make a definite prediction. Accidents can happen. I'll fight my usual way and try for a knockout.' Manager Eddie Mead said the way he hoped the fight would go was that Henry would win by a knockout in about the ninth or tenth round. Eddie had made application for a neutral referee and the name of Georges Carpentier was brought up, but in the end the champion's party settled for the board's man, Wilfred Smith.

Eddie did win one argument, however, over the question of hand bandages. He asked for an extra yard or so with the understanding that Roderick have the same. This was granted and the way was clear to the big fight. There had been one international problem, however.

'While the fighters were sweating it out in the gym, Johnny Best received a call from the Madison Square Garden Corporation informing him that unless Roderick agreed to defend the title against an American of their choice, assuming that Ernie won over Armstrong, there would be no fight.

'Johnny called in the lawyers to sort this one out, but they didn't have the answer. Johnny himself had it all along! Learning of Eddie Mead's passion for beef stew, something Armstrong's manager had been unable to get since arriving in London, Johnny whisked him off to Stone's Chop House

CHAPTER TEN

in Panton Street and sat him down in front of the finest beef stew they could serve up. That did it! So far as Eddie Mead was concerned, Johnny Best was top man, everyone else could go to yon place. Armstrong would defend the welterweight title against Ernie Roderick at Harringay Arena on 25 May 1939, no strings attached. Henry would get a purse said to be between £7,500 and £10,000. For his end Roderick would pick up around £1,500.'[96]

One thing was to mar this battle of the century … the fans stayed away in droves, and on that Thursday night only about 5,000 were in the spacious arena. Less than half full!

'While no fault whatsoever could be found with the match itself, it was the situation of the venue that made the promotion show a loss. Ernie Roderick had been boxing for many years, but could not be expected to prove such a draw in the south as he was in the north.

'Furthermore, so many wonderful tales had reached us about Henry Armstrong that it must be assumed the average fight-goer imagined that Ernie's chances were altogether too meagre. They stayed away to their subsequent sorrow. Those who stayed away missed seeing a phenomenal exhibition of non-stop battling such as may never again be witnessed. They also missed a game and courageous display by Ernie Roderick that will never be forgotten. I shall always be personally indebted to Johnny Best for having provided the opportunity for me to see Henry Armstrong in action – the personification of perpetual motion.

---

96 Eddie Baxter, *Boxing News*, London, 16 July 1965.

'But "Homicide Henry" was no ordinary person. Built superbly for his style of fighting, he had, so it transpired, an exceedingly large heart which it was necessary to work up to a fast beat before its owner could employ his limbs at the great pace he demanded of them, and also get the power behind his speedy punching. While the challenger was making his way to the ringside, the champion was indulging in a fast spell of shadow-boxing in his dressing room. As he came along the aisle to his corner, Henry was jigging on his toes and punching the air with either hand, and he kept this up after he had climbed through the ropes. Except for the moment when he stood still for the fastening of the gloves, Armstrong was perpetually on the move,' wrote *Boxing News* editor Gilbert E. Odd. [97]

United Press reported: 'With a hurricane of red leather that left his game opponent blood-smeared and groggy, Henry Armstrong of Los Angeles, Thursday night retained his world welterweight championship by winning an easy 15-round decision over Ernie Roderick of Liverpool at Harringay Indoor Stadium. Armstrong made his sixth successful defence of the 147-pound crown. He registered his 46th straight ring victory despite the handicap of nearly 11 pounds. Henry weighed 135 to Roderick's 145¾.

'The heavier and taller challenger never had a chance, despite his empire-wide reputation and his 23 straight previous victories. He failed to win a single round, although he fought on even terms in the first when still fresh – before he started to wilt under the terrific pace of the champion. The fans in the arena were amazed at Armstrong's perpetual

---
[97] Gilbert E Odd, *Ring Battles of the Century*, 1948.

motion mauling. American observers said he never fought so hard before. Perhaps he was inspired by the fact that his baby daughter, Lanetta, was lying in the arms of her mother, Lily May, at the ringside. Never before had they been at one of his fights.

'They started the fight at an impossible pace, with Roderick launching a barrage of left jabs to Henry's face, trying to fend off Armstrong's plunging attack. Armstrong bore in, receiving a few of the jabs, but picking off most of them with his gloves and forearms. The first round was even. Henry won the second and the third with his terrific pace and went on to win the fourth, fifth and sixth with the same whirlwind onslaught. Roderick appeared to be tiring somewhat as early as the fourth.

'Henry was banging him and then tying him up, preventing Ernie from taking advantage of his longer reach. At times, the bewildered Englishman stood in mid-ring and covered his head to prevent the rain of blows from rocking him. Armstrong continued to batter Ernie in the sixth, seventh and eighth, with the challenger attempting to counter now and then. Henry continued his attack in the ninth, but Roderick was keeping away better. Armstrong said after the bout that it must have been Roderick's height that prevented him from being kayoed. He thought that his blows might have lost some of their zing when travelling at such an upward angle toward Ernie's head.'[98]

Sportswriter Drew Middleton was at the ringside that night, reporting: 'There were no knockdowns, but Armstrong

---

98 United Press, *Nevada State Journal*, 26 May 1939.

did everything else. He opened a cut under Roderick's left eye and raised a mouse the size of a walnut over Roderick's right peeper. Four times – in the sixth, ninth, 11th, and 15th – Roderick seemed on the verge of a kayo. Each time the Briton's courage saved him. Especially open to Hank's whistling right hook, he would take it, shake his head and stand open to take three or four more. Henry, uncut on the face, but bleeding a little from an old wound inside his mouth, said after the fight, "He was a fine game boy. I'm sorry I couldn't put up a better fight, but both my hands are sore and bruised."

'The crowd, disappointing in size, didn't know what to make of Hank. In the first round Roderick stood him off, jabbing in the traditional style of British fighters. But in the second, Henry bulled his way in. Roderick had no defence. Hank would come swarming in, shooting his left to Roderick's Gibraltar-like chin and pounding his right to the body. By the time the 15 rounds were over and Ernie was breathless and blood-stained, there was a patch of red over his kidneys the size of a pie plate.

'For about two minutes of the 11th round Roderick came on. He started to lift left uppercuts to Armstrong's body and head and just for a moment Hank was stopped. Promptly, he switched and started to stay away, sending long lefts and rights to Roderick's head. They connected. Roderick pulled up his hands and started to jab back, and the fight was lost.'[99]

Associated Press reported from London: 'Henry Armstrong, who badly bruised both his hands in punching Ernie Roderick's "Gibraltar" jaw, will take a complete rest

---

99 Drew Middleton, *Ironwood Daily Globe*, Michigan, 26 May 1939.

CHAPTER TEN

until he goes into training about the middle of July for his second fight with Lou Ambers in New York on 9 August. An easy victor last night, Armstrong nevertheless damaged his hands so seriously he will consult doctors here and in Paris. Trainer Harry Armstrong said apparently no bones were broken, but the hands were swollen and a complete rest was required.

'Armstrong was acclaimed by the British press as a sensational and thorough winner. After a balky first round, he took command of the fight and never was headed. Referee Wilfred Smith said it was the cleanest championship bout he ever had seen. Armstrong carried away $46,800, the largest purse ever paid to a fighter in this country, but the *London Daily Mail* said today that not more than 5,000 attended the fight and "the promoters have lost several thousand pounds."'[100]

'And so it went on,' reported Gilbert E. Odd, 'with the crowd wondering how much more of it the British champion could take. After being subjected to a lengthy assault on the ropes in the seventh round, Ernie opened out and fought back with such superb courage that even the poker-faced American was surprised. The crowd roared in appreciation and the noise was such that no one heard the bell that ended the round and the referee had to tear Armstrong off his opponent.

'Henry did slow down a trifle in the 11th and for the first time Roderick was able to take the initiative. He slung a left to the body that caused Henry to break off an attack and, seeing that he had hurt his man, Ernie followed up his advantage. Several more lefts to the body had the American backing away

---

100 *Sarasota Herald Tribune,* Florida, 26 May 1939.

and, tiring as he was, the challenger pulled out all he had got in an effort to score a decisive victory. But the bulk of his energy had been expended and, although he took the round, Roderick could not land anything like a winning wallop.

'They pushed his head into a bucket of water when he got back to his corner, but Armstrong took a swig from a bottle of rum and brandy and came out for the 12th with his vigour renewed. It was all Armstrong in the last two rounds. Roderick did his best to ward off the avalanche of blows. The crowd cheered him loudly as he stood up to the terrific bombardment, but it must have been a nightmare for him. The final gong saw the verdict go to the title-holder, and while still in the ring he was presented with a gold trophy emblematic of his title status, a trophy befitting a truly great champion.'[101]

'It was a good fight, but not too hard for the champ; he battered Roderick for 15 rounds, and then toured England and crossed the Channel to take a look at Paris. To a world-famous champion, flush with money, it was a tour of triumph. Henry met Marcel Cerdan, the great French middleweight, and he shook hands with Maurice Chevalier. The crowds cheered him, wherever he went.

'But they had also begun cheering something and someone else. The clouds of war were settling over Europe. Troops were marching, and the French were getting ready for it. They had begun to forget the visiting champ when he sailed for home. But Henry should worry. Eddie Mead put $20,000 in his hand – his share of the profits of the Roderick fight. Money, money, money!'[102]

---

101 Gilbert E. Odd, *Ring Battles of the Century*, 1948.
102 Henry Armstrong, *Gloves, Glory and God*, 1957.

Chapter Eleven

BACK IN New York City, Henry was having the same problem with Uncle Mike Jacobs, who was offering him $40,000 to fight a rematch with Lou Ambers at the Yankee Stadium on 22 August. Henry packed his gear and was off to Pompton Lakes in New Jersey, the training camp he shared with Joe Louis. A week before the fight, veteran columnist Grantland Rice visited the camp and wrote up his view of the lightweight champion, who also held the welterweight title, having surrendered the featherweight title.

'Henry Armstrong can lay claim to the record that he has a pair of hands that have hit heads and human bodies more often than any pair of hands ever known to boxing,' wrote the scribe. 'His two hands have struck almost as many times against the human frame as Paderewski's have hammered piano keys. Armstrong throws something like 60 punches a minute or 180 punches in a round. He admits he can't keep any record of the blows he delivers, as he keeps both hands working at top speed from start to finish. He is sure, however, that he has piled up more than 200 punches of one type or another in several single rounds.

'The answer to all this is inevitable. Hammering Henry's hands are not what they used to be. His swollen knuckles that I looked at some weeks ago have receded considerably and now look about normal. But the punishment they have taken through the last few years has been heavy. Armstrong hasn't any worry about his legs carrying him at the same pace through 15 rounds. "They never felt better," he said. "They can go any distance. The thing that tired me in the last Ambers fight was my cut lip and the flow of blood that ran down my throat. It wasn't my legs or my arms. It wasn't the punches I threw."

'Armstrong is the one fighter I have seen who could throw more punches than Harry Greb. And Greb could throw more than his share. Armstrong goes on beyond Greb. The Hammerer takes no vacations after action begins. None at all. This is the main hurdle that Ambers has to handle … As the case stands now the Hammerer still seems to carry a little too much leeway on the offensive side.'[103]

Sixty miles from his Broadway beat, Associated Press sports editor Dillon Graham was at Carmel, in New York state, to watch Lou Ambers go through his paces. 'For almost a month now Lou has trained here where stars of the theatre used to speak their lines. Still a youngster despite his years of fighting, Lou likely is in the best shape of his career.

'"Henry will find Lou a changed fighter," says Al Weill, Lou's portly manager, "far more formidable than the fellow he was lucky to beat last August. Lou's a puncher now. And I have to thank Armstrong for that. Here's the story. Three years ago Lou knocked out a fighter named Tony Scarpati. Tony hit his head on the canvas when he fell. He died a day

---

103 Grantland Rice, *Washington Evening Star*, 17 August 1939.

CHAPTER ELEVEN

or so later. That took something out of Lou. He always had the fear that if he hit too hard he might again kill a man. Lou went along to the top and won the lightweight championship, but he remained a boxer, a fellow without a really devastating punch. Then came his fight with Hank.

'"Armstrong is not the cleanest fighter in the world and he tried a bunch of tricks on Lou. And he won the decision and took away Lou's title. Now Lou values that title above anything else. He's got plenty of money. But he wants the title back. And so Lou has shaken off his old fear of hurting a rival and is in there slugging. His punches are shorter and stiffer. I wouldn't be surprised if he stopped Armstrong."'[104]

NEA Service sports editor Harry Grayson wrote from Pompton Lakes, New Jersey: 'Amazing Henry Armstrong, under trying circumstances, is as fit as hands can make him for his 15-round lightweight title defence against Lou Ambers at Yankee Stadium, 22 August.

'Every time you see Armstrong you wonder how long he can keep going. The answer still seems to be indefinitely, although he hasn't quit marching forward and throwing punches for seven years. He is the most relentless attacker since Terrible Terry McGovern. But Armstrong had vastly more on his mind than the willing Ambers and energy expended so recklessly in the past when he started training at Dr Joe Bier's old colonial home here.

'There was the problem of making weight ... the bugaloo of all fighting men. His protracted lay-off, since the Ernie Roderick affair in London, a record for time off for the busy

---

104 Dillon Graham, *Abilene Reporter News*, Texas, 20 August 1939.

Armstrong, shot his poundage up to 143. At one stage of the proceedings, rotund Eddie Mead, who put Homicide Hank in the more important money and kept him there, was seriously considering forfeiting the lightweight leadership and having the young savages fight for the welter wreath, which Armstrong also holds by dint of having handed Barney Ross the licking of his life.

'But Armstrong, an old hand at weight-making since his feather days, finally got over the hump and now expects to, and appears capable of, coming in at 134½ as strong as John Montague. He long has been handicapped by bad hands. They could not be jammed up with an industrious and tough bloke like Ambers in the offing. Scars about Armstrong's eyes had to be guarded. He could not afford to go to the post with any hint of the old gash in his lower lip which nearly cost him his first fight with Ambers. Armstrong has gone through fights with sponges on the faces of his destructive fists.

'Breaks ... bruises ... cuts ... clouts ... weight-making ... burned up energy. Nothing seems able to stop remarkable Henry Armstrong.'[105]

Veteran promoter/manager Jack Hurley had this to say: 'The New York Commission – having had the foresight to force Henry Armstrong and Lou Ambers to sign for a welterweight championship match in September – would have you believe that Armstrong is only defending his lightweight championship Tuesday night. This is strictly the phonas-bolonus, because if Ambers wins he automatically becomes – and will be recognised – as the lightweight and

---

105 Harry Grayson, *Ada Evening News*, Oklahoma, 21 August 1939.

CHAPTER ELEVEN

welterweight champion, signed articles and commission opinion notwithstanding.

'Personally I can see no cause for alarm, because Armstrong, who has won his last 46 fights, will undoubtedly belt the honourable commission out of a ticklish predicament. Ambers's clowning style may cause Armstrong some concern, but rip-tearing Henry will eventually take command, land the most punches and go on to a popular victory. It is rumoured that should Ambers fail in his bid to regain his lightweight crown, he will retire and marry his childhood sweetheart, Miss Margaret "Tootsie" Celio of Herkimer, NY. Well, what are they waiting for? Strike up the band!'[106]

Columnist Lawton Carver recalled the first fight in his preview of the rematch. 'That was a fight for you, as bloody, fierce and brutal a piece of business as you'd care to see, with two little guys whanging away at each other for the full distance of 15 rounds and with Armstrong the winner but staggering into the wrong corner at the finish. So, going on that for what it's worth, another quite valiant stand by both of them is to be expected tomorrow night.

'Two things enter into that, reading from left to right, one being that some fear Armstrong really has outgrown the division and is taking off strength with his weight to get down to 135 pounds, the other concerning his hands. They went bad on him a couple of years ago and rapidly have been getting no better. He could blow this fight. Ambers is tough and game and has won nine straight, five by knockouts, since he was outpointed by Armstrong, who did just win last time on a

---

106 Jack Hurley, *Billings Gazette*, Montana, 21 August 1939.

split decision. On Armstrong's behalf it might be said that he doesn't figure to sustain any such cut as he did before, when he was weakened by the loss of blood. Anyhow, it ought to be good, barring disappointments.'[107]

Grantland Rice wrote a day before the fight: 'Henry Armstrong has a style all his own, they say. Well, nobody fights like Armstrong now, but somebody did once. Armstrong copied the style from a little fellow named Davey Abad, who was just a pretty good featherweight a few years ago. Eddie Mead told me about it at Pompton Lakes.

'Abad was boxing Benny Bass. Armstrong and some other kids sneaked in to see the fight. Abad won and made a terrific impression on Henry. From then on, he was Henry's hero. He tried to copy Abad's style, but he didn't make much progress. Finally, when he caught up with Davey in Los Angeles and started to box with him, he got it.

'Henry was coming on and Davey was going back by the time they fought. Henry won the first fight, Abad won the second, and the third time they fought Henry gave him a terrible beating. Abad's face was punched out of shape and his head was lopsided when the fight ended. Armstrong felt badly about having given such a licking to a boy who had been his hero and who had helped him so much. He went to Abad's dressing room and told him he was sorry, and all Abad said was, "All right, Henry. You are a good fighter now. It's all right."

'There may be a hint in that for young men ambitious to beat Armstrong – and that goes for Lou Ambers, who will try

---

107 Lawton Carver, *Atlantic News Telegraph,* Iowa, 21 August 1939.

to beat him tomorrow night. The way to beat him, apparently, is to fight him at his own style. But now that Abad is through, nobody else has that style and in order to perfect it to the degree Henry has, a boy must have as much speed, strength and endurance as he has – and I haven't seen anybody so far that has that, either.'[108]

'You Don't Say! – by Mac' was a column that ran in the *Dunkirk Evening Observer,* New York, on 17 March 1939: 'Hammering Henry Armstrong, the small edition of Joe Louis, has another beating-up coming to him during the month of June. He's meeting Lou Ambers, the Herkimer Holocaust, for the second time. Now Henry perhaps will win the decision over Lou, but you know as well as I do that Hammering Henry will have taken another beating of his life while whipping Lou. He took one from Lou and he can take another.

'Lou Ambers is a gamester. He has, perhaps, just as much intestinal fortitude as Henry has tied up in his little frame. He loves to fight and he likes to make money. Henry is tough and Lou knows it ... The boys who witnessed the last scrap are still talking about that fight. No one who saw the affair has said that the melee wasn't the toughest thing shown in a ring in this country since time began. Henry, with his mouth and face a bloody pulp, his eyes virtually closed, kept on despite it all. He was adjudged the best.

'Lou did not escape either. He too, took to his bed and stayed there for a week or so. His cuts had to be sewn up.

---

108 Grantland Rice, *Evening Star,* Washington DC, 21 August 1939.

HENRY ARMSTRONG

His face was slashed and sliced, his eyes black as coal. He openly admitted it was the hardest fight of his career and one which he thought he had won. But in his dressing room he didn't care who had won. All he wanted was rest, cool water and someone to rub his aching joints and body. Lou vowed, after he recuperated, that he'd meet Henry again and beat him. "I'll trim that man if it kills me," said Lou, and he meant it.

'It'll be a fight, gentlemen, the likes of which you and I have never seen.'[109]

In his syndicated column on the day of the fight, Grantland Rice was reminding his readers: 'It will be the second time around for Henry Armstrong and Lou Ambers tonight in the Yankee Stadium. Armstrong, who took the lightweight championship from Ambers a year ago, is favoured to win again. In their fight last summer, the issue was close – so close there were many who thought Ambers won. I thought the decision was right and that Armstrong had won. But there was room for argument. Henry had to go to a doctor's office to have some fancy stitching done on his lower lip and both eyelids. Ambers went to his hotel where, until two o'clock in the morning, he was host at a party of his friends. I know because I saw him there. If the hammering about the body he had taken and the hooks that had exploded against his chin had hurt him, he gave no sign of it.

'For Henry it must be said that he came through heroically under a terrific handicap: two bad hands and a mouth that had been cut during a sparring drill and had been lacerated

---
[109] *Dunkirk Evening Observer*, New York, 17 March 1939.

by Lou's uppercuts. Sick and scarcely able to breathe, he kept banging away – and when he had finished, he was the lightweight champion of the world.

'He has had a rest of three months or so and to those who feared that the unaccustomed lay-off would hurt him, he gave an impressive answer by the sharpness with which he boxed and the speed with which he punched. I saw Ambers at Carmel and I must say that he wasn't as impressive as Armstrong was at Pompton Lakes, but then he never is, especially in his training bouts. The urge to fight is strong in both of them and when they meet head on again they should put on a roaring battle in the old lightweight tradition, which is one of the best the ring has to offer.'[110]

Henry McLemore headed his column 'Mack the Quack Studies Case of Henry Armstrong'. The United Press sportswriter wrote: 'The outcome of the Lou Ambers–Henry Armstrong fight is a subject that doctors, not sportswriters, should discuss. It is a topic that lends itself more to the austerity of a clinic than to the hubbub of the city room, to the aroma of formaldehyde than to the ripe smell of printers' ink. Thus, needing a physician's measured advice, I had made arrangements with my family physician to look Armstrong over. But he didn't have time.

'Therefore, I, who have difficulty distinguishing between a bottle of aspirin and a compound fracture, am forced to list the merits and demerits of these 135-pounders. I am forced to give you Armstrong, whose name isn't that at all. Actually, it is Jackson. But if it were McIntyre or Van Buren or Smith

---

110 Grantland Rice, *Amarillo Globe*, Texas, 22 August 1939.

or Cohen – he still would be one of the ten greatest fighters this country ever has known.

'The last time Armstrong fought Ambers, most of you thought the bout was close. Take it from Referee Arthur Donovan, who was nearer Armstrong that night than you or I or anyone but Ambers, Henry won 12 of 15 rounds. Only pride kept him from winning all 15. In an early round Ambers hit him in the mouth with an uppercut and opened a gash of frightful proportions. Blood poured from it like oil from a gusher. The spectators never saw a drop. Round after round Armstrong swallowed it, fighting off nausea.

'They say Ambers never loses to the same man twice. Ambers isn't facing the same man the second time tonight. The Armstrong he fought the first time was drinking blood all through the last six rounds. Tonight – if the hands are right – there may be no last six rounds.'[111]

---

111   Henry McLemore, *Racine Journal Times*, Wisconsin, 22 August 1939.

Chapter Twelve

IN HIS preview of the return fight between Henry Armstrong and Lou Ambers on 22 August 1939, columnist John Lardner reported a recent radio interview featuring Armstrong and Ambers, stating: 'You got the idea that they loved each other like brothers. You also got the idea that the fight, if any, would take place between their managers, Mr Fat Edward Mead and Mr Alphonse "Weskit" Weill, who have been exhaling pure brimstone for nearly a week now.

'"Let Weill beware of putting the customary iron 'gimmick' in Ambers's glove," bawled Mr. Mead a couple of days ago, "or I will tear him limb from limb!"

'"Let Mead have a care," hollered Mr. Weill. "If he pulls any of his famous dirty stuff in this fight I will shave his ears off."

'All that prevents the two managers from replacing their boys in battle for the full 15 rounds is the fact that tonight's fight is billed for the lightweight championship of the world. Neither Mr Mead nor Mr Weill can get close enough to the lightweight limit to shake hands with it. Mr Mead represents two lightweights statistically speaking, and Mr Weill is the gross equivalent of one lightweight and three-quarters.'[112]

---

112 John Lardner, *Washington Evening Star*, Washington DC, 22 August 1939.

'Eddie Mead was a fat man,' sports editor Art Cohn of the *Oakland Tribune* wrote. 'By fat I mean he weighed 300 pounds. And every ounce of it was happy.'

Al Weill was what *New Yorker* columnist Joe Liebling called 'of the build referred to in ready-made clothing stores as a portly, which means not quite a stout. There is an implication of at least one kind of recklessness about a fat man; he lets himself go when he eats. A portly man, on the other hand, is a man who would like to be fat but restrains himself.'

Lardner added, 'Mr Armstrong and Mr Ambers will shed brotherly love with their bathrobes and do the real fighting of the evening the second the bell rings. Poets and troubadours in their spare time, they spill blood when they get down to business. Both are good, both are tough, and neither of them likes the other. Ambers is a cutting puncher. He doesn't hit hard, though his right uppercut is no spray of talcum powder. But he slits and tears, and Armstrong's hide is by no means one whole piece of cloth as we go to press. There's a scar here and a stitch there.

'Twenty-three stitches were embroidered into the region of Henry's mouth immediately after his first fight with Ambers. Ambers opened the wound simply because he was hitting Henry repeatedly in the last part of the fight and Henry was not hitting him at all. Lou rallied because he had more stamina, stronger legs, and a little bit more science than the winner.

'In other words, he can do it again, cut or no cut. He will meet a fresh Armstrong, but this will be a fresh Ambers – younger than Henry, and more ambitious and stronger in the matter of endurance, though naturally his

CHAPTER TWELVE

"spot" strength, his vitamin quotient, does not compare with Armstrong's.'[113]

'Last August Henry the Hammer was a 1-3 favourite over Lou, but at the finish of the gory fray in Madison Square Garden he was suffering from a badly cut lip, had swallowed a lot of blood and was a pretty sick young man. If the fight had gone a few rounds longer, Luigi D'Ambrosio might still be lightweight champion. What's more, Armstrong, whose way of fighting is to hit the other guy hard, often found Ambers was one rival who wouldn't stay hit. Lou was down twice in the early rounds, but he finished so strongly a lot of fans booed the verdict.

'It may be the same story on Tuesday, but there have been several sound reasons advanced why Ambers should make a much better showing. They've been so good the odds have faded from 1-3 to 5-7 against Armstrong. The first is the possibility Henry's hands may give way. The Hammer has won 46 consecutive fights, 39 by knockouts, and it's obvious he's had to hit a lot of people to do that. When he fights, he tears in and flings punches, careless of where they land, and he's cracked his mitts badly at times. He came back from his last fight against Ernie Roderick in England with his left hand in a cast. Henry claims the hand is as sound as ever now, but there's a chance it won't stand the punishment of 15 rounds.

'Then Ambers never has been known to lose a return bout. He won them from such guys as Tony Canzoneri and Fritzie Zivic, who broke his jaw once, and Pedro Montanez.

---
[113] John Lardner, *Washington Evening Star*, 22 August 1939.

He figures on preserving this record against Armstrong and with that in mind has been trying to develop a punch that will put the Hammer down for keeps.'[114]

'The usual pre-fight rumours of "business" drifted along Bash Boulevard today on the eve of Henry Armstrong's lightweight title defence against Lou Ambers, but even the betting men weren't the slightest bit interested. As you know, this betting fraternity takes very good care not to catch cold in its pocketbook. So, when the odds-layers came right out in meeting and continued to lay 7-5 that Armstrong would be "winnah and still champeen" when the 15-round tea party is over in Yankee Stadium tomorrow, you just laughed off the "whispers."

'In the present case, any such talk is as far-fetched as a flying trip to the moon. The two principals, each of whom wound up training yesterday in A1 condition, have too much in the pot to pass the dice now. The 135-pound crown is second only to the heavyweight trinket as a means of putting steak on the table, so there wouldn't be a reason in the world for Armstrong to give it up without the toughest kind of a struggle. And as for Ambers getting the championship as a gift – well, little Lou is a mean little man in any ring, and, up to now, every time the Herkimer Hurricane has climbed between the ropes, he has put out every lick of effort. Hammerin' Henry dethroned Little Lou just a year ago this month in a bloody fight as close as the skin on a grape.'[115]

'At the end of that fight, Armstrong recalled, "This had to be in the 15th. I looked up and the Garden just completely

---

114 Hugh S. Fullerton Jnr, *Billings Gazette*, Montana, 21 August 1939.
115 Associated Press, Ada Evening News, Oklahoma, 21 August 1939.

CHAPTER TWELVE

blacked out." Afterwards he asked, "What did he hit me with?" "He hit you with nothing," his trainer told him, "we had to take you off him. You almost knocked Ambers out!" According to *The New York Times*, the verdict was greeted with "a terrific din of jeers, boos and catcalls". According to Nat Fleischer, although Ambers had left Armstrong looking "wobbly and gory at the close of a vicious encounter", Armstrong was nevertheless "the decisive winner". The fairest verdict is surely that of Lou Ambers: "He beat me out. Like I've always said, he was the better man than I was on that night."[116]

And so it was, that August night in 1939 before 29,088 people at Yankee Stadium, who had paid a gross gate of $137,925 into Mike Jacobs's retirement fund. That night, Henry was the better man again. It was different this time though – Henry didn't get the decision. Ambers took a unanimous decision to regain the lightweight title. Controversy was ripe that night.

'The penalising by Donovan caused heated argument between every round between the two managers Al Weill and Eddie Mead. Finally Weill shouted across the ring, 'You'd better watch out if you keep that up.'

'The dissention that rent the air,' wrote Nat Fleischer, 'following the official verdict was ample proof that the fans were not satisfied that the champion had really lost. Even the scribes were divided on that point, 13 newspaper writers had given the verdict as did the three officials and I, in favour of Ambers, and 13 favouring Armstrong. Thus, Ambers, so far

---

116 Gerald Suster, *Lightning Strikes*, 1994.

as the writers were concerned, won the title by one vote – that of the *Ring* Editor, the deciding one.

'Making the weight of 135 pounds had its disadvantages for the loser. When Hank went to the Boxing Commission for the weighing-in ceremony, he had to sweat to rid himself of more than a pound. He made the 135-pound limit with Ambers scaling a pound less.

'Lou Ambers got his name into the record books as the second lightweight to win the laurels on a foul – or fouls shall I say – Herkimer Lew gained his through an interpretation of the New York rules that enabled him to win five rounds on low hits by his opponent.

'As some of the pictures in the movies and the stills show, several punches for which Henry lost a round, were just a little below the belt line, this being the case particularly in the seventh round when Referee Donovan didn't even warn Armstrong after its delivery but ordered the officials to penalise him once the round was over. The 14th round, the one which according to most of the ringside experts was won by Hank, was given to Ambers by Judge Frank Fullum. It was by far the best round of the defending champion. It was the contention of Armstrong that if Fullum had seen that round as most everybody else, his card would have read eight to seven in Hank's favour and the title would have been saved.'[117]

Tom Meany wrote in the *New York World Telegram* that 'Armstrong lost five rounds on fouls, which is a new high for a state with a no-foul rule!'

---

117 Nat Fleischer, *Ring*, November 1939.

CHAPTER TWELVE

James P. Dawson, writing in the *New York Times*, observed, 'The dispute concerning this highly exciting struggle will come over the penalties imposed upon Armstrong for infractions of the ring's rules. Applying the law more severely than ever before and certainly more painfully than ever it has been applied in a championship event, Referee Donovan penalised Armstrong no less than five rounds for foul punches. These were the second, fifth, seventh, ninth and 11th.

'Four of these rounds Armstrong won on competition beyond question. Ambers, without the foul that was called, carried the second. But there were times when the fouls were not visible, notably the second one which cost Armstrong the fifth round. On this observer's score sheet, Armstrong was the victim of an injustice, even taking into account the penalties of which he was the victim. Giving Ambers the benefit of the doubt in the five rounds he won by the ring's law enforcement, Armstrong still won the battle eight rounds to seven in the writer's opinion.

'This observer's score sheet gave Hammering Henry the fourth, sixth, eighth, tenth, 12th, 13th, 14th and 15th rounds by wide margins. To Ambers this reporter gave the first, second and third rounds on action, together with the remaining four Donovan penalised Armstrong on fouls. So it can be seen that this title was decided not on competition, but on fighting rules and ethics. Armstrong lost his title on fouls. The most that can be said for Ambers is that he fought gallantly. He waded in recklessly as the bout opened and before he was forced into a desperate retreat. But he wasn't entitled to the decision. He isn't Armstrong's master.'[118]

---

[118] James P. Dawson, *The New York Times*, 23 August 1939.

In his column 'Today's Sport Parade', Henry McLemore didn't pull his punches: 'Arthur Donovan is the new lightweight boxing champion of the world. He won the title in Yankee Stadium last night. He won it for Lou Ambers by rendering a decision as questionable as a mongrel's paternity. Donovan, who should run, not walk, to the nearest optician, gave Ambers five rounds because of low blows struck by Henry Armstrong. Not only were those blows no more damaging to Ambers than a BB gun to the Maginot line. Donovan, in watching for them, forgot to watch what Ambers was doing to Armstrong.

'I saw the new champion (Donovan Ambers, as I shall call him from here out) strike as many non-Emily Post blows as did the victim. In close, Ambers qualified for any exclusive goat society by butting from here to yonder and he never apologised when he took his elbow and hit with it. Armstrong did the same thing. What I'm trying to get at is that it was not a fight between a ruffian and Lord Fauntleroy, but a battle for a title that both men wanted.

'Armstrong was guilty of fouls, yes. But so was Ambers. As for the actual fighting, minus fouls, there was no comparison between the two men. Armstrong beat the daylights out of his pinch-faced opponent. Three times he had him rubber-legged and ready to go down and perhaps could have finished him off if his hands had been the hands of the Armstrong of two years ago. Ambers was game, fast and a sharper hitter than when he lost his title to Armstrong last year, but he threw only one punch against ten and simply isn't in Henry's class as a fighter.'[119]

---

119 Henry McLemore, *Moorhead Daily News*, Minnesota, 23 August 1939.

CHAPTER TWELVE

Sid Feder was ringside for Associated Press, writing: 'Henry Armstrong was penalised five rounds by Referee Donovan for low punching. If it hadn't been for those five heats, Hammerin' Henry would have won – and retained the title – in a waltz.

'Armstrong forced the fighting all the way. He never stopped coming forward, despite the storm of left uppercuts and hooks showered on him by the Herkimer Hurricane. Tonight's battle was regarded as the fistic natural of the year, and it was when Donovan wasn't warning Hurricane Hank for tossing punches below the belt line. The AP score card had nine rounds for the new champion and six for Henry, but five of these were those taken away by fouls, in only one of which Ambers showed a clear margin, regardless of the low punching.

'The crowd, obviously an "Ambers" house anyway, judging by its tremendous reception for Lou, was pleased with the decision. But there was a sharp divergence of ringside opinion among the boxing writers. A few believed Armstrong won the fight, despite the penalties, but most were of the opinion the rounds he lost cost Henry the title. He started slowly, but by the time the third and fourth heats came along he was in high gear. The rest of the way, he pushed back as he charged, charged and charged some more. His right eye was cut in the third, but no one seemed sure whether it was from a punch or from a clash between the heads of the two fighters.

'Ambers came out of a melee in the fourth with a cut left eye and he slipped to the floor, but was up before a count. Blood continued to pour from Ambers' cut eye in the fifth, which went to Lou on a foul, and the sixth saw more gore, this time from both battlers. Armstrong's right eye was opened again and he was cut in the mouth by a short left. Both were tiring fast in the eighth and ninth, but they came on again in the later heats with more steam.'[120]

'From the opening gong – when the little coast windmill sidled from his corner, left shoulder high and body quivering like gelatin, and started those tireless arms in motion – there wasn't a dull moment,' recorded Whitney Martin. 'Although lacking the knockdown thrills of their earlier meeting, it would be difficult to match for sheer sustained action and merciless punishment inflicted by bobbing heads and flailing fists. Armstrong started to bleed from a cut eye in the third round. Ambers' eyebrow crimsoned in the fourth and from that point on it was the gory spectacle of two little warriors slugging and pushing and mauling in their own blood, neither conceding a thing.

'In the head-to-head exchanges, Armstrong with his short, jolting blows, usually had the best of it. But when Ambers jigged away and started sharpshooting he set the pace, his left hook often catching the eternally stalking Armstrong off balance. Neither fighter appeared in serious trouble at any time. Ambers often would take Armstrong's best punches with hands down, bobbing and ducking and grinning through it all. The second, fifth, seventh, ninth and 11th rounds were taken from Armstrong because of low blows. The irony of it was that little "Perpetual Motion" turned in his best rounds later, after the fight apparently already had been won. Ambers said later he was hurt on a couple of occasions, but couldn't recall just when they were. The low blows, he said, did not

---

120 Sid Feder, *Montana Helena Independent*, 23 August 1939.

CHAPTER TWELVE

bother him much. Armstrong complained of what he claimed were Ambers's thumbing tactics, pointing to swollen and inflamed eyes as proof.'[121]

United Press sports editor Harry Ferguson at ringside, recorded: 'You will walk many a weary mile through turnstiles leading into prize-fights before you will see anything to equal the 14th round. In the first ten seconds of it, Armstrong bulled Ambers to the ropes and there they stayed in one spot for the remaining two minutes and 50 seconds of the round. Neither tried to duck or block a punch. Neither tried to box. They were a couple of kids in a back alley, slugging it out and forgetting all the science and cunning that had been drummed into their heads by managers and trainers. Armstrong belted Ambers in the belly and Ambers slugged Armstrong in the jaw. And there they stayed and bled and took it as though their shoes were rooted into the canvas.

'The customers almost saw a double header. Eddie Mead was screaming bloody murder at Donovan every time the referee took a round away from Henry for fouling. Between rounds he would run over to Donovan, making furious motions as though he was going to throw a punch. Donovan shooed him back into the corner, but when the bout was over Mead really exploded in the dressing room. "They stole it from us," Mead yelled. "I'll beef so loud and long about this that there'll be no more boxing in New York in 90 days."'[122]

'Al Jolson, the Hollywood movie star who once owned Armstrong's contract, raised a rumpus at the ringside as Armstrong lost his lightweight crown. Throughout the bout,

---
121 Whitney Martin, *Washington DC Evening Star*, 23 August 1939.
122 Harry Ferguson, *Moorhead Daily News*, Minnesota, 23 August 1939.

as Donovan repeatedly penalised Armstrong for low blows, Al and a group of friends kept yelling, "That's all right, Henry, they are going to take it anyway," and shouted at Donovan to "let them alone." Other fans near the ringside were screaming "fake" and "it's no use Henry, it is in the bag." Despite the fact that their favourite had gone down to defeat, Harlem behaved beautifully following the Armstrong–Ambers fight here Tuesday night. The usual pandemonium which travels in the wake of an Armstrong battle was noticeably absent. But neither was there a single incident which suggested poor sportsmanship. Lenox and Seventh Avenues, the presence of hundreds of Elks to augment the thousands of Harlemites notwithstanding, were quiet except for an occasional comment on the gameness of both boys.'[123]

Ambers was lucky in his corner where he had Charlie Goldman and Whitey Bimstein, top men in the beak-busting trade. Whitey was talking to sportswriter Barney Nagler in Stillman's Gym one day in 1950 and said he didn't know how many fighters he had trained in 34 years in the business, maybe 7,500. "'I guess my favourite was Lou Ambers, he was the easiest to handle. You didn't have to drive him. My job with him was to keep him from working too much. Funny thing was how Ambers would get cranky when it came close to a fight. Nice kid, but he would get so cranky you couldn't go near him."

'Analysing Henry Armstrong, Goldman said, "Lou Ambers was a very good in-fighter, so we had him stay close to Henry and dig in little short punches. If you backed off

---

123 *Baltimore Afro-American*, 24 August 1939.

CHAPTER TWELVE

with Henry when he was good, it was certain suicide. He'd crowd you, then throw a powerful overhand right that would knock anybody out.'"[124]

'A third meeting between Henry Armstrong and Lou Ambers hung in the balance today while Armstrong's manager Eddie Mead charged that there had been skulduggery in last night's fight. Claiming that the lightweight title was "stolen" from his man, Mead threatened to carry his charge to Albany and blow the boxing set-up in New York "wide open."

'Contracts already had been signed for Armstrong to defend his welter title against Ambers within 60 days in case Lou won the lightweight championship, and promoter Mike Jacobs announced that 1 November and Madison Square Garden would be the time and place. "Why should I let Henry risk his other title against Ambers?" Mead asked. "Wouldn't it be just as easy for them to steal it as they did the lightweight title? I'm not in this business for my health you know, and world championships don't grow on trees."

'Mead was furious at Referee Arthur Donovan for taking five rounds away from Armstrong because of fouls. Claiming that three weeks ago he had been warned "something would happen" to Henry last night, Mead quoted one of the boxing commissioners as saying that "Armstrong would lose six rounds on fouls." "That was three weeks ago, mind you, and how could he know that if something wasn't phoney?" Mead asked. "Ambers," he charged, "was fouling every round for 15 rounds. "Look at Henry's eyes," he continued. "Ambers doesn't punch hard enough to do that kind of damage. He kept his

---
124 Barney Nagler, *Ring*, September 1950.

thumbs in Henry's eyes in every round, and if Donovan thinks that's fair fighting he ought to read the rule books again.'"[125]

'Obviously a rubber match was in order. Champion Ambers married his sweetheart, honeymooned in Hawaii and then signed to defend against Armstrong again, the bout to take place on 1 December. Armstrong claimed illness and had the match postponed. Ambers continued to train but Armstrong postponed it twice more before it was cancelled.

'A long while later, Mrs Margaret Ambers told reporter John E. Heany that after the men had retired from the ring, Armstrong paid a friendly visit to her home and told her that he had staged the delays because he had not wanted to fight her husband again. For his part, Ambers averred that Armstrong gave him his toughest fights, declaring, "He wasn't smart enough, but he was good."'[126]

'Talk about Ambers having won two titles,' said Nat Fleischer, 'despite the agreement to fight for one, is nonsense. If the boys had been fighting for the welter crown and Ambers had scaled within the lightweight limit as he did in their last encounter, and had been returned the winner, then there could be no doubt about both crowns belonging to Lou regardless of agreements. But in view of the fact that to fight for the lightweight title Armstrong was penalised and forced to make a weight far below the welter limit, he cannot be deprived of his welterweight crown. Common sense rules that case.'[127]

---

125 Leslie Avery, *Moorhead Daily News*, Minnesota, 24 August 1939.
126 Gerald Suster, *Lightning Strikes*, 1994.
127 Nat Fleischer, *Ring*, November 1939.

Chapter Thirteen

FAT EDDIE Mead was a worried man. The horses were running out of the money and his bookie was hoping he would take his bets to some other guy. Henry's purse for the Ambers fight came to $46,558.74 but that was soon gone after the boys split it up. Even his star fighter was down to his last title. Henry Armstrong was at one time the one and only fighter to win and hold three world titles at the same time. But he had grown out of the featherweight 126-pound class, Lou Ambers and Referee Arthur Donovan had taken his lightweight title away, but he was still welterweight champion of the world. Henry was tentatively matched to defend that title against Ambers in December in the Garden, but Eddie Mead was already looking on the dark side, telling reporters, 'Wouldn't it be just as easy to steal it as they did the lightweight title?'

In the beginning of October it was six weeks since Henry's last fight with Ambers and the injuries to his mouth and eyes were healing nicely. Fat Eddie got out his address book and reached for the telephone. He may have been overweight but his mind still functioned as always and he soon had made calls to Des Moines, Minneapolis, Seattle, Los Angeles and Denver. Then he called Henry and told him to pack a bag, they were going places. Mead and Company was going back to work!

Three of the five bouts were scheduled for ten rounds, including one in California, where 15-round contests were not allowed, but all were bona fide title defences. First stop was Des Moines, where Armstrong was matched with Al Manfredo of Fresno, California. Ten months earlier, Henry had stopped Manfredo in three rounds in a recognised title bout in Cleveland, but although the promoter and the fighters had prepared for a world-title fight, Harvey Miller, secretary of the National Boxing Association, said the NBA would not sanction it because Manfredo was not one of the top three contenders for the title.

In the bout at Riverview Park, Associated Press reported, 'Welterweight champion Henry Armstrong moved on to Minneapolis for his second ring appearance of the week following his knockout Monday night of Al Manfredo in the fourth round of a scheduled ten-round go here. The clever Manfredo, back-pedalling before the champion's relentless offensive, captured the opening round and looked good in spurts in the second and third. The Armstrong shower of leather engulfed the Californian in the fourth however, and Referee Alex Fidler stepped in to halt the carnage with a minute and 35 seconds of the round gone and Manfredo draped helplessly on the ropes.

'After the fight, Al said he had found it difficult to make the 147-pound limit and hereafter would compete as a middleweight. He weighed 146¾ to Armstrong's 141½. Hammering Hank meets Harry Scott of Washington DC in a title scrap Friday night in the Minnesota city.'[128]

---

128 *Cedar Rapids Gazette*, Des Moines, Iowa, 9 October 1939.

CHAPTER THIRTEEN

Minneapolis, 13 October, Associated Press: 'Henry Armstrong, world's welterweight champion, knocked out Howard Scott, Washington DC, in the second round of a scheduled ten-round title bout tonight. The dusky little champion moved into the attack from the first bell. He drove Scott about the ring with a shower of lefts and rights, but the Washington boy fought back gamely, although outclassed.

'Just before the end of the first round the welterweight champion cut loose with a short left hook squarely to Scott's chin and the latter tumbled to the floor. Up at the count of nine, he back-pedalled for the remainder of the round. The second round lasted one minute and 38 seconds. Armstrong weighed 141, Scott 147.'[129]

Bout number three saw Henry in Seattle to cross gloves with old foe Richie Fontaine, Missoula, Montana, this one scheduled for 15 rounds at the Civic Auditorium. They had boxed in two back-to-back bouts in 1936, Richie winning the first and losing the second a month later. The boys were featherweights back then; this time Henry weighed 139¾ to Richie's 141.

'Although Fontaine gamely carried the fight to Armstrong in the first round, there never was any doubt that the man from Los Angeles would win. Fontaine went down five times in the second round, and each time he bounced back without taking a count. Thoroughly battered and groggy, he came up for the third session and this time Armstrong went to work. Flailing both fists at the now helpless Montana scrapper, Armstrong knocked him down for counts of one and six.

---

129 Associated Press *Titusville (PA.) Herald*, 14 October 1939.

Finally after two minutes and three seconds of the third round, Fontaine's handlers threw in the towel and Referee Tommy Clark raised the dusky battler's hand.'[130]

Four days after he caused Richie Fontaine to wonder if he was in the right business, Henry was in Los Angeles to fight Jimmy Garrison at the Olympic Auditorium, ten rounds or less.

Garrison, from Kansas City, brought a pro record of 56-11-4, and had won his last five. The champion had chalked up 101 wins in his 120 bouts with 67 knockouts. The referee was George Blake, top man on the coast. A crowd of 7,000 was there to enjoy the action. They got their money's worth as the guy they called Hurricane Hank turned on the punch machine in round one and kept it going for all ten rounds to win the fight and retain his title for the fourth time in 14 days.

Armstrong started slow and took it easy with in-fighting for five rounds. He started hammering in the sixth and used a short right uppercut. The knockdown came in the eighth, but Jimmy was back on his feet within two seconds. In the tenth round Armstrong chased Garrison around the ring and pounded him with rights to the head. Mr Blake gave Henry all but one of the ten rounds. Next stop Denver and a guy called Bobby Pacho.

'There were 4,500 people in Denver's Municipal Auditorium that Tuesday night to see the 15-rounds championship bout between Armstrong and Bobby Pacho, who outweighed the champ 146 to 140. The title-holder looked trim and sharp, while Pacho did not appear to be

---

130 *Nevada State Journal*, 21 October 1939.

CHAPTER THIRTEEN

in the best of condition. As the fight started, Hammering Henry pounced upon Pacho in the Filipino's corner and kept him there during the entire round. In the second, Armstrong again crowded his foeman. Holding his head against Pacho's chest, Armstrong aimed a steady fire of short jabs. Then he straightened against the ropes and shook him with several long lefts and rights.

'The third round saw the beginning of Pacho's downfall. Armstrong hammered him against the ropes and battered him. Pacho managed to escape, only to be trapped again near Henry's corner. Pacho absorbed a dozen withering blows there. Armstrong chased his foe across the ring and connected three times with terrific left hooks to the chin. It was a wonder that Pacho was able to come out at the bell for the fourth round. He tried to make a fight of it in the final round. He shuffled out to the centre of the ring and traded blows with Hammering Henry at close quarters. With Pacho rolling helplessly along the ropes under Armstrong's merciless attack, Referee Jack Bloom stepped between the fighters and stopped the bout after little more than a minute of the fourth round.'[131]

Armstrong had defended the world's welterweight title five times within 22 days – a little over three weeks' time. He had scored a total of nine knockdowns in approximately 63 minutes and 25 seconds of fighting – a little more than 21 total rounds of actual ring combat.

It was Christmas, and in Cleveland, Ohio, that meant the annual *Cleveland News* toyshop fund promoted by Ed Bang,

---

131 *Galveston Daily News*, Texas, 31 October 1939.

sports editor of the *News*, and a 'bang' up fistic feast for the fans. The 1939 card was topped by two world champions, middleweight king Al Hostak and welterweight super-champ Hurricane Henry Armstrong, and 11,000 fans were already lining up for tickets to the arena.

'Armstrong, who two weeks ago called off a title jam with Lou Ambers because of an attack of flu, certainly has staged a most rapid recovery. Watching the sleek Negro glide around the Arena battleground last night one would never have thought he had been laid low by the flu bug. Henry was all gloves as he gave Jimmy Garrison a neat going over and after the third round one had just the faintest suspicion that the classy Armstrong could name the round for the kill.

'And this was surprising, for several months ago Jimmy Garrison gave Armstrong the toughest kind of a battle out on the Pacific coast, staying ten rounds with Hammering Hank and losing by only the scantest of margins. A no-count knockdown Henry scored in the eighth decided that battle in his favour.

'But last night Armstrong was the fast-stepping lad who at one time held three crowns – featherweight, lightweight and welterweight. He has given up all but the welter toga. Garrison travelled more or less on even terms with Armstrong in the first two rounds. The Kansas City boy made his best showing in the second when he stood toe-to-toe with Henry during almost the entire round and traded punch for punch with the dusky swinger. But that savage round sapped most of Jimmy's stamina and punching prowess. From the third round on until the finish he was just another target for Armstrong's merciless fists.

CHAPTER THIRTEEN

'Garrison took a severe battering and his face looked as if it had come into contact with a meat grinder. He was badly cut about both eyes but he stayed in there gamely until Armstrong went to work in earnest in the seventh. A slashing right flush on the jaw dropped Garrison for a nine count shortly after the round opened. He climbed back to his feet but there was a glassy look in his eyes. Swiftly Hammerin' Hank moved in and an equally torrid right connected and again Garrison was down. This time, the referee, former lightweight champion Benny Leonard, waved Armstrong to his corner. Jimmy was through for the night.

'The show attracted a gate of 10,988 fans, grossed $28,579 and dumped $10,000 into the *Cleveland News* toyshop fund. Unfortunately Henry's Cleveland caper did not go unnoticed. Commissioner D. Walker Wear of the New York State Athletic Association said today he would recommend suspension of Henry Armstrong, welterweight champion, for fighting Jimmy Garrison in Cleveland last night after failing to meet Lou Ambers in New York on 1 December. "There is no question but that Armstrong ran out on his fight with Ambers," said Wear. Armstrong contracted a cold and the bout with Ambers was cancelled. The commission cautioned the champion he should not fight Garrison.'

Armstrong's manager Eddie Mead was suspended following the September fight for his vociferous outburst when Ambers regained the lightweight title on a controversial decision.

While New York sorted itself out, Armstrong went home to St Louis to give his old hero a shot at the title. Joe Ghnouly, a 27-year-old Italian, was a ten-year veteran who once excited

Henry's admiration when he worked out in a St Louis gym, and found his heralded bolo punch to be ineffective against the champion. Henry had knocked out Lew Feldman in the first round of his last St Louis appearance and looked set to duplicate that feat when he sent Joe to the canvas three times in the opening round. Joe was dropped first by a left hook, then a left to the head and a right to the body, then he fell a third time before the bell. With the 5,000 fans on their feet, Ghnouly got on his bike for the second and third rounds, but Henry caught him in the fourth and Joe was on the deck when the bell saved him. In the fifth, Armstrong met Ghnouly with three left hooks to end his title dream.

'If he could turn back the calendar a couple of years, Pedro Montanez might lift the world welterweight championship from the Henry Armstrong he is to tackle over 15 rounds at the Garden on 24 January,' wrote Harry Grayson, then added, 'Armstrong isn't the fighter he was, but neither is Montanez. Armstrong used racial prejudice to get out of an appointment with Ceferino Garcia in Los Angeles on 22 February ... said he couldn't tackle the Filipino at Wrigley Field under the auspices of the Hollywood Post of the American Legion when that organisation refused coloured lads the right to perform in its indoor arena.

'At this late date, experts of the manly art of mangling mugs claim to have found a flaw in Armstrong's armour ... say he can no longer absorb body belts. Montanez is a vicious body puncher, but Armstrong always has protected his breadbasket well. Armstrong isn't throwing as many punches as he formerly did. Hammering Henry is gripping the canvas with his toes now ... making sure shots count.

CHAPTER THIRTEEN

'Montanez has had 54 fights in this country, every one a main event. Prior to coming to the United States from his native Puerto Rico, he went to Europe where he whipped the lightweight title-holders of a half dozen countries. Infected teeth and diseased tonsils, which have been removed, curtailed his activities a year ago. He expects to scale 146 pounds for Armstrong, which gives him an edge of eight or nine pounds.'[132]

Joe Williams was ringside for this graphic account. 'The referee stepped in and stopped the fight in the ninth round last night but there was only one round the Madison Square Garden patrons remembered. And by the same token it will be a long time before they forget it …

'One minute of the fourth round had passed when Armstrong caught Montanez against the ropes and cracked him with a right hand to the temple that shook and seemed to daze him … he stood there against the ropes helpless, blood dripping from an old cut over his right eye, and Armstrong swarmed all over him.

'Bang! Bang! Bang! One punch after another as fast as Armstrong could throw them, faster than ringsiders in the press section could tabulate them. During this violent bombardment he went down twice. He had never been on the floor and he had a fierce pride in this record. Somehow he managed to straighten up and regain a fighting posture. Once again Armstrong beat him down and on the way he fell into the lower rope in a sitting position and sat there while the referee's count gave him temporary surcease from the human

---

132 Harry Grayson, *Cumberland Evening Times*, Maryland, 18 January 1940.

fury in front of him. Nobody knows for sure exactly how many times he was hit ... For by this time Montanez was literally a human punching bag.

'This was prize fighting at its ugliest, and, paradoxically, at its emotional peak. It was a bloody, senseless, revolting slaughter, a helpless dazed, hurt fighter being hacked to pieces. There never can be anything lovely about such a spectacle, and yet it is these sickening senses that bring out human qualities which demand admiration. Out of the slaughter Montanez emerged a heroic pattern in raw courage. No fighter in our memory ever gamed his way through such a cruel, relentless, almost unending attack.

'This was the round that cost him the fight, but it was also the round which established him as a gallant fighting man.'[133]

---

133 Joe Williams, *Syracuse Herald Journal*, 25 January 1940.

Chapter Fourteen

'WITH THE possible exception of Pancho Villa, the mightiest explosive Philippine ringman shipped into the US mainland from the tiny atoll in the Pacific was bolo puncher Ceferino Garcia. Garcia led the vanguard of great Filipino scrappers that included Small Montana, Pablo Dano, Speedy Dano and Ignacio Fernandez. Managed by George Parnassus throughout his prolific career, the hard-punching 5ft 6in 145-pound keg of dynamite unleashed his fury of professional ring punishment in his debut during the year 1927. Arriving in the US in the year 1932, Garcia settled on the west coast where, during the 30s and 40s, he became a popular ring figure at the Hollywood Legion Stadium and Olympic Auditorium.'[134]

In no time at all he was fighting men like Young Corbett, Freddie Steele, Kid Azteca and Bobby Pacho. September 1935 saw the Filipino matched with welterweight champ Barney Ross in a non-title affair in San Francisco. 'Ross was the toughest fighter I ever met inside the ring,' he said. 'The first time I fought him I landed a terrific right-hand shot to his jaw and dropped him.

---

134 Jess Hernandez, *Ring*, October 1976.

'But Barney got up and beat me. He won the fight going away. He was a great champion.'

Garcia lost to Ross in Barney's Chicago home town, and in September 1937 was given a shot at Barney's world title on the Carnival of Champions, one of four world-title bouts promoted by Mike Jacobs in New York. It seemed that the Filipino's vaunted bolo punch, a cross between a right hook and an uppercut developed in cutting the sugar cane back home in Manila, was not performing too well. Given a shot at Henry Armstrong the following year, who had beaten Ross to a standstill to become welter champ, Ceferino had high hopes.

'But he was going against the fighter writer Harry Ferguson termed "the closest thing to a perpetual motion machine the US Patent Office will ever see," the fighter Gayle Talbot described to his readers: "Armstrong is not of course, a real person. Historians will know that he was a legendary character made up by some Orson Welles of the fight racket as a rival attraction to the Man from Mars.'

Ferguson wrote, 'Armstrong, the little man, 134 pounds of drive and dynamite, gave one of the great exhibitions of his great career in Madison Square Garden last night against Garcia, the big man, and won all the way. Standing in the haze of smoke at ringside, promoter Mike Jacobs announced that Armstrong, like Alexander, had whipped so many people he sighed for new worlds to conquer.'

Talbot wrote, 'Garcia lifted Henry clear off his feet with several terrific belts in the Garden last night, but all it got the husky Filipino was a beating he will remember long after he has returned to the cane fields. Armstrong, who at 134 pounds, looked like a midget before his 146½-pound rival,

CHAPTER FOURTEEN

practically knocked the daylights out of Garcia. He won nine of the 15 rounds by wide margins and lost only five, one of which was taken away from him by Referee Arthur Donovan because of a low blow.'[135]

Jack Cuddy, reporting for United Press, stated: 'Only twice during the bout did Garcia land dangerously with his whistling uppercut. He staggered Henry in the sixth round, and jarred him groggy in the 12th, bringing the crowd to its feet cheering thunderously. It was one of the few whole-throated cheers during the bout. A right uppercut smashed into Henry's reddened face and knocked him back on his heels. Armstrong's knees buckled momentarily, but he continued bobbing about and Garcia was unable to connect with that elusive target.

'Armstrong admitted that Garcia had plenty of dynamite in his bolo. He said he was staggered on three occasions. He said that the one that hurt most was in the 12th. That was the blow that closed his left eye, although it had started to swell earlier.'[136]

Parnassus started thinking. Garcia was a middleweight, and it took the Armstrong defeat to open their eyes. George, a Phoenix businessman, got Garcia back in the gym, straightened out his finances, and hired a trainer, Johnny Villaflor, who would also serve as Garcia's driver. There was no way Parnassus wanted Garcia behind the wheel of a car. His love for speed had been well documented by the California highway patrol.

---

135 *Cumberland Evening Times*, Maryland, 26 November 1938.
136 Jack Cuddy, *Nevada State Journal*, 26 November 1939.

Garcia won his next nine fights and landed a fight with Fred Apostoli, who was recognised by the New York Commission as middleweight champ. Well, he was up to the seventh round of their fight in Madison Square Garden on 2 October 1939. Garcia entered the ring a 2-1 underdog, but the ferocious Filipino controlled the action from the opening bell, knocking Apostoli down three times in the seventh round. Referee Billy Cavanaugh stopped the fight halfway through the final count and at two minutes seven seconds of the round, Ceferino Garcia was the new champion, recognised by the New York Commission and the California State Athletic Commission.

Jack Mahon wrote, 'Garcia proved in outgaming a great, game battler that he is one of the real punchers in modern ringdom. The only guy with a wallop outside of Joe Louis, Ceferino is the Louis of the smaller men.'[137]

'I left the Philippines in 1932,' he told a reporter a few days before the fight, 'and said I would never come back until I was champion.' Along with immortal flyweight champion Pancho Villa, Garcia had become the most idolised Filipino fighter of all time.

Ceferino, with his new bride Evangeline on one arm and his championship belt on the other, made his welcome home parade in Manila as crowds cheered, a national holiday was declared, and the festivities lasted for several day, and those crowds wanted to see their hero in a fight.

The local promoter got busy and Garcia went back to the gym. He was going to defend his title against Glen

---

137 Jack Mahon, *New York Times*, 3 October 1939.

Lee from Nebraska, a guy who had already given Ceferino a stiff argument in two fights, winning the first one and losing the second. Garcia used his bolo punch to good effect and the bell saved Lee from a knockout in rounds two and three. He still fancied his chances and jumped at the fight when offered.

A crowd estimated at 40,000 jammed their way into the Rizal Memorial Sports Complex in Manila on 23 December 1939 and former heavyweight champion Jack Dempsey was paid $7,500 to travel halfway around the world to referee the fight, the first world-title bout ever held in the Philippine Islands. Among the spectators were Francis B. Sayre, United States high commissioner to the Philippines, and President Manuel Quezon of the Philippines. They saw a good fight.

United Press reported: 'Ceferino Garcia, recognised by the New York State Athletic Association as middleweight champion, retained his title tonight by scoring a technical knockout over Glen Lee of Nebraska in the 13th round of a scheduled 15-rounds bout. Referee Jack Dempsey halted the contest a few seconds before the bell rang to end the 13th round. Garcia dropped Lee for a count of eight in the 13th and when the Nebraskan got up Garcia floored him again. Lee arose at the count of nine, but was in such bad shape that Dempsey halted the fight and awarded the victory to Garcia.

'Garcia, performing before a hometown crowd, gave a great demonstration of his famous bolo punch. Despite the fact that it drizzled through the fight, making the canvas slippery, Garcia fought a sure, confident bout. He drew blood from Lee's mouth in the first round and scored a total of seven knockdowns before the bout was halted. According to the UP scorecard, Garcia won every round except the first and sixth rounds which were scored even. After the bout Garcia told Lee, "I only had to give Apostoli one hook before he went down, but I gave you a million punches and you kept getting up." Garcia's claim to the title is still not clear, however, for the NBA recognise Al Hostak of Seattle as champion.'[138]

'ARMSTRONG CANCELS LOS ANGELES FIGHT' the United Press reported from New York on 16 January. 'Because of alleged racial discrimination, Henry Armstrong has cancelled at last his middleweight title fight with champion Ceferino Garcia at Los Angeles on 22 February. This ten-round title bout at Wrigley Field has been a pugilistic storm centre for many weeks since it threatened Mike Jacobs' control over his contracted champions.

'Armstrong, the Los Angeles Negro who holds the world's welterweight crown, called off the bout Sunday night after charging that the Hollywood post of the American Legion discriminated against Negro fighters.

'Armstrong cancelled the bout after long distance conversations with Los Angeles Negro leaders. These leaders informed Hammering Henry that the *Hollywood Post* had recently rejected a petition to permit Negro fighters to fight at the *Post*'s Hollywood stadium. Armstrong's manager Eddie Mead explained that Negro leather slingers never have been permitted to fight at the Hollywood stadium, although Mexicans and Filipinos were welcomed.'

Mead quoted Armstrong as saying, 'If Negro boys can't fight at the *Hollywood Post*'s stadium, why should I fight for

---

138 *Syracuse Herald*. 24 December 1939.

CHAPTER FOURTEEN

the *Post* at Wrigley Field? Coloured boys were allowed to fight in the trenches with white boys in the last world war – were allowed to give their lives for their country. Why should the Hollywood Legion discriminate against them now?'

'Promoter Charlie MacDonald, representing the *Hollywood Post*, announced this match several weeks ago. It was expected to draw close to $150,000. When it was announced, promoter Mike Jacobs – who has both Garcia and Armstrong under contract for title activities – declared he would prevent it.'[139]

Good news from Los Angeles on 1 February: 'The *Hollywood Post* of the American Legion this week ended its Jim Crow policy of refusing to permit Negro boxers to appear at the Legion Stadium. The action was the direct result of an intensive campaign of protests by Los Angeles Negro organisations, supported by labour and many progressive groups. The campaign was dramatised and given momentum last week by the statement of Henry Armstrong condemning the discrimination of the Legion – and cancelling a scheduled fight with Ceferino Garcia in which the Legion had a promotional interest.

'The sports page of the "People's World" West Coast labour and progressive paper played a major role in organising opinion and pressing for action to end the Legion's Jim Crow policy. The rising ride of protests forced the California State Athletic Committee to hold a two-day hearing on the matter. The hearing was ended when Ernest Orfilla, Legion spokesman, threw up the Jim Crow sponge and guaranteed

---
139 *Lincoln Nebraska State Journal*, 16 January 1940.

147

an ending to all discrimination at the Legion Stadium in the future.'[140]

In Los Angeles on 18 February, Jack Guenther, United Press staff correspondent, was writing, 'Life begins at 32, and for authority we refer you to George Parnassus, dealer in pugilists. Mr Parnassus has the proof right with him – Ceferino Garcia. Garcia is a middleweight boxer with a right hand that produces sleep quicker than a pint of chloroform. He has been following his trade since he was a boy of 14. Since he has just turned 32, that makes 18 years of fighting in all. Mr Parnassus holds that Garcia at 32 is a more effective workman than ever before and that, actually, his career is only beginning. By 1930 he was the welterweight champion of the Orient and in 1932 he came to the United States. He debarked with two distinctions other than his title. He was and still is the largest of all Filipino athletes, yet the most he ever weighed is 155 pounds. As well, he was the only member of the Tagologs – one of 32 Filipino tribes – to attain athletic prominence.

'Next 1 March he expects to settle an old score with a fellow townsman, Henry Armstrong, who will debut that night as a middleweight in search of his fourth crown. Armstrong never has been whipped as welter and Garcia never has lost as a middleweight. "Of course I'm prejudiced," Mr Parnassus explained, "but I truly believe Garcia should be an inspiration to young athletes. He has proven age doesn't matter, so long as a man keeps fit and trim. Think of it, 18 years of fighting and he's better than ever."'[141]

---
140 *Cleveland Call and Post,* 1 February 1940.
141 *Nevada State Journal,* 19 February 1940.

CHAPTER FOURTEEN

They weren't saying that about Henry as he prepared for the Garcia fight. 'There were those who said Henry was through – that he was now starting down the other side of the hill. He didn't think so. No fighter ever does, so long as he can fight. Henry was still welterweight champ; Garcia was a middleweight. Henry looked forward to getting that middleweight crown; it would make four titles! He wanted that victory, and bad.

'A week before the fight, he was training one morning and his trainer told him there was a meeting he was supposed to attend at the gym on Main Street.

'He went meekly to the gym, into a back room, where he found several men standing around. One of them threw a pile of bills on the table. Henry estimated quickly that it was about $15,000.

'"Take it," said the stranger. "It's all yours."

'"What for?" asked the startled Henry.

'There was a silence for a minute, and then the man said, "Look, champ, I don't know just how to give you this, but – that money's all yours if you'll let Garcia put you down in three rounds."

'Yes, that's what they meant. Take a dive! Henry saw red – He thought of all his friends along Central Avenue, in Los Angeles, betting on him and counting on him, and he really got mad.

'"I wouldn't do that for a million," he shouted. "I'm fighting Garcia on the level, as hard as I know how. If he wins he'll have to knock me out."

'They started to reason with him. He wasn't reasoning, wasn't buying any of it. "Shut up and get out of here," he told them. "If you try it again, I'll go to the FBI." They got out. He was never approached with a bribe again.'[142]

'With the money he has accumulated from nine years of battling, Henry plans to settle down quietly and start leading a literary life, like Gene Tunney. Armstrong makes it clear that he is not retiring this year because he feels he is through as a fighter, but because the atmosphere of gymnasiums, training camps and the like are not conducive to literary output.

"'It is the long training grind for fights that runs Henry crazy," Eddie Mead, Armstrong's manager, told me. "All he really needs to get ready for a scrap is five or six days. Take the one he is going to have with Ceferino Garcia here this month. He could start work a week before the fight and be in top shape. But he can't do that. With publicity being as necessary to a fight as it is, he must start a month early so that the newspaper men can write about him and the fight fans can go and see him work."

'In regard with Armstrong's fight with Garcia for the middleweight championship, Mead, one of the most sensible managers in the game, doesn't lightly dismiss the chances of the Filipino. "Garcia hits so hard that he will have a chance against anybody as long as he is able to climb into a ring," Mead said. "That bolo punch of his, which is nothing more than a dressed-up right-hand uppercut, is a killer. When Henry fought him in New York Garcia caught him at the back of the ear with the bolo in the 12th round and Henry started dropping. He managed to come out of it before falling,

---

142 Henry Armstrong, *Gloves, Glory and God*, 1957.

CHAPTER FOURTEEN

but he wouldn't have had the punch caught him on the chin. Garcia will stiffen anybody he hits squarely."'[143]

A news bulletin from Los Angeles on 18 February stated that Garcia wouldn't be hitting anybody in the near future. 'The California Boxing Commission tonight postponed the ten-round middleweight championship fight between Henry Armstrong and Ceferino Garcia to 1 March because of a rope burn on Garcia's leg. The fight was scheduled here on Thursday night. The boxing commissioners accepted the report of Dr W. L. Carver, who examined Garcia today and set the fight the following Friday.

'Garcia suffered the burn in training preparations last week. Dr Carver said the sore now "looked like a boil." The burn, or boil, on Garcia's leg will be lanced tomorrow or Tuesday, his physician said. The Filipino's leg was slightly red yesterday but he was able to work out with it. When he appeared in the gymnasium today, it was swollen from an infection which hot towels were unable to prevent. Postponement will not hurt either one, the trainers said, since Garcia will weigh around 152 and Armstrong 140 for the 160-pound title. The gate will be stimulated by bringing the event on the eve of Santa Anita's $100,000 Handicap when thousands of visitors will be in town.'[144]

When news of Garcia's rope burn reached New York, it brought a rare smile to the face of Lou Stillman. Talking to sportswriter Jack Cuddy in his world-famous gymnasium on Eighth Avenue, Lou described 'our current crop of prize-fighters as a bunch of softies.'

---
143 Henry McLemore, *South Haven Daily Tribune*, Michigan, 13 February 1940.
144 *Nevada State Journal*, 19 February 1940.

151

A week later, three important fights have been postponed or cancelled because of 1) a rope burn on middleweight champion Ceferino Garcia's right leg: 2) a boil under light-heavyweight champion Billy Conn's right arm, and 3) a touch of flu in heavyweight contender Lee Savold's right lung.

'Conn was scheduled to make a return title defence against Gus Lesnevich at Miami on Wednesday night but his boil postponed the bout. Savold was due to tangle with Bob Pastor in a 12-round bout at Madison Square Garden on Friday night but his flu knocked that out.'[145]

In his preview of Armstrong–Garcia, syndicated columnist Grantland Rice wrote: 'Hammering Henry will start swinging at every sector of Garcia's body from the waist to the top of the head. With Armstrong it will be the old matter of breaking up balance – mental and physical balance. This fight even has Al Jolson puzzled. Jolson, the "Mammy" song singer, was one of the first to put up money with Eddie Mead for the Armstrong contract. Apparently he isn't sure that Armstrong can weather some of the heavier punches he must take from a much bigger man – and a much harder hitter.

'While Armstrong can throw 300 or more punches per round in an exhibition, his limit is around 70 a minute in an actual fight. But this happens to be slightly better than a punch a second. Most of these punches carry little force. They leave no definite dent upon chin or stomach. They merely befuddle or check the other fellow's offensive. They keep him from getting set – after the old Harry Greb style, employed against Gene Tunney, Tom Gibbons and then Jack Dempsey

---

145 Jack Cuddy, *Salt Lake Tribune*, Utah, 1 March 1940.

CHAPTER FOURTEEN

in training … All in all, this battle for the middleweight championship has more than a few interesting angles as far as boxing competition is concerned. It even has the gambling element tied into a number of knots. "You bet 10 to 9," one of the leading layers told me, "and you take your pick. I haven't any pick."

'I'd say that Armstrong carries the edge. I'm still a believer in anyone who can upset balance – in any who has the superior speed. On form this should be one of the best – one of the most interesting ring contests that 1940 has to offer. It is a battle of opposites – and that always means action.'[146]

From the premier wordsmith of the press benches to a man who can talk both hind legs off a donkey, 'Dumb' Dan Morgan, only he is far from being dumb. Sportswriter Dillon Graham wrote this for Associated Press on the eve of the Armstrong–Garcia fight: 'Dumb Dan Morgan has the idea that Homicidal Hank will get a punch in the puss that'll set him to star-gazing. After exactly 37 minutes of punching the bag with his vocal chords, during which he employed several thousand quickly chosen words, some of which have not yet found their way into the dictionary, Dumb Dan managed to express his four-word opinion: "Garcia will kayo Armstrong."

'Dumb Dan Morgan, dumb as a slick red fox, has managed enough fighters to start a colony and has the voice of experience. He has had three world champions. "You gotta crowd Armstrong, stay on top of him all the time," Dan explained. "He's a great fighter with a marvellous source of stamina. Hank has to keep bullying and roughing

---

146 Grantland Rice, *The Evening Star*, Washington DC, 21 February 1940.

an opponent. As long as he can run the show and push you around and keep you off balance, he'll win. It'll take a fellow strong enough to out-bully Hank to beat him. A chap who will push against Hank and make him give ground. That's what Garcia will do. He'll have the weight advantage. Garcia should have beaten him last time. He had him ready for a knockout twice but Hank got away. Garcia was short of stamina that night. Taking off poundage to make the weight taxed his strength. This time Garcia will be at his natural middleweight poundage. He'll have his full strength and he'll lick Armstrong," Dumb Dan said.'[147]

An AP news item dated Hollywood 26 February read: 'Henry Armstrong, who comes Friday and is going after Ceferino Garcia's middleweight title, took a rest today because his trainer feared he might go stale. Harry Armstrong said, "Hammering Henry was near his best fighting pitch and would work out only briefly tomorrow and Wednesday." The fight first was scheduled for 22 February but postponed when Garcia developed a boil on his knee. Betting odds have shifted from 4-5 against Garcia to 8-5 in his favour.'[148]

---

147 Dillon Graham, *Twin Falls News*, Idaho, 28 February 1940.
148 *Ogden Standard Examiner*, 26 February 1940.

Chapter Fifteen

THE GILMORE Stadium in Los Angeles had a reported capacity of 18,000, but on that Thursday evening in March 1940, a raucous crowd of about 20,000 pushed their way in to see the championship fight between welterweight champion Henry Armstrong and Ceferino Garcia, one of the biggest Filipino fighters ever to show in the States. Garcia was recognised as middleweight champion by the New York State Athletic Association and the California Athletic Commission, and it was for that title the boys were arguing tonight. When they hit the scales at one o'clock that afternoon, neither was anywhere near the middleweight poundage, Garcia making 153½ to Armstrong's 142. Henry had already made boxing history by becoming the only fighter to win and hold three world titles simultaneously. Now he was going for his fourth title against Garcia, a guy he had beaten in November 1938 when defending his welterweight title. But now the Filipino was at his natural weight, giving him a 12-pound advantage. A big advantage!

'If Armstrong, weighing 140 or less, can whip Garcia he will stand out as the most sensational performer in the history of the ring, no matter how far back you go to Grecian and Roman fighting days,' wrote Grantland

Rice, adding, 'Garcia will pack more than ten extra pounds into action at this meeting. This means a lot more than any such discrepancy among heavyweights. Garcia, the middleweight king, is an artilleryman. He figures that one of his punches, if it lands, will more than offset ten or 20 punches thrown by Hammering Henry and his machine-gun rataplan.

"'I'll nail him on the right spot before the fight is over," Garcia tells you, "and when I do he'll know he has been hit. I've found out he can't hurt me. He's a tough fellow to tag because he always is in motion, but don't think he can't be hit. I know Armstrong can take it, but you can only take so much. He isn't going to keep me off balance for any ten rounds, even if he throws 500 punches a round. I know a lot more now than I did a year ago."

'Whatever happens, this fight has the entire West Coast pretty well churned up. For one thing, they know when Armstrong fights there'll be all the action anyone could ask for. In the second place, they know that when Garcia happens to land it isn't a matter of chucking daffodils or thistle blossoms.'[149]

Writing for United Press, Henry McLemore raised a point that didn't seem to be bothering anyone else. 'Someone whose taste in literature is bad was reading the book on California State boxing rules the other day and came across this informative and superbly written paragraph:

"'Each contestant shall wear, during such contest, gloves weighing not less than five ounces if such contestant weighs,

---

149 Grantland Rice, *The Evening Star,* Washington DC, 19 February 1940.

CHAPTER FIFTEEN

in ring attire, 145 pounds or less; six-ounce gloves if contestant weighs more than 145 pounds."

'When its full meaning became clear to him, he made for the telephone to call Eddie Mead, manager of Henry Armstrong. The cause of Mead's delight concerning the information about the five-ounce gloves is obvious. Armstrong fights Ceferino Garcia for the middleweight championship here next Friday and as Henry can't possibly weigh in at more than 140 he will be able to use the lighter gloves. Garcia, who will scale considerably more than 145 will be forced to use the heavier gloves.

'Well, some of my best friends have cauliflowered-ears and they tell me that one ounce makes one heck of a difference. Which explains why Garcia's board of control is raising such a fuss about Armstrong's lighter gloves, and even threatening to call off the fight if he is allowed to use them.

'Light gloves are a help to any fighter. There is less padding over the knuckles and any blow landed is going to be more effective. Having to carry one less ounce in either fist will be definitely to his advantage. Over ten rounds – hundreds of punches – the ounce adds up to something really important.

'The commission may be called on to settle the question this time. Because as little as an ounce sounds, it can be an important factor in a fight. It was not reported if the Commission made any decision re the Armstrong–Garcia fight.'

A similar situation occurred on 29 May 1933 when Jimmy McLarnin challenged Young Corbett III for the welterweight championship at Wrigley Field in Los Angeles. McLarnin, the Vancouver Irishman, hammered Corbett loose from the title in two minutes 37 seconds of the opening round, Referee George Blake stopping the fight after the champion had been floored three times.

'The California State law allowed boxers weighing less than 145 pounds to wear five-ounce gloves, and fighters weighing above that mark were obliged to wear gloves not lighter than six ounces. A welterweight championship match was made at 147 pounds and both the Commission and Corbett expected that six-ounce gloves would be worn by both champion and challenger on the basis that in fighting for the welterweight title Jimmy theoretically became a 147-pounder.

'But Pop Foster, McLarnin's manager, contended that in as much as Jimmy would weigh less than 145 pounds for the bout, he would be within the rules by wearing five-ounce gloves for the title scrap. Pop told the press that if White and Corbett had their way they'd be fighting with pillows. He claimed that in the presence of witnesses, when the match was made, Larry White, Corbett's manager, agreed to let Jimmy use the lighter gloves. A compromise on the gloves of five-and-a-half ounces was reached.'[150]

At noon on the day of the Armstrong–Garcia fight, chairman Jerry Giesler of the California State Athletic Commission sat down with the other four members to select the referee for the main event. Three names were on the list – George Blake, Abe Roth and Jack Kennedy, with the veteran Blake as front runner, and when the ring announcer named the 'man in charge of the action', it was Blake who climbed into the ring.

---

150 Andrew Gallimore, *The Jimmy McLarnin Story*, 2009.

CHAPTER FIFTEEN

'George Vincent Blake arrived in Los Angeles sometime during 1904 from Chicago, where he claimed to have been a boxer. He started his officiating career in San Diego and by the early 1920s he was the regular referee at Jack Doyle's Vernon Arena and the Hollywood Legion Stadium … He took an interest in young, promising Fidel LaBarba, a future Olympic gold medallist and world flyweight champion. Blake would eventually manage world bantam champion Pete Sanstol, Harry Kid Matthews, Joe Salas, Clayton Frye and Toby Vigil. Blake was known as a man of impeccable character. When he agreed to sign Sanstol, the young Norwegian cabled his parents in Oslo "that I was being managed by the biggest figure and the best-liked man in all America."'[151]

'Matchmaker Charlie McDonald announced that a sum of $35,000 was already in the till, which tops by a wide margin the previous box office sum of $21,000, which was taken ahead of the fight three years ago between Bob Pastor and Bob Nestell. The only dark outlook for the bout was the possibility of bad weather. If it rains, the crowd will be very slim as California people never venture to sports events in the rain. While the fighters rested, awaiting the weighing-in ceremony at noon, Friday, the rival managers, Eddie Mead of Armstrong and George Parnasssus of Garcia, continued a word battle.

"'I hope Armstrong doesn't slip and unhinge his sacre-jilliback or whatever it was that happened to him in New York," Parnassus declared, recalling the pre-fight injury to Henry before the 1938 engagement between the two fighters. And

---

151 *BoxRec*, December 1952.

Mead retorted, "Don't worry about Armstrong. You'd better watch out for your Filipino. He's liable to get his sacroiliac broke all to pieces in the ring."[152]

'In March 1940, when he stepped into the ring at the Gilmore Stadium, George Blake was 71 years old, and already thinking of retiring. Right now he had a fight to referee. Seconds out!

'Round one: Adopting his customary attacks Hammerin' Henry bored in shooting short punches to the body from a crouch. Garcia laced his opponent around the head. Armstrong stuck his head in the Filipino's chest, flailing away with both hands. Garcia scored effectively with right and left uppercuts. The referee cautioned Armstrong for butting with his head. Each landed a vicious body punch toward the end of the round. The Filipino landed the hardest punches.

'Round Two: Armstrong drove in flailing wildly but ineffectively. He scored twice with left hooks to the jaw but Garcia came back with a battering two-handed attack that had Henry backing. Garcia landed two looping rights to the body and each scored with short rights to the stomach. Armstrong backed Garcia into a corner and rained punches on the Filipino. Henry whipped over two left hooks to the face and continued to batter Garcia as the bell ended the session. Garcia returned to his corner with blood flowing from a cut over his right eye.

'Round Three: They continued the furious pace, Armstrong spearing for Garcia's patched-up eye. He tossed ten punches to the Filipino's one in a wild melee that had

---

152 *Baltimore Afro-American*, Maryland, 2 March 1940.

the fans cheering wildly. Garcia rallied to drive in two husky rights to the body, but he was quickly crowded back into the ropes. Garcia's eye was bleeding again as he took punch after punch to the face and midsection. The Filipino's body punch landed on Armstrong's left side and spun him into the ropes but he came back swinging with both hands. Garcia was crowded into a corner taking punches as the round ended.'[153]

'Round Four: Armstrong's left eye is beginning to swell as the round starts, and Garcia helps the matter with a big right. Head-to-head they stand, banging away like lumberjacks attacking an old oak. Again Armstrong is warned for butting. Another left hook sends blood flying from Garcia's eye. Hank is grunting with every punch as he drives Ceferino to the corner again and the barrage has the champ's face covered in red from the hammering.

'Round Five: Armstrong rushes out and begins throwing punches well before he is in range and few land. Garcia begins to box on the outside where he is strongest. A mean left to the face followed by a right to the body by Garcia was the first effective combination of the round, and Ceferino tries to circle the centre of the ring with Armstrong attached to him like a bad cold. The pace slows for a minute, then they are back toe to toe. Armstrong lands a few down under and the round ends with Armstrong's eye swollen the size of a golf ball. Garcia's round.

'Round Six: Between rounds the corner seconds cut Armstrong's eye to relieve the swelling. The exchanges continued in the centre of the ring with no one taking the

---

153 *Cumberland News* Maryland, 2 March 1940.

upper hand until Garcia landed a big left hook to the body. The flurries reopened the bleeding in Ceferino's eye and Armstrong begins to hold his elbows high, blocking many of the blows coming at him and protecting his eye which is swelling again. Armstrong lands three big left hooks and covers from a series of uppercuts to his chest and chin. Round is even at the end.'[154]

'It was a mauling battle for the middleweight title, so crammed with blows that referee George Blake did not once have to step in to separate the two. It was a rough battle in which Armstrong had two rounds taken away from him for low punches and elbow punches, and in which Garcia was warned by the referee after the fourth round to "lay off" those kidney punches. Armstrong was the aggressor throughout, swarming all over Garcia and keeping the fighting at such close range that the title-holder had no chance to deliver his famous "bolo punch," a long looping right. Garcia's manager claimed that two boils on his fighter's left leg slowed the champion down.'[155]

'Round Seven: Armstrong's left eye was almost closed as they came out for the seventh; Garcia adopted new tactics to shove his rival back with one hand and punch with the other. It worked a couple of times until Armstrong brought his elbows closer to his body. Garcia was more at ease and landed repeatedly. Armstrong beat a tattoo on Garcia's body. The Filipino continued shooting for the face. He landed hard a couple of times, receipted for a sharp left hook that made the blood flow again as the round ended.

---

154 Keith Terceira, *BOXINGSCENE*, 26 February 2008.
155 *Moline Daily Dispatch*, Illinois, 2 March 1940.

CHAPTER FIFTEEN

'Round Eight: They were flailing away at each other head-to-head as soon as the round opened. Garcia scored several times at long range, twice landing with strong right uppercuts. Henry's elbowing and head-butting tactics brought shouts of disapproval, but the referee said nothing. Armstrong landed lefts and rights on Garcia's chin as he backed the latter into the ropes. The Filipino weathered the barrage and came back with a two-fisted attack of his own that had Armstrong halted in his tracks as the bell clanged.

'Round Nine: Armstrong peered through his one good eye and started swinging as soon as they came together. The swift pace was telling on both, but they never ceased pounding. Garcia's bolo punch started from the canvas, grazing Armstrong's chin with no damage. Armstrong was landing occasionally and missing more frequently. He cracked Garcia's jaw with a right and left, drove two rights to the body and took a right to the midsection in return. As in most of the other rounds, the Filipino was fighting off the ropes at the bell. Armstrong's round.

'Round Ten: With the crowd on its feet, the two met in the centre of the ring for the bloody tenth, hardly touching gloves, and went at it toe to toe, blow for blow. Armstrong, for once throwing punches from long range, moved into a lead. Garcia scored with a right to the chin and Armstrong retaliated with a steady tattoo on his opponent's face and body. Garcia got in two effective rights to the chin but for the most part his blows were landing on Armstrong's elbows. Armstrong landed rights and lefts to the face.

'They were banging away after the bell ended the last round. Armstrong landed at least half a dozen punches to the body after the bell while Garcia raised his hands over his head.'[156]

'The champion bled from mouth and nose almost from the start, while Armstrong's left eye started closing early in the fight. In the last two rounds the soggy flying fists of both gladiators were spraying blood over the newspapermen in the press row. It was one of the most savage bouts ever seen in a California ring and one that wrecked the little brown bomber's dream of capturing a fourth title in his spectacular career. When referee Blake managed to stop them fighting after the final bell, he threw up both hands for his draw decision at the finish. The referee took one round away from Armstrong for low punches – the fifth – and twice warned him for illegal use of his elbows and shoulders.'[157]

'Both fighters were badly cut up and Parnassus claimed an injured left hand would necessitate a postponement of a scheduled match with Ken Overlin in New York. "You'd need a baseball bat and a knife to fight that guy Armstrong," snapped Parnassus as he looked over the champ's bruises and bumps in the dressing room after the fight. When Eddie Mead, Armstrong's manager, heard that, he laughed and said maliciously, "That gang is a bunch of cry-babies." Henry himself bore many marks of the battle and he complained of a bad right arm. Mead said X-rays would be taken today to determine whether or not any serious injury had been sustained.'[158]

'Armstrong came rolling down the stretch and had the bout been scheduled for the recognised championship route

---

156 *Uniontown Morning Herald*, Pennsylvania, 2 March 1940.
157 *Salt Lake Tribune*, Utah, 2 March 1940.
158 *Moline Daily Dispatch*, Illinois, 2 March 1940.

CHAPTER FIFTEEN

of 15 rounds he probably would have won even easier if not by a clean knockout. In California the decision is entirely up to the referee. Blake, former manager of Fidel LaBarba and recognised as one of the country's most dependable third men, never officially announced his decision. He left the ring immediately after the tenth-round bell and sent back his message – to Garcia and Armstrong alike. The fight was no financial wow but it was a magnificent social success. The flower of filmdom was packed around the ringside, packed so tightly the cinema cream soured the press section. One was fearful of hitting his typewriter lest he bruised an orchid.'[159]

'Armstrong skirted the rules when he weighed in wearing a water-soaked towel around his waist and two lead weights taped to his hips. The California commission required all boxers to be within 12 pounds of their opponent. With the heavy towel and weights, Armstrong scaled 11½ pounds less than Garcia. Blake's decision, though met with some scepticism, did not come under much of an attack from either corner or the boxing writers.' Eddie Borden wrote in the *Ring*: 'The affair could have been stopped on several occasions because of eye injuries suffered by either principal had referee George Blake desired to do so. Blake is an official who enjoys an unimpeachable reputation, and since he called the bout an even affair, you can be assured that was his honest opinion.'[160]

This was George Blake's last assignment as a referee, according to his obituary in the *New York Times* on 21 December 1952.

---

159 Henry McLemore, *Coshocton Tribune*, Ohio, 2 March 1940.
160 Roger Mooney, *Ring*, April 1994.

Chapter Sixteen

HENRY MCLEMORE from Los Angeles for United Press wrote on 2 March 1940: 'I hit the Henry Armstrong–Ceferino Garcia fight for the middleweight championship right on the nose. I said well in advance that it would end in a ten-round draw. But I am not bragging, even though I am a man who does not make the correct selection very often.

'Because this was no draw.

'Armstrong won it easily, so easily, in fact, that even the gatecrashers, who helped swell the small crowd of this great production, must have known from their perches just this side of Fresno that there could be no honest doubt of the decision. I am not a man who puts himself up as a ring expert, but neither do I sell pencils on the corner; in short, I am not blind, and from where I sat with other members of the press in the front row, Armstrong won six rounds, lost two and got an even break in two others. This is what I saw.

'What referee George Blake saw is something he will reveal probably only in his memoirs.

'How on earth he could see this as an even fight is beyond even my comprehension. Apparently, he didn't make up his mind until he was over his third wheat cake at the Brown Derby, because I will swear to you that no official announcement either by Blake or anyone else ever was made as to the decision.

'This correspondent had to tap a man on the shoulder to find out what the Blake verdict was. Fortunately, the man who I touched was Jerry Giesler, criminal lawyer, and chairman of the California boxing association. Giesler whispered to me, sotto voce, that Blake had decided on a draw.'[161]

'The performance of referee Blake was a subject for discussion in the press room of the *Oakland Tribune*, where sports editor Art Cohn was listening to Jimmy Duffy, the Bay city's only boxing referee. "Well," Duffy was saying, "according to all the newspaper reports, Blake admitted that he penalised Armstrong heavily for illegal tactics and took the fifth round away from him because of low blows. Obviously, California's No. 1 referee is so damn good that he doesn't have to obey California's boxing rules, but can make his own."

'"Meaning what?" Cohn asked.

'"Meaning this," snapped Duffy. "There is no California boxing rule that permits a referee to penalise a fighter for a foul by taking the round away from him. The rules provide that we must warn him for illegal tactics, can disqualify him and stop the bout for repeated violations and even recommend fines after the bout … but we CANNOT punish him by awarding the round to his opponent."

'So speaks Jimmy Duffy, licensed referee in the State of California.'[162]

'Ceferino Garcia's face looked like he had been trying to pound stakes with it after his bruising fight with Henry

---

161 Henry McLemore, *Santa Ana Register*, California, 2 March 1940.
162 *Oakland Tribune*, California, 3 March 1940.

Armstrong on Friday night. Armstrong was unmarked, save for a puffed eye. The Filipino exhibited a boil on the calf of his right leg which was swollen and pained him throughout the fight, and cut down his speed and effectiveness.

'Garcia reviewed the ten-round draw somewhat bitterly. He said Armstrong elbowed him and butted. Armstrong appeared satisfied with the judgement of referee George Blake. He said he thought he had won the middleweight crown, but if the referee decided otherwise, he was not going to complain.'[163]

'From champion Al Hostak in Seattle came a taunt of "shame" today at the failure of his middleweight title rival Ceferino Garcia, to defeat the smaller Henry Armstrong in their fight last night. "If the Filipino can't lick a little guy like Armstrong," commented Hostak, "he ought to be ashamed of himself. Boy, I'd like to get this hand out of the cast." Hostak, recognised as world middleweight champion in 46 states, fractured one of his fists recently in a non-title fight he dropped to Tony Zale in Chicago.'[164]

'Garcia didn't win by a knockout. It was a wild swinging fight for ten rounds, but neither man went down. Henry was sure he would get the decision; he was dumbfounded when the referee left the ring without casting a vote! The referee said it was too close. The referee took two rounds from Henry on what he said were fouls. Nobody else thought so. The press booed the decision, and so did the fans. But Henry did not get the title. He still thinks he was robbed, and so did a lot of others.'[165]

---
163 *Salt Lake Tribune,* Utah, 3 March 1940.
164 *Santa Ana Register,* California, 2 March 1940.
165 Henry Armstrong, *Gloves, Glory and God,* 1957.

CHAPTER SIXTEEN

Had the gamblers who couldn't get Henry to take a dive in the Garcia fight got to the referee, the unimpeachable George Blake? Henry even thought that the boxing commissioners didn't want him to win another title. They had talked to Mike Jacobs about monopolising the titles.

Whatever, Henry still had the welterweight title, he and Eddie could still make money with that, the last of his three major ring titles. And his name was still good at the box office.

Two months after the Garcia fight, Henry defended his welterweight title against 30-year-old Paul Junior, 194-bout veteran from Lewiston, Maine, at the Boston Garden before 16,469 spectators who paid a gate of $33,855. The packed house was only 33 less than the all-time New England record set by Jim Maloney–Tom Heeney in 1930. The champ picked up a nice bonus in his $15,000 purse and was in control most of the bout.

'Armstrong was master of the situation from start to finish. In the opening round he sent Junior to the canvas twice and had the Maine welterweight staggering wild-eyed when the bell sounded. King Henry coasted for the next four rounds, baffling Junior with his bobbing and weaving and his peculiar head-to-head, shoulder-to-shoulder infighting. In the sixth two lefts and a right from Armstrong sent Junior to the canvas again for the count of nine. After a minute of the seventh round, a slashing left hook dropped Junior for nine again. Another barrage of lefts and rights drove Junior across the ring. He went down, got up at the count of four and staggered along the ring in practical oblivion until referee Johnny Martin stopped the bout. Junior was accompanied by about 5,000 of his Maine admirers.

'The body of Owen F. Shields, 71, of Saco Maine, who dropped dead at Boston Garden while watching a preliminary to the Armstrong–Junior welterweight championship fight, today was returned home. Shields was sitting with his son, Fred H. Shields of Kennebunk, Maine, when he was stricken with a heart attack.'[166]

A month later, Eddie had his boy back in the Boston Garden for another 15-round title bout against Ralph (Rough House) Zanelli of Lewiston. Reporter Lydia T. Brown watched Zanelli in training and he told her, 'I'll go up to Boston Friday night and whip Armstrong to a frazzle.' In his 55-bout pro career Zanelli had never met another fighter like Hammerin' Hank Armstrong. He was in for a shock!

'For the second time in a month, Henry Armstrong, 140 Los Angeles, welterweight champion of the world, today had successfully defended his crown in the ring at Boston Garden before 16,000 fans. Armstrong was declared the winner by a technical knockout over Ralph "Rough House" Zanelli 145½, Providence, R.I., after one minute 30 seconds of fighting in the fifth round of a scheduled 15-round bout.

'In the second, third and fifth rounds, Armstrong dropped Zanelli for lengthy knockdowns. In the fifth and final frame, the challenger went to the canvas for counts of nine and eight before Referee Johnny Martin stopped the fight.'[167]

United Press reported from Boston on 25 May: 'World welterweight champion Henry Armstrong, who has earned nearly $700,000 in eight years of professional boxing, vowed today he would send lightweight king Lew Jenkins "home

---

[166] *Lowell Sun*, Mass., 27 April 1940.
[167] *Burton Post*, 25 May 1940.

CHAPTER SIXTEEN

on the range" when they meet in a 12-round non-title bout at New York on 17 July. The sepia superman added $6,849 to his bankroll in scoring a fifth-round technical knockout over Ralph Zanelli, and though manager Eddie Mead said he was satisfied with Armstrong's showing against the game Italian youth, he mapped extensive training plans for the bout with Jenkins who recently knocked out Lou Ambers.'[168]

'Lew Jenkins, of Sweetwater, Texas, is toying with the idea that he can whip Henry Armstrong since his kayo of Lou Ambers. When they meet on 17 July, Sweetwater's sweetheart is sure to turn sour. In case Henry should lose his last title, he plans to retire, for the once holder of three world championships is definitely fed up with the bold, bizarre bickering rings of the fistic racket ... Lorenzo Pack, Chicago heavyweight and Henry Armstrong collaborated on a lyric which they are trying to have published ... Pedro Montanez was injured in an auto smash-up in Puerto Rico where he has been vacationing since his battle with Armstrong.'[169]

Some guys never learn! 'Paul Junior's second attempt in two months to wrest the world's welterweight boxing crown from the ebony brow of Henry Armstrong had failed dismally today as the battle-worn Lewiston veteran nursed the wounds of a third-round technical knockout at the hands of the tireless champion here last night. After tame mauling for two rounds, in which Junior had succeeded in cuffing Armstrong lightly about the head, the Californian loosed a barrage of his famous trip-hammer rights which sprawled the challenger four times in the third round. Three of the four were for nine counts

---
168 *Taylor Daily Press*, Texas, 26 May 1940.
169 *Baltimore Afro-American*, 25 May 1940.

and on the fourth referee Johnny Martin performed an act of mercy by halting any further mayhem.

'Armstrong weight 144, Junior 142½.

'In their first meeting in Boston, Armstrong pounded out a seven-round technical knockout, but only after Junior had inflicted a mild degree of punishment in the third, fourth and fifth rounds. At the end of the abbreviated scrap last night, the battlers presented a picture of contrasts. Junior obviously was tired and hurt, Armstrong as fresh as though he had just finished a brief session of shadow boxing. About 5,000 fans jammed Portland's Exposition Hall to watch Maine's first world championship fight. The fight for Armstrong was a tune-up for his title clash with Lew Jenkins in New York next month.'[170]

On 25 May 1940 Mike Jacobs announced that Henry Armstrong, 147-pound boss, will meet Lew Jenkins, newly crowned lightweight champion in a 12-round non-title bout on 17 July. The bout will be held at the Polo Grounds in New York. Hymie Caplin, manager of Jenkins, met with Eddie Mead, Armstrong's manager, and made arrangements for the fight. The weight has been set at 138 pounds so as not to jeopardise Jenkins's crown.

After watching Armstrong training at Greenwood Lake, New York, Harry Grayson predicted in his column: 'Unless Henry Armstrong gets away from right-hand punches better than he has in training, Lew Jenkins will hand the welterweight champion his first knockout in their 12-round handicap match at the Polo Grounds next Wednesday. Armstrong insists he

---

170 *Biddeford Daily Journal*, Maine, 22 June 1940.

CHAPTER SIXTEEN

was hit only one solid wallop in 25 rounds with Ceferino Garcia, but sparring partners couldn't miss his head, and he is making a grave mistake if he is comparing the speed and accuracy of the Filipino's round-house rights with that of the lightweight leader.

'As more than one competent critic has observed before, Armstrong's "slip" is showing, and in the end he may have the same excuse as that offered for Lou Ambers when Jenkins so quickly tagged him ... the weight. Armstrong's best weight is now the 144½ pounds he scaled for Paul Junior in Bangor a month ago. Trying to get down to 140 became such a problem that Eddie Mead considered forfeiting the $2,500 he posted and give it up as a too dangerous, if not hopeless, job. Jenkins expects to come in at 134 pounds.

'It's the old, old story ... one coming, the other going ... a hungry, vicious fighter with the urge against one who has had it all. Jenkins is riding the crest of the wave. He is unbeaten since striking his stride in Manhattan ... has won ten in a row, seven by knockout. He cuts easily, but no easier than the battle-scarred Armstrong. But the main point is that Henry Armstrong no longer seems able to get under, or otherwise away from right-hand punches. And Lou Ambers and a dozen others testify that being struck by Lew Jenkins' right is like being kicked in the head by one of those cavalry horses the Thin Man used to ride on the Texas plains.'[171]

New York newspaperman Lester Bromberg remembered Lew Jenkins in a *Ring* magazine feature in November 1958: 'Floyd Patterson was training for his fight with Roy Harris in

---

171 Harry Grayson, *Lowell Sun*, Mass., 15 July 1940.

a chromium plated camp at Oceanside, California. In walked a man who evoked memories – Lew Jenkins, the Texan who won the lightweight championship. "This sort of place makes me jealous," Lew drawled. "I got nobody to blame," he added. "I chased myself out of the big time before I had a chance to appreciate it … crazy, drunk and plain stupid. I didn't have the brains to know what an honour it was to have a champion's training camp."

'One of the finest lightweight punchers of all time, he burst onto the New York scene in the summer of 1939. Within seven months he was world's lightweight champion. His light burned brightly for about a year and a half despite his efforts to drown it in alcohol. When everything caught up with him soon thereafter, his title went, his fame, his money too. He seemed headed for the bottom – and he barely missed it.

'Al Weill, manager of Lou Ambers, was banking on that Texas reputation of Jenkins for carousing when he took him on for a title fight in the Garden on 10 May 1940. But Jenkins amazed Ambers with his right-hand thunderbolts. He stiffened Ambers in the third round.

'Jenkins had gone to Grossinger's in the Catskills near New York to train for a fight with Henry Armstrong. Instead of working hard, he had carried on wildly. "I didn't know what I was doing up there. I never went to bed before 2am and I got up only in time to go to the bar. I knew I was going to lose the fight and I didn't care."'[172]

Katie cared; she was married to Lew at the time and she was as tough as he was, used to drive stock cars in races

---

172 Lester Bromberg, *Ring*, November 1958.

around Dallas, Texas. 'Katie took Lew back to New York City, driving through the night. They went to Stillman's Gymnasium, where Hymie joined them. "I'll knock him out early – he can be hit and never has been hit by what I throw," Lew said at Stillman's.

'Before the fight, Armstrong said, "I still believe the same general ideas, and that's to keep 'em off balance. They have to be set to nail you hard, and I try to keep 'em from getting set. No fighter off balance is going to hurt you much. I know how hard Jenkins can hit … but if you keep on crowding in and never stop, they can't take aim and let you have it."

'Just a breeze,' Lew stated a few hours before the fight. The oddsmakers made world welterweight champion Henry Armstrong a 9-5 favourite over the world lightweight champion, Lew. If the public knew about his carousing and drinking, Lew would have had few backers even at much better odds. Wilbur Wood of the *New York Sun* summed up the fight: 'Henry Armstrong isn't half the fighter he used to be, and Lew Jenkins isn't half the fighter he was supposed to be.'[173]

Unbeknown to the 23,306 fight fans eagerly waiting for the fight to begin, there was drama backstage and it looked as though there wasn't going to be a fight at all, not in the ring anyway. Eddie Mead was threatening to call the fight off if any changes were made to the bandages on Armstrong's fists. Mead and Caplin had agreed two days before the fight to use 10ft of bandage on each hand of their fighter. But a commission inspector watched the men have their bandages

---

173 Gene Pantalone, *From Boxing Ring to Battlefield*, 2018.

put on and promptly turned thumbs down. The commission rules called for 7½ft on each hand. He wouldn't allow the ten yards and informed chairman John J. Phelan, who ordered the fight off.

'"OK," Eddie Mead countered, "then there'll be no fight." Phelan ordered promoter Mike Jacobs to announce the fight was off. "Announce it yourself," Mike grumbled. "You're stopping it." The general returned to his ringside seat and gave it a second thought. Then he picked up his special ringside phone, called the dressing rooms and told the inspectors to "let Armstrong's bandages alone and let Jenkins use the same amount."'[174]

The fighters were soon in the ring and the crowd settled down as referee Arthur Donovan called the warriors to ring centre. Champion welterweight Armstrong had weighed in at 139 pounds to 135½ for champion lightweight Lew Jenkins. The contest was a non-title affair and they were boxing 12 rounds, not the usual 147 pounds over 15 rounds.

'Jenkins was boss of the ranch for the first two sessions, during which his well-directed punches seldom missed their mark. While Henry's attempts were mostly wild punches that couldn't land, Jenkins kept tossing them ceaselessly at Hank's jaw and as the moving target rushed incessantly forward, the target was met with unerring accuracy. But Henry's blows to the body seemed to take considerable steam out of Jenkins and in the third, which like the first two sessions he won, his margin was not so big.

---

174 Sid Feder, *Valley Morning Star*, Harlingen, Texas, 19 July 1940.

'While Henry's misses didn't sap any of his vitality, those of his rival proved costly. When he came out of his corner for the fourth round, he no longer was able to mix it with his ever-active opponent. His reserve power had been exhausted in that effort to score a knockout in the early rounds. The long-leverage punches that had done damage to other rivals, couldn't land on the boring-in welter king whose body smashes now began to take their toll and to weaken the Texan champ.'[175]

'Jenkins started fast,' wrote Harry Ferguson. 'Rights and lefts rattled off Armstrong's head, a savage right uppercut set him back on his heels. In came Armstrong, bobbing, weaving, crouching and throwing those short vicious hooks to the head that stunned Jenkins into a coma and made him a sleep-walker under the hot lights. In the second round, too, Jenkins slammed his right and his left to the head and won the round.

'Jenkins hit the floor first in the fourth round when Armstrong got him against the ropes and sent sledge-hammer rights and lefts to the head. Lew got up at the count of nine and weathered the round, but worse trouble was ahead in the fifth. He came out fighting but the hurricane again blew him down with rights and lefts to the head. Jenkins was up at the count of one and immediately was pounded to the canvas again. This time he stayed down until the count of nine and then got up to be saved by the bell.

'They worked hard over Jenkins between rounds but when they sent him out for the sixth the storm warnings were up

---

175 Nat Fleischer, *Ring*, October 1940.

and the hurricane was in full force. Armstrong bobbed in for the kill. Hooks to the head dropped Jenkins, but he got up at the count of one. Armstrong slugged him again and once more the Texas gamecock hit the deck. But this time he stayed down for a nine count. When he got up his legs were gone, his arms were dead, his brain was numb, but his heart said "go on". So he stood there while Armstrong floored him once more for a count of nine. The merciful clang of the bell then sent Jenkins to his corner, wobbling like a longshoreman on Saturday night. He sat down, then pitched off his stool. That was enough for everybody, including Referee Donovan.

'Henry Armstrong blew his man down at the Polo Grounds last night in a bout that proved nothing except that the little man from Los Angeles is pound for pound one of the greatest fighters of all time.'[176]

---

176 Harry Ferguson, *Tucson Daily Citizen*, Arizona, 18 July 1940.

Chapter Seventeen

'THE NEW York boxing commission today ordered promoter Mike Jacobs to withhold the purses of Lew Jenkins and Henry Armstrong, who fought last night at the Polo Grounds. No immediate reason was given, but the commission announced it would meet tomorrow and ordered all persons connected with the fight to appear before it. The order was contained in a letter to Jacobs from John J. Phelan, chairman of the New York commission. One puzzling feature was that the letter was dated yesterday and apparently was written before the fight.

'Jacobs was angry when he received the letter today and threatened to withdraw from boxing after the Billy Conn–Bob Pastor fight next month. Some thought the commission might be attempting to hold part of each fighter's purse as a forfeit. Armstrong and Jenkins have promised the commission in writing that they will make the next defence of their welterweight and lightweight championships in New York state. The forfeit would be for the purpose of enforcing the agreement.'[177]

---

177 *Tucson Daily Citizen*, Arizona, 18 July 1940.

The fight didn't please everyone ... For United Press, Henry McLemore wrote, 'You'll have to dig in the records until your thumbs are dusty to uncover a poorer lightweight champion of the world than Lew Jenkins ... It was Armstrong's worst fight in three years. His punches lacked the old snap, the sharpness was gone from his legs, and during the first two rounds he only went through the motions.

'Furthermore, he got hit often. During the first six minutes Henry's jaw played snare drum to the sticks of Jenkins's fists, but the only effect was to make Armstrong snort a little louder, shake his head a little faster, and bore in a little more resolutely. Then Jenkins ran out of punches. Arm weary, a little sick in his stomach from the blows, Armstrong had sunk in his middle, and a bit discouraged because the best blows he possessed had no noticeable effect. Jenkins resigned. He started falling down and staggering up, falling down and staggering up. Six times he went down before the finish, and I'll swear to you that not one of the falls was due to a clean, hard punch from Armstrong's fists.

'You don't have to take my word for this. You can have the word of Eddie Mead, manager of Armstrong. "It was the worst fight I ever saw Henry fight," Mead said in the dressing room. "The Armstrong of two years ago would have run Jenkins right on past El Paso in one round."

'Armstrong, if one is to rate him on last night's performance, is only half the fighter he was two years ago. But an Armstrong only 50 per cent efficient is too good for any of the light boys around today.'[178]

---

178 Henry McLemore, *San Mateo Times*, California, 18 July 1940.

CHAPTER SEVENTEEN

It was September 1940 and Henry was defending his welterweight title for the 19th time since upsetting Barney Ross in May 1938. He was in the nation's capital, Washington DC at Griffith Stadium to accept the challenge of local 33-year-old veteran Phil Furr and there was a good crowd of 15,000 in the stands when referee Ray Bowen got them away. Shortly before the main event started, Heine Miller, secretary of the District Boxing Commission, was approached by Eddie Mead, manager of the champion, who demanded a substitute for Mr Bowen. Mead said he understood Bowen might lose his head in an exciting exchange and he didn't want his meal ticket rendered null and void by an error in judgement. Miller refused to make a change and Bowen proved to be an excellent choice.

'Washington DC 23 September 1940 – Henry Armstrong, welterweight champion of the world, tonight knocked out Phil Furr, of Washington, after one minute and 45 seconds of the fourth round of a scheduled 15-round title fight. Armstrong weighed 146, Furr was a pound heavier. The little champion could hardly have had an easier evening. Fighting cautiously in the first two rounds, Armstrong opened up in the third and after a minute he dropped the Washington boy with one of his chopping rights. Furr got up at the count of one but he was hurt and dazed. As the fourth began, Furr tried to stay in close, but Armstrong began pulling away and pounding Furr with rights and lefts.

'One of Henry's rights then caught Furr on the head and he dropped – hurt but not out. Furr took a nine count, jumped up and tried to reach Armstrong with a left but missed by feet. Moving in with lightning-like swiftness, Armstrong then smacked Furr with a devastating right. The challenger didn't sag this time – he dropped. He crawled around on the floor as the count went through to the final "nine and out" and referee Ray Bowen raised Armstrong's hand in victory. As the fight ended the champion was breathing easily and made a short address to the crowd.'[179]

From ringside, Lewis F. Atchison reported: 'Henry Armstrong may have gone back some in the last year, but you couldn't prove it by the 15,000 fans who saw him beat a rhumba on Phil Furr's tattooed torso and finally knock him out in the fourth of a scheduled 15-round bout last night at the Griffith Stadium.

'There's plenty of steam in the old boilers still and the welterweight champion intends to keep up the pressure until Christmas or a month or so thereafter, then hang the mahogany mittens on some handy nail as a keepsake. He'd like to quit after boxing on the annual Christmas Fund card at Cleveland, but the alluring prospect of a good money shot may keep him on the treadmill until spring. After that, he's through definitely – he says.

'Armstrong couldn't put his finger on a particular day and say, "That's when I'm through" because sitting in the front row – on a freebie – was that sinister character known to the trade and his intimate friends as Mike Jacobs. The gent with the loose-leaf teeth is the hobgoblin who keeps the National Boxing Association in a continual stew by his refusal to unhand any of the top-notch ringmen he has under contract.

---

179 *Bluefield Daily Telegraph*, West Virginia, 24 September 1940.

CHAPTER SEVENTEEN

'Uncle Mike stood up to take a bow but sat right down again. He wouldn't commit himself, but Armstrong evidently had inside information and outlined it briefly as follows: Lew Jenkins, lightweight champion in New York vs. Pete Lello. Jenkins is being brought back to satisfy everybody he is a good fighter – a genuine champion, and if he survives this brand of competition he'll be re-matched with Armstrong. This is the money shot Armstrong figures may keep him active longer than he originally planned, but it will be well worth waiting for.'[180]

The money shot Henry was waiting for came as an offer from Mike Jacobs to defend his title in the Garden against Fritzie Zivic of Pittsburgh on 4 October 1940. It was not welcome news for everyone. MARYLAND TAKES ACTION AGAINST HENRY ARMSTRONG ran a headline in the *Baltimore Afro-American* on 1 October: 'Asserting that it was "time to stop the tying up of boxers and smash monopolies," the Maryland State Boxing Commission declared Henry Armstrong's welterweight championship vacant today. Stanley Scherr, the commission chairman, said the move was directed against the "New York Boxing Monopoly" in general, and by taking this stand Maryland became the first state to oppose "the powers that be." It's doubtful that Mike Jacobs lost any of his beauty sleep over this announcement. He had a show at the Garden in a couple of days, time to check the box-office.'

Fritzie Zivic was born on 8 May 1913, the youngest son of immigrant parents; his father was Croatian, his mother

---
180 Lewis F Atchison, *Evening Star,* Washington DC, 24 September 1940.

Mary Kepele was Slovenian. They named the boy Ferdinand Henry John Zivich. As a boy, he followed the example of his four elder brothers, who boxed and became known as the Fighting Zivics. Pete and Jack, the first and second born, boxed in the 1920 Antwerp Olympics. The kid would become Fritzie Zivic when he turned professional in 1931. Recalling his youth growing up in the rough, tough, crowded Ninth Ward of Lawrenceville, Zivic would say, 'You either had to fight or stay in the house. We went out. We weren't the toughest family in the neighbourhood but we ranked up close to the top.'

'His father ran a saloon,' wrote sportswriter Jack Cuddy, 'and whenever a bit of bouncing was necessary, Pop merely whistled and down from upstairs swarmed the five Zivic brothers with fists flying. Fritzie says, "I was just a little tyke then, so I used to hammer and bite at deadbeats' legs while the other four belted at their chins. It was good training."'

Looking at the forthcoming title battle with Armstrong, Cuddy wrote, 'Fritzie is formidable because he's fast, strong, smart, tough and a hard puncher. He knocked out 65 of his 149 opponents and broke Lew Ambers's jaw in 1935. Although taller than Armstrong, Fritzie too has slender legs and the muscular torso of a middleweight. The last of the Zivics was given the chance to bring his family its first title because he won an over-the-weight decision from Sammy Angott, the NBA lightweight king, on 29 August. Moreover, he delights in rough tactics.'[181]

---

181 Jack Cuddy, *Madison Wisconsin State Journal*, 2 October 1940.

CHAPTER SEVENTEEN

'I'd hit guys low,' admitted Zivic, 'choke 'em or give 'em the head. My best punch was a left hook to you-know-where.'

There were many among the 12,081 fans who pushed their way into Madison Square Garden that October night who remembered too many of the Pittsburgh lad's early reverses as a professional. Practically everybody beat Ferdinand, who took the name Fritzie when he joined the money ranks.

'But the youngest and last of the Five Fighting Zivics got going in 1937 when he knocked out Johnny Jadick and repulsed Bobby Pacho and Chuck Woods. And then, as brother Jack, a fine lightweight in his day, remarked at the time, Fritzie had fighting blood put in his veins. Fritzie nearly died of pneumonia. It was Jack's blood in a transfusion that turned the tide. Doctors said Fritzie would never fight again, but he was back in the thick of things on Christmas night of that year, 1937, when he dropped a decision to Tommy Bland.'[182]

'Along Scrambled Ear Avenue, there has been an unwritten rule the past couple of years – "Never bet against The Hammer,"' wrote Sid Feder. 'Knowing this, and appreciating the fact that those acquainted in, and with, the business of bashing beaks rarely invest their coconuts unless they've picked apart every angle, it is surprising, to say the least, to find several of our leading citizens getting off The Hammer now. As you've guessed by now, The Hammer is Henry Armstrong.

'He defends his world welterweight championship against Fritzie Zivic in Madison Square Garden tomorrow night. Up to now, Henry the Hammer never has given anyone cause to

---
182 Harry Grayson, *Racine Journal Times*, Wisconsin, 20 October 1940.

185

switch from the rule mentioned above. So, it's only natural that you raise your eyebrows when some of the better boxing minds – fellows like James Joy Johnston, Johnny Ray, Chris Dundee, and even the honest brakeman Lou Diamond – figure it may be just too bad for The Hammer this time. For instance, take Jimmy Johnston. He's probably the best free-style conversationalist on the avenue. And the ex-Boy Bandit frankly fears for the little buzz-saw.

'"This Zivic is a rough, tough guy who can take a good punch and throw one," James Joy explains. "Yes, sir, Henry better not stick his head up carelessly tomorrow night, or he'll get it knocked off."

'Then there's Dundee, a newcomer among the Jacobs Beach "Brains" and manager of Ken Overlin, world middleweight champion of New York and California. He's even planning to "take the price" and put a little bit down.'[183]

A few days before the Zivic–Armstrong fight in the Garden, a reporter cornered Luke Carney, 'a well-padded gent' who managed the fighting careers of the five Zivic boys. '"Fritzie is the last and the youngest of the brothers," Carney began. "The first two, Jack and Pete, started earning a living in the ring shortly after the war; Joe, the oldest brother, started fighting around that time but he quit after a few fights in favour of a baseball career, and Eddie, who is next to Fritzie, is still battling occasionally." Carney then related how Jack was the only man to knock out Lew Tendler, a great southpaw who would have been champion if he could have licked Benny Leonard. "Pete almost had a title fight. In 1922 he was all set

---

[183] Sid Feder, *Tucson Daily Citizen*, Arizona, 3 October 1940.

CHAPTER SEVENTEEN

to meet Joe Lynch for the bantamweight crown until someone gave us the business at the last minute.

'"Eddie never had an opportunity to fight for a title. Armstrong knocked him out in the fourth round in 1937 or 1938 and Fritzie is out to revenge his brother's loss. Henry might as well know here and now that we're going to win next Friday."'[184]

Pugilistic history doesn't recall another family with as many as five brothers boxing as professionals. Two years earlier, March 1938, they made the journey from Pittsburgh to Detroit to cheer Eddie on as he made his fight with Armstrong. 'The world featherweight champion weighed 135 pounds, the lightweight limit, as he scored a technical knockout in the fourth round over Eddie Zivic of Pittsburgh here last night. The Pittsburgher was never down but absorbed terrific punishment before his seconds tossed in the towel.'[185]

The boys were around the ringside that October night in Madison Square Garden, the bets were down, and, as Luke Carney told that reporter, 'we're going to win'.

Now the fighters were in the ring and renowned announcer Harry Balogh was introducing the officials appointed by the New York State Athletic Commission … Judges John Potter, Marty Monroe, Referee Arthur Donovan.

'When hostilities got under way,' wrote Joseph C Nichols, 'Armstrong moved forward in his characteristic manner, but his fire was wild, and Zivic clipped him with short punches through the first and second rounds. In the third, Armstrong managed to find the range and, resting his head on the

---
184 *Chester Times*, Pennsylvania, 1 October 1940.
185 *Burlington Daily Hawk Eye Gazette*, 26 March 1938.

Pittsburgher's left shoulder, proceeded to belabour the body with a two-handed tattoo. He kept up this line of attack in the fourth and fifth, but at the end of the fifth it was apparent that his eyes, if the fight went the limit, would give him trouble. It was then that the swelling was evident.

'Zivic conserved his strength surprisingly well. Pacing himself splendidly and standing up under Armstrong's hardest punches, the durable Zivic, exhibited a willingness to trade with his foe when such strategy seemed expedient and to stay away and stab effectively with a long left hand when that course appeared the better one to pursue.

'Zivic capitalised on Armstrong's wild eagerness by stabbing the champion repeatedly in the sixth and seventh, but the next two rounds saw Armstrong more than hold his own.

'Henry was on his way out as early as the eighth round when Zivic, fighting a cool, heady battle, cut both of the fading champion's eyes and never let up banging away at them … In the 11th round the defending title-holder was blind to all intents and purposes. As he returned to his corner at the end of each round he would murmur prayerfully, "Oh, if I could only see."'[186]

'Youngest of the five fighting Zivic brothers, he began to pace himself in the third round. And when he started this pacing business – taking it easy and merely letting Armstrong pound him, with only short, sharp uppercuts to the chin in rebuttal – every one of the 12,081 cash customers in the Garden figured Fritzie was through. But Fritzie wasn't through. He was just getting set for the first 15-round fight

---

186 Joseph C Nichols, *The New York Times*, 5 October 1940.

CHAPTER SEVENTEEN

in his career. Although Fritzie had fought 149 professional opponents, he never had gone more than ten heats. Hence, he was carrying a great psychological burden he carried to perfection.

'It was perfection because Fritzie beat Armstrong at his own game – at infighting. Although no foul blows were struck, both used rough tactics with plenty of heading and elbowing. But Fritzie always stood at an angle, where Armstrong's whistling hooks would glance off his head, meanwhile shooting a variety of uppercuts to Henry's head and body. Never in any fight has a crowd witnessed such a range of uppercuts as the brown-haired, pug-nosed Pittsburgher used. In close, they were short chugs to chin and brow. At middle distance they were semi-bolos that knocked Armstrong back on his heels. And at long range they were full bolos that crashed into Armstrong's belly. In the tenth round, for example, Fritzie drove one of those bolos into Henry's midriff with such power that poor Hank was almost jack-knifed.

'Bleeding from gashes above both eyes, from his left cheek, from mouth and nose, Hurricane Hank explained later in the dressing room that he could not see out of his left eye after the third round, and that he was virtually blinded in both eyes after the tenth – with blood from his brows.'[187]

'To most writers, the Armstrong–Zivic thing was just another title defence for Armstrong. It was his 20th, and, as in the other 19 cases, was expected to end in a hurry or via the decision route. We who took it in over the radio had the idea, at least for the first few rounds, that it would be

---

[187] Jack Cuddy, *San Mateo Times*, California, 5 October 1940.

Armstrong again. In fact, Sam Taub gave the impression at the time that the champ was on his way to a quick victory, and wire dispatches bear him out that the new titlist was really in trouble on more than one occasion. As usual, Armstrong threw more blows than any human could keep track of, but Zivic's heavier hitting told the story.'[188]

Pat Robinson was ringside for the International News Service to send the following report: 'There are some sports events so unforgettably thrilling they remain etched in the memory forever. Jack Dempsey being knocked out of the ring by Luis Firpo. Man o' War racing John P. Grier to defeat in the stretch. Babe Ruth calling his shot in a World Series. Old Pete Alexander shuffling into fan Tony Lazzeri with the bases loaded. Glenn Cunningham breaking a world record.

'All memories that linger but none of them more soul-stirring than the sight of little Henry Armstrong, battered, bruised and blinded, marching into his doom against the flaying fists of Fritzie Zivic in Madison Square Garden last night. Yes, Henry lost his welterweight title after 15 of the most vicious rounds ever fought, but he lost like a true champion should. There was no doubt as to the victor. The crowd sensed as early as the tenth round that a new champion was in the making, but that crowd stayed to cheer the game little fellow who gave it all he had and still lost.

'Henry was on his way as early as the eighth round when Zivic, fighting a cool heady battle, cut both of the fading champion's eyes and never let up banging away at them. Zivic did just what he said he'd do – cut the old scar tissue over

---

188 Harvey Rockwell, *San Mateo Times*, 5 October 1940.

CHAPTER SEVENTEEN

Henry's eyes, blind him and then finish. He didn't quite finish him.'[189]

'Henry answered the bell for the 15th round with a wild rush, almost sweeping Zivic off his feet. But Zivic backed away, slashing and cutting. Just as the bell was about to ring for the end of the fight, he landed a hard right on Henry's jaw and the champ went headlong to the canvas – the first time he had been knocked down in his championship career. The bell saved him from the count; his seconds ran out and dragged him to his corner.

'Caswell Adams said next day in the *New York Herald Tribune*, "And then, from exhaustion as much as from a wallop, Armstrong fell and the bell rang, and one of the greatest chapters in fistic history was clapped shut. Armstrong won't be able to fight again for four months, and maybe never will again, but he went out the way the best do – fighting."

'Adams was wrong in guessing that Henry would not fight again for four months, or maybe never again. Henry rested less than two months, letting the eyes heal and the strength come back, and then he started training – for another bout with Zivic.'[190]

---

189 Pat Robinson, *Lowell Sun,* Mass, 5 October 1940.
190 Henry Armstrong, *Gloves, Glory and God,* 1957.

Chapter Eighteen

'LET OTHERS, more maudlin than I,' wrote Alan Ward, 'bemoan the sad fate which has befallen the GREATEST prize-fighter of his generation, Henry Armstrong. Let others weep figurative tears that a rank outsider not only won Henry's welterweight championship, but gave Hammerin' Hank a whipping from which he probably never will recover. For my part, I'm inclined to say "Goody, goody," and express the fervent hope Armstrong has learned his lesson and will retire to his annuities and the bosom of his family, and leave prize-fighting for younger (but not MORE courageous) men.

'And in saying this I am prompted by a deep admiration and friendship for Henry Armstrong. I knew Armstrong when he was a hollow-cheeked lad who wore cast-off clothes and didn't eat regularly. He'd fight for peanuts here, and in other parts of California, and even then he was the same stout-hearted little gentleman he is today. Success hasn't spoiled Henry. He's well in the chips and able to have pork chops seven days a week if he so minds. He can afford to buy a half dozen tailor-made suits at a crack and 20 neckties.

'But good food and fancy duds can't be completely enjoyed by a man, young in years if old in ring experience, whose brain is foggy, who bounces when he walks and whose eyes can't

CHAPTER EIGHTEEN

properly focus. Oh, Armstrong isn't in any such condition at present. But he is quite apt to be if he absorbs one or two more lacings like the one handed to him Friday night in New York.

'C'mon, Henry, be a smart chap and quit while you're still right up there at the top of the heap.'[191]

'One of the many celebrities at the Pittsburgh–Washington game at Forbes Field yesterday was Fritzie Zivic, the new welterweight king. Fritzie, Pittsburgh's pug-nosed likable boxer, received a tremendous ovation from the 25,200 fans when he was introduced as "the world's new welterweight king."

'Zivic said after the game yesterday that he promises to be as active a champion as the man he dethroned in a roaring battle at New York last Friday night – Henry Armstrong. Never one to walk away from a good brawl, Fritzie promises to take on all challengers now that he has ascended to the top of the heap in the 147-pound division, victor over one of the roughest, toughest champions who ever entered a ring. One of Zivic's first acts after winning the title was to sign for a return match on 17 January with Armstrong.

'Veteran of 150 ring battles, the broad-shouldered Zivic was a heavy underdog when he entered the ring against Armstrong, one time holder of three titles. When he left, Hammerin' Henry was a battered hulk; Fritzie was virtually unmarked. The 27-year-old is Pittsburgh's second current champion. His friend, Billy Conn, holds the light-heavyweight title and aspires to the throne of heavyweight champion Joe Louis. A businessman at heart – Zivic has a hand in several businesses – Fritzie will revel in the increased income the

---

191 Alan Ward, *Oakland Tribune*, California, 7 October 1940.

title will bring. But the championship also means much from a purely sentimental angle to the champion and his family. Despite years in the ring, his four brothers, Jack, Pete, Joe and Eddie, never succeeded in winning a title. Now they have one.'[192]

'They'll drive nails in your coffin more quickly in boxing than in any other sport,' Jack Cuddy wrote for United Press. 'One losing fight, and you're a bum – you're washed up. Henry Armstrong got licked Friday night by Fritzie Zivic in such fashion that they took away the last of Armstrong's titles, the welterweight crown. That was a just decision. There's no question about that. We are predicting now that Armstrong will knock out Zivic within ten rounds of this return melee. We know that Armstrong still has at least one good fight in his body, and that he will turn in that fight on 17 January after three and a half months of rest. Zivic won Friday night's bout impressively, but closely. The referee and one of the judges voted eight rounds for Fritzie against seven for Armstrong. In other words, if Zivic hadn't won the last two heats – when Hurricane Hank was blinded by brow bruises and blood – Zivic would have lost. The wise boys of Jacobs Beach say Armstrong, now 27 years old, is but a whisper of the great fighter. That's where they're wrong.

'Armstrong ... is still one of the most formidable fighters in any division. His performance on Friday night proved that. Even though outsmarted and blinded by a sturdy lad, the dusky dynamo was still punching when he went down. Remember this: the next time Armstrong meets Zivic, a fresher

---

192 *Monessen Daily Independent,* Pennsylvania, 7 October 1940.

CHAPTER EIGHTEEN

Armstrong will give Zivic no chance to pace himself. An informed Armstrong who made a certain significant mistake by inches will not err again. This refreshed and smartened Armstrong will knock out Zivic within ten rounds.'[193]

From New York, there was news that Henry Armstrong was scheduled to undergo a second eye operation within a week. 'Armstrong had an inch of superfluous skin removed from over his left eye on Tuesday by Dr Alexander Schiff who intends to perform a similar operation over the right eye. After the second operation, Armstrong will return to his home in California for several weeks of rest and then will go to Hot Springs, Arkansas, to get in shape for a return title bout with Fritzie Zivic on 17 January in New York.'[194]

On 19 October, columnist John Lardner reported: 'Henry Armstrong has just been taken to the hospital for an operation on the scarred and puffy region around his famous eyes, which used to glare balefully upward at the enemy's chest, the whites rolling below as Henry tucked his chin down and came jogging into action. If they can't get those eyes open to stay, then Little Vitamins, as the boys sometime call him in the trade, is doomed to retirement. But give him just 50 per cent daylight, says Henry, and he'll still be back for the blood of Fritzie Zivic, the tough Croat, on 17 January.

'Mr Zivic shut up Henry's eyes and collared his welterweight title the week before last. I missed the fight but they tell me it was one of the best of recent years between little men, a long crescendo of brutal excitement that ended with the champion blind and beaten, but still throwing his fists in

---
193 Jack Cuddy, *Madison Wisconsin State Journal*, 9 October 1940.
194 *Dubuque Telegraph Herald*, Iowa, 16 October 1940.

the hope of finding the unseen foe. The result did not surprise little Henry. A few weeks ago he fought a character named Phil Furr in Washington. He knocked Mr Furr quite cold, but in the process his face got in the way of several random gloves.

"'I can't see so well," he said afterward. "They're beginning to catch up with me." That of course is the sensible time for a man to quit the business, but Jack Dempsey is the only fighter I remember offhand who got out of there quickly when he thought his eyes were in danger.

'If the operation on Hank Armstrong is successful, I suppose they will have to let him fight Zivic again. As a matter of fact, give him a fairly good job of eye repair and he is quite likely to beat the tough Croat.'[195]

News from Hot Springs, Arkansas, 24 November, where Armstrong was thinking out loud about his future in and out of the boxing ring: 'Henry Armstrong, the game little battler who once held three boxing titles simultaneously, said today he would fight about four more bouts and then swap the boxing gloves for an orchestra leader's baton. Those remaining fights, Hammerin' Hank carefully explained, depend on how well his injured eyes bear up during each match. At any rate, the end of his ring days is close at hand.

"'That's definite," he declared, "I'm not fooling myself. I'm coming like Old Black Joe – slow. May not get there at all. We get old, see, and you get cut up."

'As soon as the curtain falls on his ring career, Armstrong says he's going to organise his own orchestra and he will be its vocalist.

---

195 John Lardner, *Butte Montana Standard*, 20 October 1940.

CHAPTER EIGHTEEN

'"I've always loved music," he commented. He greeted his interviewers from a piano bench where he was fingering the keys. The dusky little fighter said he already had collaborated on the lyric of one song and was interested in composing. The little maestro-to-be isn't worrying about the outcome of his musical venture. He said investments of his ring earnings would bring him $300 or $400 monthly for the rest of his life, adding, "That oughta be enough to get along on."

'Armstrong, who will be 28 next month, hasn't had a fight since he had his left eye operated on for removal of surplus tissue from battle scars. The veteran of more than 300 bouts will enter the ring again on 17 January in New York's Madison Square Garden to meet Fritzie Zivic, who relieved Armstrong of the welterweight title. He plans to stay here three weeks and work off some surplus weight before getting down to serious training.'[196]

December arrives with thoughts of Christmas, but for many sportswriters it was a chance to fill their columns with a review of the year just gone and the one to come. Pat Robinson went looking for Nat Rogers. 'Rogers, a dark, silent little man with watchful eyes, is matchmaker for Mike Jacobs's 20th Century Club, the largest boxing club in the world. Nat probably knows as much about fighters as any man on earth. He could tell you off-hand the condition of their back teeth, the state of their tonsils and whether they liked poached eggs for breakfast. A year ago he predicted five ring titles would change hands in 1940. Five ring titles did change hands in 1940.

---

196 *Butte Montana Standard*, 25 November 1940.

'Therefore, when he told us on Thursday that not one champion was a sure bet to retain his crown in 1941 we did not scoff at the forecast as we did a year ago. "In looking to the future, you must remember there are no supermen in boxing," declared Nat. "They can all be taken, that goes for Joe Louis as well as any palooka. In fact, I think Joe is a sure bet to lose his title to Billy Conn next June! I think Billy will outspeed and outbox Joe and win the decision ... Fritzie Zivic looks fairly safe on his welterweight throne but he is by no means a sure bet. If Henry Armstrong has regained his stuff after his long lay-off he may win back the title. That's the general set-up right now but before many months have passed you will see many new faces and many new stars climbing through the ropes in Madison Square Garden. This coming year is going to be about the most active the game ever knew."'[197]

December found Mr Armstrong back in New York to receive some good news. Sid Feder wrote: 'For his contribution to boxing in losing as well as winning, Henry Armstrong, on Tuesday, was awarded the Edward J Neil memorial trophy which annually honours the memory of the Associated Press boxing writer and war correspondent who was killed in Spain. In naming Armstrong unanimously, the New York Boxing Writers' association considered his gallant showing in losing his welterweight championship to Fritzie Zivic two months ago as much as the fact he is the only ringman in fistic history to hold three world titles simultaneously.

'The third annual award of this plaque will be made at the writers' annual dinner on 9 January at Ruppert's

---

[197] Pat Robinson, *Dubuque Telegraph Herald*, Iowa, 26 December 1940.

CHAPTER EIGHTEEN

Brewery. Armstrong follows Jack Dempsey and Billy Conn as winners of the award, which goes to the man who has done the most for boxing each year. Only two other fighters, Louis and Max Baer, received consideration with Armstrong for the award. After considerable discussion, the association voted unanimously in favour of Henry who came from St Louis originally, but more recently has fought out of Los Angeles.

'Armstrong returns to the fistic wars on 17 January to meet Zivic in Madison Square Garden in an attempt to regain his welterweight crown. He lost a one-sided 15-round decision to the Pittsburgher on 4 October, and at the final bell, with both eyes punched closed so that he couldn't see his rival, he was still on the aggressive, moving forward blindly and throwing punches.'[198]

New York, 21 December – 'Promoter Mike Jacobs must have had an uneasy minute or two last night while the announcer was gathering up the slips and discovering that Fritzie Zivic and Lew Jenkins had fought themselves a ten-round draw in the Garden. Mike already had Zivic signed to defend his welterweight title against Henry Armstrong on 17 January and that would have been a fine one to try to ballyhoo if Fritzie had dropped a duke to Jenkins, the cadaverous lightweight champ. And Zivic came very close to that. All that saved him was a determined rally in the last four stanzas.

'Steve Hamas, one of the judges, called it even after the other two officials had given a split verdict. Referee George Wallish thought Jenkins won it. A bulging crowd of 17,000

---

198 Sid Feder, *Lincoln Nebraska State Journal*, 4 December 1940.

didn't see a single knockdown, even though Jenkins planted his noted right on Zivic's features many a time. Fritzie of the dented nose came out of it unmarked, but Jenkins suffered cuts over both eyes and looked pretty well used up at the finish. Of the two, Zivic was the bigger disappointment. A 1-2 favourite at fight time, the Pittsburgh veteran had practically no right at all and only his superior infighting enabled him to hold Jenkins for the first five rounds. The referee warned him repeatedly for doing funny things in the clinches, but took no rounds away from him.'[199]

'Mike Jacobs has arranged in a hurry for three important fights involving four champions. He signed Billy Conn, light-heavyweight champion for a heavyweight title match in June with champion Joe Louis. He virtually forced Fritzie Zivic, welterweight ruler, to go through with a return title tilt with Henry Armstrong on 17 January, despite Zivic's questionable showing against Lew Jenkins on Friday night. He closed for Jenkins to meet the Zivic–Armstrong winner in February. He had to put plenty of pressure on Zivic before Fritzie agreed to go through with the Armstrong match instead of taking a long rest as manager Luke Carney desired. Carney thought Zivic needed a vacation after his uncertain performance in last night's ten-round draw with Jenkins at Madison Square Garden.'[200]

'Lawton Carver, of International News Service, posted his Christmas greetings to a group of sportsmen, including Billy Conn, baseball's Jimmy Wilson, golfer Sam Snead, and Henry Armstrong, the little man who did things in the prize

---
199 Gayle Talbot, *Hagerstown Daily Mail*, Maryland, 21 December 1940.
200 *Nevada State Journal*, 23 December 1940.

CHAPTER EIGHTEEN

ring that made even the old-timers forget their heroes – he's arriving on Tuesday to start a new campaign against Fritzie Zivic, who took his last title away from him.

'On the same sports page was an interesting interview with Lou Ambers. The former lightweight champion, launching his campaign as a welterweight, says he expects to wrest that championship from Henry Armstrong before August. "I know Fritzie Zivic is champion now, but Armstrong will beat him and take the title when they meet on 17 January," said the former lightweight king. "Zivic won't do it again – not against the new Armstrong." Ambers has just arrived back from Hot Springs where he has been boiling out preparatory to launching his welter campaign. Armstrong was at the Springs also and Larruping Lou met him almost daily on his early morning hikes.

'Armstrong looks like a man-killer now. Since he fought Zivic, he's had an operation on his eyes which had too much scar tissue. Now they're perfect again. And his rest since October has made him strong as a bull. The old Armstrong had the style to beat Zivic, but not the eyes and strength. The new Armstrong has everything.'[201]

Sid Feder was talking to welterweight champion Fritzie Zivic on Wednesday, 15 January, two days before he was to defend his title against former champ Henry Armstrong. 'The way Fritzie Zivic figures it out, you wouldn't expect a millionaire to trade his bankroll for a job driving a truck, would you? Well, Fritzie explained today, then there's no reason you can expect him to give up his world welterweight

---

201 *Dubuque Telegraph Herald*, Iowa, 24 December 1940.

201

championship to Henry Armstrong in Madison Square Garden Friday night, just because Henry is supposed to have an extra special incentive to win.

"'If you're talking about reasons for winning," pointed out the youngest of the five flying Zivics out of Pittsburgh, "then don't go any farther than little Fritzie. Look, I kicked around the ham-and-egg spots for seven years. I fought for coffee and cake money so often that the first time I saw caviar I asked a guy why they were serving little ball bearings and how do you eat them? Before I beat Sammy Angott last summer, in which I was paid $4,000, I had never received more than $2,500 for a fight in my life. And up to then I'd been fighting seven years and had been to the post about 130 times.

"'All of a sudden I'm in the chips. In my last four bouts, counting the one I beat Armstrong to win the title, I've gotten $30,000. Say, despite the money I've made since winning the title, I'm still a hungry fighter. Because then I didn't know any better. I didn't know there was that kind of money around loose. I want to tell you this – Fritzie is through as a ham-and-egger, and I'll knock out Armstrong in about ten rounds Friday to prove it."

'Zivic is in even finer condition that he was for his first tussle with Hennery the Hammer. He was down to 147 pounds after his final three-round session today.'[202]

---

[202] Sid Feder, *Titusville Herald*, Pennsylvania, 16 January 1941.

Chapter Nineteen

PROMOTER MIKE Jacobs let it be known that Friday's fight figures to be the outstanding financial success of the season. It was learned the advance sales totals nearly $30,000 and that no one in on the promotion would be at all surprised if the gate goes well over $50,000. It actually came out at $78,242 paid by a record-breaking crowd of 23,190.

'The defeat he had been handed by Zivic hurt Henry's heart more than his eyes,' he wrote in his autobiography. 'He could not and would not admit that he was through, even though he was aware of the fact that his reflexes were not what they used to be, that he didn't seem able to punch as hard as he had a year ago, that his timing was off and that his legs had got tired too fast. He was still sure he could take Zivic.

'Something else was rankling in his heart, too. More and more he kept thinking about preaching. That Voice from somewhere beyond kept coming back. It was aggravating – like a little splinter under your fingernail; it wouldn't let him alone. Nobody was putting any pressure on him, about this – nobody but that insistent, tireless Voice from somewhere. He trained hard for Zivic; this was *it*.

'When he climbed into the ring at Madison Square Garden on the night of 17 January 1941, he looked out on the biggest fight crowd in the history of the Garden. Mike Jacobs had even sold *standing*: there were over 23,000 in the seats and in the aisles, and rumour had it that 10,000 were milling around in the streets outside. It was an Armstrong crowd; here were his friends, his old fans, his pals from Harlem, come to cheer the old warrior. They had bet 8-5 on him to win. It almost made him cry.'[203]

Leading members of the press brigade were beginning to change horses, to wonder if Henry Armstrong still had something in the tank or was he running on empty? 'Prize fighters almost never vary when it comes time to hang up the gloves,' wrote the *Washington Evening Star*. 'We are thinking at the moment of Henry Armstrong, who will climb into the ring again tomorrow night at Madison Square Garden. Last year, September to be specific, he said there would be no next year in the ring for Henry Armstrong.

'This was when he came to Washington to fight Phil Furr in the Variety Club show. He was sitting in his little dressing room at Turner's Arena and having his hands taped. "I'm just about finished," he said, "I'm getting afraid of my eyes. This fight, another in New York with Fritzie Zivic in October, and probably a third on the Cleveland Christmas show … and then it'll be quits." Hammering Henry got by Furr easily enough, but Zivic didn't roll over for him. On the contrary, Zivic handed him a terrific beating, almost knocking him out in the final round.

'His hemstitched eyes were ripped open again and the lacings which held together his mouth on the inside came

---

203 Henry Armstrong, *Gloves, Glory and God*, 1957.

CHAPTER NINETEEN

apart. He underwent operations ... new stitches ... eye tests ... and three months' rest.

'He had a close call. Now he's coming back again. Why do they do it? For one thing, pride is a factor. Pride and quick money. Prize fighters rarely quit when they are champions. Instead they wait until they are dethroned and then they keep trying to regain their thrones so they can quit. That undoubtedly is one of the reasons why Armstrong is going to try again. He was great once and Zivic never was an outstanding champion. He could hit and he's made of all heart. But in the other corner will be a slashing fellow who is younger and anxious for some of that big money that Armstrong has been getting. And, most of all, a fellow who isn't held together by catgut lacings.'[204]

Lawton Carver for INS said: 'Along the pugilistic byways today you could pick up such morsels of gossip as the one to the effect that Armstrong is through and knows it, but is going to bat just one more time in the hope that he can retire as an undefeated champion. And you hear also that he is making this fight for his ill manager, Eddie Mead, who needs a payday ... In the meantime, Zivic, one of those tough, slow-seasoning veterans with a fair sort of punch, a great will to win and a ruthlessness with his thumbs and elbows, has come on to look like the kind of fellow who might do it to Armstrong all over again. Having given Armstrong his lumps before, Zivic simply doesn't see how he can miss this time.'[205]

From Gayle Talbot of Associated Press: 'If Zivic trounces him again, then it's adios to one of the greatest of modern

---
204 *Washington Evening Star*, 16 January 1941.
205 Lawton Carver, *Cedar Rapids Gazette*, Iowa, 16 January 1941.

fighting men. Though Armstrong probably will go into the 15-rounder a slight favourite in the wagering, he is by no means an overwhelming choice of those who qualify as experts. Such an old stager as James Joy Johnston, for instance, has predicted that Zivic will wear Armstrong down and knock him out by the tenth.

'This ringsider, in his choice of Henry to win back his championship Friday night, should be accepted without reason like the weather. However, if a reason is demanded, then it becomes a painful duty to recall Zivic's recent performance against Lew Jenkins. Fritzie was extremely lucky to earn a draw, and if Armstrong can't beat this kind of fighting he ought to retire.'[206]

Harry Ferguson for United Press: 'Henry Armstrong, once the greatest fighter pound for pound in the business, makes what may be his last stand against welterweight champion Fritzie Zivic in the Garden tonight. He has been stripped of all his titles; his eyes are scarred from surgeons' knives; Eddie Mead, his manager, lies ill and won't be in the corner shouting encouragement; and Armstrong faces a rough, tough clouter who blinded him with blood in their last fight. But the legend of the human windmill's fighting heart rose above these blows of fate today, and the cold-blooded bookies made him a 7½ to 5 favourite to regain the title he lost to Zivic.

'Whether Armstrong wins or loses, the ringside customers are going to get their $11.50 worth. If he wins, they will yell themselves hoarse for one of the most popular fighters who ever pulled on leather.

---

206 Gayle Talbot, *Mason City Globe Gazette*, Iowa, 17 January 1941.

CHAPTER NINETEEN

'If he loses, they can tell in the years to come – when his name is bracketed with Leonard and Gans and McAuliffe in the book of the great – how they saw him give it one more try on a cold January evening in 1941. They can take away a memory of Henry snorting and moving forward to give and take punishment.

'An astonishing little fighter, Henry Armstrong, once a three-way title-holder, came to the end of the road last night, but before he did he gave the boys something to remember him by, one last dramatic flare-up that had the packed Garden rocking with sadistic roars, roars that deafened writer Joe Williams as he hammered these words through his typewriter.

'Referee Arthur Donovan had gone over to Armstrong's corner at the end of the tenth round to scrutinise the condition of his bleeding, lacerated eyes. It was the third such trip the referee had made. Completing his examination this time, the referee said, "One more round, Henry. If you can't do it in one more I'll have to stop it."

'The fighter nodded his head and tapped the heels of his gloves together impatiently. His nervous feet performed the pattern of a jig as he sat on the stool. Fighting a cool, wisely planned fight, Fritzie Zivic had all but blinded Armstrong with long left jabs and short, cutting uppercuts. The only way he could lose was by a knockout. This was the situation when the bell sounded to start the 11th round. What was left of a long and spectacular career depended on the round coming up.

'It was a round that will long be remembered by the thousands who thronged the Garden. With both eyes closing and his face a bloody smear, Armstrong, for the first time during the fight, was the old Armstrong, a human dynamo, moving relentlessly forward, throwing punches in a steady stream, angry, desperate streams, fighting his heart out. For a full two minutes he was strangely young and vibrant again, a pulse-beating picture of the youngster who came here years ago to amaze ringsiders with his inexhaustible stamina and insolent indifference to punishment.'[207]

'The career of one of the greatest little fighters the ring has seen came to an abrupt and bloody end last night when they guided Henry Armstrong's uncertain feet down the steps from the Madison Square Garden ring for the last time,' wrote Gayle Talbot. A crowd of more than 23,000, the biggest ever to jam its way into the Eighth Avenue arena for a boxing match, fittingly was on hand to stand and cheer the little man as he groped his way, nearly blinded, to the dressing room and fistic oblivion. The end came mercifully, after 52 seconds of fighting in the 12th round, when Donovan, hearkening to the roar of "stop it" from the crowd, took Armstrong in his arms protectively and led the little fighter to his corner.

'Dr Alexander Schiff, who examined Armstrong after the fight, said the cuts around his eyes would not endanger his sight. In an adjoining cubicle sat Zivic, his face unmarked, and said it was a comparatively easy victory, easier than his first over Armstrong last October. Some thought Zivic was less than brilliant in slashing Henry into his final defeat and said that Armstrong, in his prime, would have taken the youngest of the Zivics apart. That might have been true. But Zivic, for the night and the particular job, was almost the perfect

---

207 Joe Williams, *Syracuse Herald Journal*, 18 January 1941.

CHAPTER NINETEEN

workman. Eddie Mead, Armstrong's manager, did not see or hear the downfall of his little friend and idol. Bedded with a heart illness, he was given a heavy sleeping potion before the bout began and was awakened only to be told the result. Ray Arcel, a top man in any corner, took Eddie's place at Henry's shoulder.'[208]

'Zivic took command in the first round and kept it by waging a crafty battle. The best weapon in his arsenal was one of the fanciest uppercuts ever seen hereabouts. That uppercut tore Armstrong's face into shreds, rocked his brain and reeled his senses until referee Arthur Donovan stepped in after 33 minutes and 52 seconds of fighting.

'Donovan had given him one more round to come back. It meant that Armstrong had 180 speeding seconds, three precious minutes to regain the last of the world championships he once held. Into the short period between the clang of two bells, he called on what little reserve was left after 350 bruising fights. He forgot about the crowd. His world had narrowed to what he could see through a crimson haze between two slits of eyes, and all he could see was the blurred figure of Zivic in black tights moving in for the kill.

'Armstrong tore in. He belted a left hook to the head, slammed a right to the jaw and drove Zivic to the ropes. He kept him there because when you have a man on the ropes you can be blinded and still hit him. Armstrong poured in lefts to the head and rights to the body. The crowd came out of their chairs and loosed a roar that drowned out the soggy smack of Armstrong's gloves. A woman in the fifth row threw away her

---

208 Gayle Talbot, *Kalispell Daily Inter-Lake*, Montana, 18 January 1941.

hat. Men who had never met before slapped one another on the back and howled themselves hoarse. And still Armstrong poured it on. Donovan finally tore him away from Zivic when the bell rang and the crowd sank back into their seats, limp and happy. Hammerin' Hank had done them proud.'[209]

The man for United Press recorded: 'At the opening gong, Armstrong used new ring tactics. He came out in semi-crouch, flat-footed and tried to shuffle within range of Zivic's body, instead of using his former juggling, snorting method of attack. Zivic stood back and jabbed at Henry's wide-open face until he had the former champion's brows well reddened, then he looped in uppercuts and opened a gash in Henry's lower lip before the battle was two minutes old. He shook Armstrong with several hard rights in the second session, but Armstrong rallied to fight back in a corner. He staggered Fritzie twice with hard hooks to the head in the third but suffered a gash under his right eye.

'Pug-nosed Fritzie kept his blacksmith's right arm over his liver and caught most of the body blows there. In the sixth session a right uppercut dropped Armstrong to the canvas on one knee for no count. Henry's left eye was opened in the seventh and he took such a bad battering in the eighth that referee Donovan examined his cuts between rounds.

'Zivic suffered a bad gash behind his right ear in the ninth. At the close of the 11th Donovan called the commission physician, Dr William H. Walker, into the ring. He permitted Armstrong to go out for the 12th but Armstrong was in such pitiful condition that Donovan halted the bout in that session.

---

209 *Dubuque Telegraph Herald*, 19 January 1941.

CHAPTER NINETEEN

'Armstrong scaled 140½ to Zivic's 145¾. Zivic, who had wagered $2,000 on the chances of his own victory, said in the dressing room, "The hardest punch I gave him was in the fourth – to the liver. He hurt me in that same round with a right to the body. I injured my left hand in the tenth."'[210]

James P Douglas of the *New York Times* was moved to write, 'Through the 11th round he pulled the crowd to their feet in as glorious a rally as this observer has seen in 25 years of attendance at these ring battles. The former champion hammered Zivic all over the ring. He pelted the title-holder with lefts and rights to the body, plied him with savage thrusts of the left and wicked right smashes to the face and head. Repeatedly, Armstrong grazed the jaw with desperate rights, blows with which he hoped to turn the tide of crushing defeat that was engulfing him. For two minutes Armstrong went berserk. He was a fighting maniac in the one flash he gave of the Hammering Henry of old. It was glorious, spectacular while it lasted. Zivic was too busy trying to defend himself in this unlooked-for charge to launch a counterfire.

'But then Zivic stepped to the attack and through the last minute of the 11th round he hammered and punched Armstrong mercilessly with short, choppy but stinging lefts and rights that ripped open old wounds and started a flow of blood. Henry started the 12th as if to press his dynamic recovery. But he had given all his strength in that 11th-round stand. He shuffled into a barrage of straight lefts, a criss-cross of lefts and rights, punishing, cutting blows. He tried a roundhouse right for the jaw, missed and slipped. Up he came,

---
210 *Madison Wisconsin State Journal*, 18 January 1941.

facing his foe, charging recklessly, only to be pelted by Zivic's shower of blows. When Donovan realised what Armstrong must have known but would not admit, the referee stepped between the fighters and waved an end to the battle, and Armstrong's career.'[211]

'It was all over. The last chance had gone glimmering, and Henry Armstrong was definitely out of the "big time". Yet, when the fighters left the ring, the cheers for Henry were louder than those for Zivic. The crowd was still with him, even in defeat. In the dressing room, Harry hovered over him like a heart-broken brother, his eyes filled with tears, his hands moving tenderly over the swollen, shapeless face and head. The reporters came pounding at the door; Harry held them off. He said Henry would go into business now. This was for sure: he wouldn't fight any more.

'They got Henry over to Dr Schiff's office, where the "Doc" looked at him in utter silence, shaking his head. Just before they left the dressing room, Zivic came in. He took Henry's hand and said slowly, "Henry, you're the greatest champ that ever lived." Then the lights went out in the Garden and the place was still.

'Henry missed one familiar figure in his corner that night: Eddie Mead wasn't there. Eddie had had a heart attack, and on doctor's orders he listened to the fight over the radio. In Dr Schiff's office, Henry found Eddie stretched out on a couch, his eyes filled with tears. He reached out and took Henry's hand. He said slowly, "It's all over Hank. You'll never have to go through with anything like this again. You go home now,

---

211 James P. Douglas, *New York Times*, 18 January 1941.

CHAPTER NINETEEN

to California, and get a good long rest with your family and your friends. You've earned it, boy." Then Dr Schiff came and led Henry over to the operating table where he began to cut away the scar tissue that had been building up around the eyes and to stitch the bleeding eyes and mouth.'[212]

---

212 Henry Armstrong, *Gloves, Glory and God*, 1957.

Chapter Twenty

'THE FIGHT mob said "so long" to gallant little Henry Armstrong today as his conqueror, welterweight champion Fritzie Zivic, left for a Florida vacation before picking up his fistic trade again, probably against lightweight champion Lew Jenkins in March.

'At the same time a thorough search of the records disclosed that the crowd of 23,190 fans who packed Madison Square Garden like a giant sardine can last night not only was greater than ever for a Garden fight, but was the largest turnout ever for an event in the big sports arena. The previous high for a professional fight was marked by the 21,712 who saw Jimmy McLarnin outpoint Ray Miller in 1929. Tony Canzoneri and Al Singer fought before 21,617 before that, and since then Primo Carnera and Big Boy Pedersen attracted 21,171. A Golden Gloves amateur show once drew 22,000.

'There was no change of mind about Henry's retirement today as promoter Mike Jacobs sent him a $16,530 pay cheque as his share of the gross gate of $78,242.46 and the net of $66,817. His personal physician, Dr Alexander Schiff, looked over the great little fighting man's eyes again and reported that until the swelling goes down he would be unable to take the necessary stitches in the wounds they suffered last night.

CHAPTER TWENTY

In a week or so, Henry will visit his home in Los Angeles and then will return to take up a business career either in wine or whisky.

'Financially he is comfortably fixed with annuities estimated at $9,000 from the approximately $350,000 he has earned in the ring.

'Zivic, meantime, picked up $19,836.60 for his successful defence of the welterweight title and left with promoter Mike Jacobs and light-heavyweight champion Billy Conn for a stay in Florida.'[213]

Some six years later, about February 1947, Fritzie was back in New York talking to Red Smith, columnist for the *Herald Tribune*, and he was recalling his fight with Henry Armstrong, the first one, when he won the welterweight title. 'You remember that Cadillac,' he said to Smith. 'Ever since I was a kid, that's what I always wanted. I figured then I'd be a success. So the day I'm fighting Henry Armstrong for the title in New York, I go and look at the biggest Cadillac I can find. That night Henry's giving it to me pretty good and I can see that Cadillac rollin' farther and farther away from me.

'Henry's givin' me the elbows and the shoulders and the top of the head, and I can give that stuff back pretty good, but I don't dare to or maybe they'll throw me out of the ring. Well, in the seventh round I give him the head a couple times and choke him a couple times and use the elbow some, and the referee says, "If you guys want to fight that way, it's okay with me."

---

213 *Evening Star* Washington DC, 19 January 1941.

'"Hot damn!" I told Luke Carney in my corner. "Watch me go now." And from there out I saw that Cadillac turn around and come rollin' back.'[214]

On a day in April 1959, Henry Armstrong dropped into the *Ring* magazine offices in Madison Square Garden. Writer Ted Carroll recorded: 'Looking very well indeed, Henry Armstrong, the great old "Triple Champion" himself, strolled into the *Ring* office one day last month to renew old acquaintances and "pass the time of day." The pleasant-mannered, well-spoken one-time ring great hasn't changed a great deal in appearance since his rip-roaring boxing days. Grotesquely wide shouldered as of yore, bespectacled but otherwise unmarked, well dressed and apparently unworried, Henry, a fluid, engaging conversationalist, regaled the *Ring* staff and editor Nat Fleischer for several hours with flashbacks of his wondrous boxing career.

'Armstrong voiced wonderment over the present plight of his one-time nemesis Fritzie Zivic, of whom he is very fond. "When I read about Fritzie working as a labourer I felt kinda bad. He had lots of tricks in the ring but there never was a sweller guy outside of it. What in the world did he do with all his money, but then who am I to ask that question?" whimsically philosophised Henry.'

'Like many fighters, Henry ... was doomed to wind up with far too little of the half million dollars or so in purses garnered through his ring career.

'If this bothers him, he shows little evidence of it, as again, like most fighters, he has no regrets and insists he

---

[214] *The Book of Boxing* Ed., WC Heinz & Nathan Ward, 1999.

CHAPTER TWENTY

wouldn't trade his fighting experiences for all the gold in Fort Knox.

'Eddie Mead was a very good manager and I have no complaints. I feel he meant well, but he just wasn't made to handle the kind of money we were getting. I should have watched over my own money, but I didn't. That was my mistake. I didn't know how to take care of money any more than Mead did. He ran through a couple of fortunes of his own before he went through mine.'[215]

Henry's interest in Zivic's financial problems was triggered by an article in *Ring*'s April 1959 issue, written by Al Buck: 'Newspapers carried the story that Zivic, former world welterweight champion, was broke and reduced to swinging a pick and shovel on a road crew of the Allegheny County highways department. In 17 years in the ring, Zivic earned a fortune. When he retired he owned a $40,000 house, complete with a swimming pool. Today he shovels for $1.70 an hour. His weekly pay amounts to about $70.

'He lives with his family in a modest apartment, rented of course. Tough? No doubt it is, but what has boxing to do with it? Nothing. Bad investments ruined Zivic, just as they have ruined ball players, bankers and others. He would never have had the $40,000 house, the swimming pool and all that goes with them if, back in 1940, he hadn't won the world welterweight title from Henry Armstrong.

'Zivic was in business long before he retired from boxing. I recall Fritzie arriving from Pittsburgh for a Garden fight. He came in a station wagon on which was painted, "Fritzie

---
215 Ted Carroll, *Ring*, May 1959.

Zivic & Sons, Wholesale Nuts." This was no gag. The Zivics were in the nut business, selling walnuts, peanuts, hazelnuts and whatnuts.

'Zivic tried promoting fights in old Hickey Park at Pittsburgh. More recently he tried selling used cars. Now he's working on the county roads. A fellow and his family have to eat. The ex-welterweight champion is an object of pity in some quarters. Still it can't be said boxing is responsible for his plight. What would Fritzie have been without boxing? Most likely an unknown, unsung worker in the steel mills.'[216]

'Starting in 1940 the Armstrong engine started to lose steam and he began to slow down. Former heavyweight champion Jack Johnson was of the opinion that "nobody ever wasted energy like that boy. There is no way in the world he could have lasted any longer than he did fighting that way."'[217]

Historian Bert Randolph Sugar wrote: 'No one who ever saw this fighter will ever forget him: a nonstop punching machine, his style more rhythmic than headlong, his matchstick legs akimbo, his arms crossed in front of his face. His likes will never be seen again.'[218]

Henry Armstrong would be seen again, but it would be 16 months before America's fight fans saw him back in the professional ring, and it was a woman who talked him into it.

Her name was Emma Lou Jackson and she was Henry's sister-in-law. She had been a constant in Henry's corner ever since he came home with a black eye and a broken nose as a kid fighter trying to break into boxing. "Why don't you

---
216 Al Buck, *Ring*, April 1959.
217 Jack Johnson, *Ring*, April 1941.
218 Bert Randolph Sugar, *Boxing's Greatest Fighters*, 2006.

stop all this fighting, Henry?" she said. "Get these wild notions out of your head. Become a preacher." "I'm not ready to become a preacher yet," he answered slowly. "Someday, maybe …"'[219]

'After the second fight with Fritzie Zivic, when Henry was about ready to start for California, he went looking for Eddie Mead and asked about some money. Eddie had borrowed from Henry when his pockets were empty; and Henry figured it was time to pay a little something back. He trusted Eddie Mead as he would have trusted his own father. But it was the same old story with Eddie, an inveterate horseplayer; the nags were all running backwards these days, he aimed to pay Henry back some day but he didn't know when that day would be.

'So Henry cashed in some bonds and bought himself a beautiful new Cadillac, and started for home, early in February. First things first: he had to go to St Louis and say goodbye to Sis Lou. He found her reading her Bible by the light of three little candles, and she was delighted to see him. Emma Lou was religious, from her head to her toes. She spoke to Henry before he could speak.

'"Come on in, brother. I've been waiting for you. And I've got great news for you. Right now you think you're through, but you're not. You are going back to the ring, and you'll make more money than ever."

'Henry couldn't, wouldn't believe it. Doc Schiff had warned him never to fight again, that if he did his eyes would be cut to ribbons, and he'd be blind. Emma Lou laughed.

---

[219] Henry Armstrong, *Gloves, Glory and God*, 1957.

"'Don't you believe it, brother. You just go on out to California like he said, and rest yourself. And trust God. He's a great healer. In three months He'll make you as good as new. I know. He told me so. Just put the thought of getting hurt out of your mind; it won't happen. You'll make a comeback, and in all the fights you have in the comeback, you'll never get a scratch. God says so. Why don't you listen to Him, Henry?"

'Why didn't he listen? The Voice, again! They stood there looking wistfully at the little glimmering candles, and a little candle began to glimmer, to flicker and grow brighter in the heart of Henry Armstrong. Back in California, he rested awhile. He checked his assets. Not so good! He would have to do *something*.'[220]

When word got around the fight business that Henry was free and looking for work, the guys started to come around with their propositions. Joe Glaser, a big guy in the music business, got him fixed up with Don Redman's orchestra in Detroit, told Henry he could make a lot of money. It wasn't for Henry. He quit after two weeks, borrowed on some life insurance annuities, and went home. Lee Lewis, a famous publicity man, got Henry back in the ring refereeing fights up and down the West coast. It lasted seven months and he was off home again.

Movie tough guy George Raft had the ex-champ touring army camps staging exhibitions for the soldiers. This was more like it, he was getting back in the ring, getting into condition, and it meant doing something for the boys in the army. Just after the Barney Ross fight in 1938, Eddie Mead

---

220 Henry Armstrong, *Gloves, Glory and God*, 1957.

CHAPTER TWENTY

had introduced his boy to Freddie Sommers, who sent Henry out with a soft-ball team, booking him all over the country. When that flopped, Freddie had another idea. What about a comeback! Have a few warm-up fights then go after some big names. This was more like what Henry had in mind. But in May of 1942, Henry was saddened by the news that Eddie Mead had died of a heart attack.

'Los Angeles, 27 May – Five thousand fight fans stood silent as the timer's bell sounded ten times in memory of Eddie Mead, who piloted Henry Armstrong to three world championships. Standing in the centre of the ring was Armstrong, who came to the Olympic Auditorium last night to see George Latka, Gray, Indiana, lightweight outbox Richie Lemos of Los Angeles. It was in the same ring that Mead and Armstrong began their fistic association several years ago. Mead died of a heart attack in New York on Monday.'[221]

'Eddie Mead had a memory for a face and a name. He'd have been a great politician, for it takes more of that "hail fellow, well met," business to get along in the scrap racket than most politicians own. And Eddie had it in abundance. A sharp man with the percentage figures when lining up a fight, was Eddie, but as open-hearted as a book otherwise, and that's how he made such friends as George Raft and Al Jolson, who bought Henry Armstrong's contract and practically made a present of the document to Mead. Yes, Jolson kicked eventually for his cut on Armstrong, whereupon Raft bought the entire sheet of paper and turned it over to Mead.'[222]

---

221 *El Paso Herald Post*, Texas, 27 May 1942.
222 Rex Hess, *Mansfield News Journal*, 27 May 1942, Ohio.

A New York Irishman, Eddie Mead was 49 when he died in May 1942. Before he met up with Henry Armstrong, Mead had managed Joe Lynch, who twice won the bantamweight championship in the roaring twenties. 'Eddie had won three fortunes in boxing,' Henry would recall, 'and he had lost a lot of it betting on the horses. He just couldn't stay away from the tracks. He even bought himself a horse and entered him in a race. The horse was a has-been, he wasn't supposed to have a chance in any race. But – in this race he pulled the upset of the century, and outran the field! Listening in over the radio, Eddie was as stunned as the rest of them when the nag came in – but not stunned enough to forget to reach for his winnings. The excitement started his heart pumping. He started for Dr Schiff's office on 54th Street, and dropped dead in front of the doctor's office.

'It was a terrible blow to Henry; he had learned to lean on Eddie, heavily. But there was nothing to do now but to get himself a new manager – which he did, in George Moore. Moore – was good, he knew his way around.'[223]

Friends of Mead said that Eddie had wired Armstrong just the night before, pleading with him to abandon any hopes of a comeback to the ring. But it was too late. Emma Lou had already planted the idea in Henry's head and he had been training at a Dude Ranch in California. Now, with Moore handling his business, Henry Armstrong was back in the fight business.

---

223 Henry Armstrong, *Gloves, Glory and God*, 1957.

Chapter Twenty-One

MOORE BROUGHT Henry back to the fight business on the first day of June in 1942, going against Irish Johnny Taylor at the San Jose Auditorium and the place was packed to see what the former triple-champion had left. He had enough to beat Taylor inside four rounds. Referee Clayton Frye stepped in after Armstrong left Johnny draped on the ropes after taking a right, two lefts and another right to the button.

'Even a layoff of more than a year hasn't made a zephyr of the hurricane,' wrote Alan Ward in the *Oakland Tribune*. 'Hurricane Henry Armstrong, one of the greatest fighters ever to don a boxing glove, today had proved he still is capable of whipping a lot of welterweights. When Taylor got back to the dressing room and looked in the mirror he saw a cut on his left cheek, a hint of a black eye, and the start of a cauliflower ear.

'"I've been fighting 12 years," he said, "under 18 different names, and that's the first cauliflower ear I ever got. I still can't get over it, the great Armstrong slugging me, whacking me for three heats without knocking me down. And all he gets is $470 which he has to cut with his manager. But what the hell, I didn't even get $200. We're both washed up. The only difference between us is I know it." Jimmy Murray, the Oakland matchmaker, spoke up. "Johnny," he growled, "you're the proof Armstrong still packs a terrific wallop. This is his first fight since January 17, 1940. That was 17 months ago. Who else but a great fighter could have looked so good after a layoff like that?'[224]

Three weeks later, Henry fought Sheik Rangel at the Oakland Auditorium in a fight that had ringside observer Alan Ward writing, 'Hollywood popularised a few adjectives which logically can be borrowed to designate a fight held in this city last night. The superlatives are "terrific, colossal and gigantic," and any words less indicative of the ultimate in art or endeavour wouldn't do justice to that ten-round fight at the auditorium between Henry Armstrong and Sheik Rangel, won by Armstrong.

'One had to witness those ten rounds of bruising, ceaseless punching to really appreciate that a classic of prize fighting had been unfolded … any such ring performance previously witnessed by this writer paled into insignificance when compared with the Armstrong–Rangel Donnybrook. Had an observer doubted the potency of Armstrong's blows during those ten dramatic rounds he had but to inspect the grotesque visage of Rangel when it was over.

'The Fresno Steamroller will be days erasing the souvenirs of combat … and it will be weeks before he is in proper condition for additional fighting. His right eye was badly slashed and swollen shut. His left peeper was similarly out of shape. His lips were broken and twisted and his nose was almost twice its normal size.

---

224 *Oakland Tribune,* California, 2 June 1942.

CHAPTER TWENTY-ONE

'It can be said Armstrong's comeback bout – his recent four-round technical kayo of Irish Johnny Taylor really didn't count – was more than successful. It was impressive. The great little battler displayed all of the amazing vitality, the unstinted aggression and sharp, cutting punching which gave him three world titles and a permanent niche in Fistiana's Hall of Fame.'[225]

If Henry had any ideas about setting off any crackers on Independence Day, young Reuben Shank had celebratory ideas of his own. 'At the Municipal Auditorium in Denver, the best welterweight prospect in the Rockies took all Henry had to offer in the sixth round, bounced off the floor after a nine count and finished fast to win a unanimous decision. "This comeback stuff isn't so easy," muttered Henry, "but I thought I had him." So did the sportswriters at the ringside who marked their cards in favour of Hammerin' Hank by a wide margin. Armstrong, who weighed 145½ to 149 for Shank, said "he would like to meet Shank in a neutral city" and thought the decision "hurt Shank's reputation."'[226]

A couple of weeks later Henry was in Sacramento to see off the Oakland entry Joe Ybarra within three rounds. 'Showing more punch than in his three previous comeback bouts, Hammerin' Henry Armstrong scored a third-round technical knockout in a scheduled ten-rounder Monday night. Whaling away in his two-fisted style, the game Armstrong cut Ybarra's lip in the first round, put him down for a five count in the second and was battering him badly when Referee Johnny Lotsey stopped the encounter in the third.

---
225 Alan Ward, *Oakland Tribune*, California, 25 June 1942.
226 *Ogden Standard Examiner*, Utah, 4 July 1942.

225

'"Hope to have Armstrong signed for an August bout in Ogden within 48 hours," said promoter Ben Petre today in a wire to the *Standard Examiner* sports department. Armstrong made his fourth stop in his comeback campaign last night in Sacramento. The 'L' Street arena was jammed for the Armstrong–Ybarra ten-round headliner.

'Armstrong stopped Ybarra in the third round. He had Ybarra on the floor four times before the bout was finally terminated in the third round. "Armstrong has packed 'em in everywhere on his comeback attempt," said Petre. "He is in great shape and will attract a record throng in Utah if he accepts terms."

'Last fall Armstrong was signed to meet Jackie Burke in Ogden. He suffered a finger injury in a car crash in Oklahoma and the bout was cancelled. Burke was chosen from a field of ten boxers and the match at that time was "red hot". "My first concern is to get Armstrong on the line," said Petre. "After that I'll decide just who will be his opponent."'[227]

'Warming up for the Burke fight, Armstrong scored a seven-round technical knockout over Aldo Spoldi of New York. The Los Angeles man won every round by a comfortable margin and made a punching bag of Spoldi, whose only reward was the big hand he received from a crowd which filled the ten thousand-seat Civic Auditorium in San Francisco.

'Armstrong had met Spoldi before – in New York five years ago – but not nearly so decisively as last night. The Italian went down three times in the seventh for counts of

---

227 *Ogden Standard Examiner*, 21 July 1942.

CHAPTER TWENTY-ONE

eight, seven and five before the bout was stopped by Referee Frank Carter.'[228]

The Utah city of Ogden was buzzing over the Armstrong–Burke fight, set for John Affleck Park. The advance sale for tickets was reported heavy when Armstrong and manager George Moore checked in at the Porters and Waiters club ten days before the fight. Hank would work out at Hillfield on Friday and Saturday and perform at Ogden Arsenal on Monday.

'The scheduled ten-round fistic feature between Armstrong and Jackie Burke, Ogden switchman Tuesday night will be staged Thursday night. Inclement weather caused the postponement. Maxie Baer, referee and former world heavyweight champion, will remain over for the headliner. Burke and Armstrong weighed-in Tuesday. Each man tipped the scales at 145 pounds. Baer weighed-in at 244 pounds, 35 pounds heavier than when he beat Carnera for the title in 1934. Big brother Buddy was there and he hit the scales only seven pounds heavier.

'Promoter Ben Petre bumped into a new headache late Tuesday and the argument was not decided today. Henry Armstrong insists on wearing six-ounce gloves for the contest, while Burke wants to don eight-ounce gloves. "I'll even battle Burke barehanded if he cares to," said Armstrong today. "I'm in fine shape and believe the delay will help both Burke and myself." Burke engaged in a light drill during the rainstorm on Tuesday and reported he will be as keen as a razor when the bell sounds on Thursday night.'[229]

---

228 *Reno Evening Gazette*, 4 August 1942.
229 Matt B Wise, *Ogden Standard Examiner*, 12 August 1942.

227

'In an industry noted for its overindulgence in self-confidence, Armstrong's attitude is refreshing. He told columnist Stubby Currence, "I really am not interested in getting to the top again for a big eastern fight. I'll be satisfied to fight a lot of boys out this way and pick up what I can. The money I make this time will be used more wisely."

'Henry, one-time triple champion, is in the throes now. He is making his attempt at an opportune time, however. The war has thinned the ranks of real crowd pleasers and that's where Henry was always 1-A. Henry, close to 30, knows what he is doing: he's picking his opponents carefully.'[230]

Ogden, Utah, 14 August, INS reported: 'Henry Armstrong, who three days ago declared he was fighting "just to keep from getting flabby", today conceded that he definitely was "on the comeback trail" after his ten-round decision over Jackie Burke of Ogden. Hammerin' Hank came out of a crouch in Affleck Park last night to display some of his former speed and punch to bash the Utah welterweight to the floor three times. In the eighth, Burke went down for counts of six and nine, but in the ninth he climbed back to his feet immediately after the knockdown, although groggy.

'After being awarded the decision by Referee Max Baer, Armstrong said he hoped to land a title fight with Fred (Red) Cochrane, welter champ. Earlier in the week he had denied title aspirations and declared he was fighting just for the fun of it and to keep in trim.'[231]

Jackie Burke didn't think it was just for fun, having to pick himself off the canvas five times before the final bell sounded.

---
230 Stubby Currence, *Bluefield Daily Telegraph*, 7 August 1942.
231 *Moline Daily Dispatch*, Moline Illinois, 14 August 1942.

CHAPTER TWENTY-ONE

But he impressed *Ogden Standard Examiner* reporter William Smiley who wrote, 'It was a fight that will stay in the memories of Ogden fans for many years. Burke and Armstrong put on one of the finest head-to-shoulder slugfests this part of the country has ever witnessed, and kept the crowd roaring throughout.

'Strong legs and piston-like arm action of the Ogden switchman prevented the former triple champion from getting anything like a kayo punch into action. Fans will gossip for years of the toe-to-toe infighting of the two battlers – vicious, jarring jabs that continued for round after round without let-up. Burke lost the fight to Armstrong, but every ringsider and bleacherite of the nearly 4,000 assembled there was proud of the way in which he lost to a man who has become almost legendary in the ring. "I say again," said George Moore, manager of Armstrong, "Hammerin' Hank is the next welterweight champion."'[232]

A couple of weeks later, the 'almost ring legend' took a close look at his bank book. It didn't look too good. Bad investments had cut into it. There had been a Chinese restaurant in Hollywood, in which Henry invested $7,000; it went bad. All Henry got out of that was one good filet mignon steak.

'Discouraged, he and Eddie then got into a motion picture deal. Henry was the "hero" of the film, which was shot in Long Island City. It was called "Keep Punching" but it was no knockout. Henry is still punching, trying to get back what he put into that one. How much he put in, he'll never know!

---

232 William Smiley, *Ogden Standard Examiner*, Utah, 14 August 1942.

229

He thought of these "flops" and of other ex-champs who had gone into business, to safeguard their winnings. Some had done well – Jack Dempsey, Harry Wills, Jimmy McLarnin, for instance. But there was also Sam Langford, who died destitute and blind; George Godfrey, the "Black Shadow", who died in a shack in Los Angeles; and Ad Wolgast, who died in a mental institution. You never knew how you'd end up in this game. Henry still thought he'd come out well, rich, in the end.'[233]

He quit dreaming and went back to the gym. Two weeks after the Burke fight, Henry was in Oakland to fight Rodolfo Ramirez. 'In the wake of Oakland's greatest fight crowd, which jammed the Civic Auditorium to the rafters last night to see Henry Armstrong score an eight-round knockout over Rodolfo Ramirez, came the announcement this morning that Armstrong's next local opponent will be Earl Turner. Matchmaker John Sylvester has the bout signed for the night of 30 September and has visions of equalling or exceeding the $18,766.29 worth of customers who saw Armstrong thoroughly master the little Mexican.

'Don Shields, chief inspector for the State Boxing Commission, is authority for the statement that the 8,201 customers who last night enriched the coffers of promoter Tommy Simpson, is the greatest crowd ever to witness an indoor fight in Oakland. Also said Shields, the gross of $18,766.29 is the largest ever paid for an indoor fight here at prices of one, two and three dollars. The net receipts, after deduction of State and Federal taxes, was $16,204.90, of

---

233 Henry Armstrong, *Gloves, Glory and God*, 1957.

CHAPTER TWENTY-ONE

which Armstrong received $4,861 and Ramirez $4,051. It was the largest cheque the former triple title holder has received since starting his comeback campaign.

'George Parnassus, the wily and excitable manager of the Mexican, complained repeatedly to Referee Johnny Lotsey because of Armstrong's use of his head, elbows and shoulders. It is true, as Parnassus claims, that Armstrong used his head, shoulders and elbows. But it is equally as true that he hit Ramirez 10,000 times with his fists and it was the gloves on the end of his tireless, piston-like arms that won the verdict. A left hook and right cross to the head brought the bout to a dramatic end.'[234]

They didn't have big fights in Pittman. They didn't have any fights in Pittman. Not even on a Saturday night. Excitement? Well, Pittman was a small residential neighbourhood located about six miles from Downtown Las Vegas and nine miles from the Strip. But there was a September night in 1942 when garish posters were pasted up outside the local arena: 'BOXING! MONDAY NIGHT. 10 ROUNDS-HENRY ARMSTRONG v. CECILIO LOZADA Come early!'

Even in that small Nevada town they had heard about Henry Armstrong. The guy won three world championships! The only fighter to ever hold three world titles simultaneously. They called him 'Homicide Hank' and he was still a good fighter even though on a comeback. They expected him to beat this Lozada guy, probably knock him out. Armstrong didn't knock Lozada out, the Nevada Commission doctor

---

234 Lee Dunbar, *Oakland Tribune*, California, 27 August.

did when Cecilio failed the physical. The promoter made a few calls and found Irish Johnny Taylor ready and willing to face Armstrong.

'At a recent testimonial dinner for Henry in Oakland, the ex-champ said that in all his life, "he never meant to harm anyone". While Henry was all in earnest, Alan Ward, *Oakland Tribune* sportswriter and master of ceremonies, pointed out that he doubted if Hank lived up to his intentions that night he fought Irish Johnny Taylor, the handsome Oakland pugilist, whom he kayoed in practically nothing flat, after meting out a short-lived but savage beating.

'To this statement, Mr Taylor, who was present, added a loud "Amen!"'[235]

'They say a boxer isn't entitled to any more money than he can draw through the gate. On Labour Day Henry Armstrong stopped Irish Johnny Taylor in three rounds at Pittman, Nevada, near Las Vegas. Only 585 fans attended.'[236]

Bob Ingram, writing in the *El Paso Herald and Post*, had good news for the fighters: 'Go to California. There's plenty of gold in the Golden State for the men who swap punches in the ring ... Jimmy Erwin, El Paso promoter, has returned from California and was amazed at the lush business in the boxing trade. He saw fights at Oakland, San Francisco and Hollywood, the three main boxing centres in California. He was floored by what he saw. Hollywood, reports Mr Erwin, has had 32 consecutive sellouts, and it takes a crowd paying

---
235 Hal Wood, United Press Staff Correspondent, *Oakland Tribune*, 15 February 1945.
236 *Ogden Standard Examiner*, 10 September 1942.

CHAPTER TWENTY-ONE

$6,500 to make a sell-out there. Henry Armstrong, who recently started a comeback, drew $18,000 in an Oakland fight last week.

'Never have conditions more favoured a comeback attempt by an old champion, considered through, as they have for Hammering Henry. He's back in the big dough. Promoter Erwin went to California expressly to see the following fighters and try to get them signed for local rings: Fred Apostoli, Ceferino Garcia, Ken Overlin, Armstrong and Manuel Ortiz. Apostoli and Overlin are in the navy, Garcia has quit the ring for good, having turned down an offer of $2,500 recently to meet Tiger Jones in San Francisco. Mr Erwin reports his managers are still excited about Ortiz winning the bantam title from Lou Salica and are letting their fighter bask in the glory of a champion.

'That leaves only Armstrong among the Big Five. George Moore, his manager, told promoter Erwin that Armstrong was booked solid until 28 October. He promised the local matchmaker Armstrong's services about that time, which will not be advantageous to Erwin. The Juarez Bullring is the only place Armstrong could be shown to his full advantage here, and it will be too cold to hold night outdoor fights the latter part of October or first of November.'[237]

It was warm enough in the Civic Auditorium at San Francisco when Henry came charging down the aisle and climbed into the ring to face Leo Rodak, former amateur star from Chicago, in the ten rounds main event. A pro since 1933, Leo had won 73 of his 102 fights but only five by kayo, which

---

[237] Bob Ingram, *El Paso Herald and Post,* Texas, 8 September 1942.

was lucky for the ex-triple champ, as Alan Ward noticed from his ringside seat:

'If Earl Turner, slated for a ten-rounder with Armstrong in Oakland on the night of 30 September, was present at the San Francisco Auditorium last evening, he probably noticed Hammering Hank was a mark for a right-hand uppercut. Henry, although scoring an eighth-round technical knockout over Leo Rodak of Chicago, receipted for that blow too many times for comfort, Armstrong's comfort.

'Fortunately for Henry, who looked none too impressive beating Rodak, the Chicagoan didn't possess a sufficiently heavy punch to break an egg. Had he a socker of, say, Turner's ability, the outcome of Promoter Benny Ford's headliner may have been different. It was no considerable beating but a cut left eye which caused Rodak to lose by a TKO. In fact, the fans booed lustily the action of referee Frankie Brown. Armstrong would have won the decision hands down had the fight gone the limit.

'The bout's final round was the best of the eight and at the conclusion the crowd was in a lather of excitement. Rodak, apparently recovered from two non-count knockdowns in the second and third rounds, waded into Armstrong with both hands. Armstrong briefly was confused by the onslaught! Then he got mad. He fought harder and more bitterly in the final 45 seconds of the frame than at any previous period during the match. On Henry's behalf it can be said he forced the fight all the way.'[238]

---

238 Alan Ward, *Oakland Tribune*, 15 September 1942.

CHAPTER TWENTY-ONE

Art Cohn, sports editor of the *Oakland Tribune*, had called Earl Turner a great, great amateur, so what was he doing sharing the ring with Henry Armstrong? He wasn't boxing, and if he was Henry didn't notice. The highly touted schoolboy from Richmond had won 16 of his 25 professional bouts. Armstrong brought a 117-15-8 record to the ring and was already hailed as the world's greatest fighter, having won and held three world championships simultaneously. Promoter Johnny Sylvester must have figured the kid had a chance with the ex-champ, and so did some of the capacity crowd, who paid $21,442 to pack the Oakland Auditorium that September night in 1942.

This thing could only go one way. It ended after two minutes nine seconds of round four as Armstrong, still warming up, sent Turner crashing to the canvas out cold. 'He wasn't right,' apologised Fred Roberts, one of his two managers. 'He couldn't get started. His punches had no sting. He wasn't right.'

'The story of the Richmond Bubble is a tragedy in leather,' wrote Art Cohn. 'He might have been welterweight champion of the world. But he isn't – and never will be. Apparently, the kid has everything except a fighting heart. This much, though, he would have gone much farther properly handled. It is a pity he was ruined.

'"The boy is a good prospect and he has a fine left hook," Armstrong said afterwards, but Henry has always been a gracious winner.'[239]

---

239 Art Cohn, *Oakland Tribune*, 1 October 1942.

HENRY ARMSTRONG

And for most of his fighting career, Henry Armstrong had been a winner. In 1937 he won 27 consecutive fights, all but one by knockout ... he faced 17 champions throughout his career and defeated 15 of them ... When Lou Ambers regained the lightweight title from Armstrong in 1939 it was Henry's first defeat in 46 bouts.

And he was still winning fights in 1942.

Chapter Twenty-Two

HIS SQUARE name was Juan Bautista Zurita Ferrer, born in Veracruz, Mexico, in May 1917, and they claimed he started fighting when he was a ten-year-old kid; he probably didn't want to go to school. Aged 17, he followed his brother Benjamin as a professional fighter, and he was a good one. By April of 1945, manager Jimmy Fitten brought Ike Williams to Mexico City to fight his boy for the lightweight title and the fight was recognised by the National Boxing Association. Juan didn't win that one because Williams was a great fighter. Three years earlier he had fought another great fighter.

By October 1942, Henry had no titles left, but he was still hungry so he carried on fighting. Manager George Moore booked him into the Olympic Auditorium in Los Angeles, a ten-round main event with Juan Zurita, a popular Mexican lightweight with the fans there. Zurita had won 109 of his 140 fights and claimed the Mexican lightweight title.

'Armstrong started slow in last night's scheduled ten-rounder with Zurita, but peppered the Mexican late in the second round with a flurry of blows and dropped him with a right to the jaw. The ten-count caught Zurita on one knee struggling to rise. Zurita won the first round easily and held the margin in the first part of the second before Armstrong began throwing his heavy punches. Armstrong had trouble meeting the 142-pound weight limit and appeared slower at first than Zurita, who weighed 135. It was Henry's second victory over the Mexican, having knocked him out in four rounds in August 1936.

'Since beginning his comeback in June of 1942, Armstrong had won ten of 11 fights, losing a hometown decision to Reuben Shank in Denver. "I'm dead serious about this comeback and I'm confident that I can regain the world's welterweight and lightweight crowns. I want to get Zivic and Cochrane in the ring. I'll beat 'em both." Armstrong has kicked the daylights out of the old athletic adage: "They never come back." Sure, Armstrong has lost some of his brilliance that carried him to three world's championships ... but if he can get Sammy Angott and Red Cochrane into the roped arena, he will deliver enough ability to regain the lightweight and welterweight championships. Credit for Armstrong's comeback must go to George Moore, his manager. Moore succeeded in getting Hank on the comeback trail, but not until after Hank had spent two months in northern Arizona getting into shape.'[240]

If there was one guy Henry Armstrong wanted back in the ring with him, it was Fritzie Zivic, the Pittsburgh Croat who had sent him into retirement after two brutal beatings that saw the last of Henry's world titles leave his grasp. In the 22 months since taking Armstrong's welterweight title, Zivic had lost seven of his 27 bouts, including the loss of the title just six

---

240 Al Warden, *Ogden Standard Examiner*, 27 October 1942.

CHAPTER TWENTY-TWO

months after whipping Armstrong, Freddie 'Red' Cochrane pulling an upset in his New Jersey backyard.

Whether manager George Moore had any doubts when he signed for the Zivic bout, to be held in the Civic Auditorium at San Francisco three months after Henry's first defeat by Fritzie and two weeks after the Zurita bout, they were quickly dashed by the confident Armstrong. Talking to columnist John Lardner, the ex-champ was thinking nothing less than victory.

'He was just a nasty fighter, just a foul fighter. He did everything foul and, of course, when he got me, he got me when I was tired and I should have been resting but my manager wanted that money quick. When he fought Lew Jenkins, Zivic showed that punches in the body can hurt him. He winced every time Jenkins hit him in the middle. Well now, I can hit much harder in the body than Jenkins and I can hit five times as often. Along about the time Zivic figures he will start getting the range on my face, I will have him so hurt and discouraged he won't feel like lifting his hands. What I aim to do is keep Zivic so busy protecting himself that he won't have time to work on me.'[241]

On 26 October, Associated Press reported from San Francisco: 'Henry Armstrong, the little tornado, gets his long awaited chance tomorrow night. He squares off at the Civic Auditorium with Fritzie Zivic, the tough Pittsburgh boy who beat him out of his welterweight title a couple of years ago and battered him into retirement. The ten-round bout is the most attractive ring engagement lined up

---
241 John Lardner, *Washington Evening Star*, 25 October 1942.

here in years and, with an $8 top, is expected to draw more than $30,000.

'Zivic, as confident as the day, late in 1940, when he lifted the last of Armstrong's world crowns from Armstrong's head, predicted he would give his opponent another lacing. In his two New York meetings with Armstrong, he won the title in 15 rounds, then stopped the former champ in 12 rounds a few months afterwards.

'Armstrong's handlers claimed a badly cut eye cost him both fights. The dusky warrior has had no difficulty with his eyes since operations removed growth over then and several doctors have pronounced him physically fit. He has won all but one bout in his comeback campaign, most of them by knockouts, technical or straight. Zivic long since has lost his championship but undoubtedly is the number-one challenger for it.'[242]

'Armstrong is certain he can whip the fellow who twice defeated him ... and both of those defeats could be charged far more to badly slashed eyes than to physical punishment. It is significant in his several matches since he launched his comeback Armstrong has not received even the suspicion of a cut eye. Betting on the ring natural, which figures to do $30,000 worth of business and create a new indoor gate receipt record for San Francisco, continues to be at even money.

'A couple of months ago Armstrong stopped Aldo Spoldi without trouble, but he did the job in such a handy fashion he won the regard of the San Francisco fans. Oakland will turn out in force for the transbay classic. Hundreds of dollars'

---

242 *Montana Helena Independent*, 26 October 1942.

CHAPTER TWENTY-TWO

worth of tickets for the show have been sold on this side of the bay.'[243]

San Francisco promoter Benny Ford knew he was on to a winner when he signed Henry Armstrong for his main event at the Civic Auditorium. Armstrong sells tickets, Fritzie Zivic was not a box office draw. It was Henry Armstrong who drew the biggest fight crowd in 14 years as 12,000 jammed their way into the arena that Monday night in October 1942. The A to Z of the welterweight division was on show, Armstrong and Zivic.

Henry had trained hard for this one, this was one he had to win.

'But Zivic, weighing in at 147½, four pounds heavier than Armstrong, took the first round with chopping rights and lefts. Armstrong then came back to win the second round, reverting to the windmill tactics, which made him the only boxer in ring history to hold three titles. The third was evenly fought, but Armstrong took the next three rounds and was outslugged by Zivic in the seventh. Armstrong took rounds eight and nine but ended the tenth a bit battered by heavy blows from Zivic.

'Although there were no knockdowns, Henry levelled a continuous barrage of rights and lefts to Fritzie's head throughout the bout and twice had Zivic staggering. However, the judges handed Armstrong a unanimous decision and rekindled hopes of his backers that Henry will get to the top again. The United Press score sheet gave Hammerin' Hank seven rounds, Zivic one, and called two even. The

---

243 Alan Ward, *Oakland Tribune*, 26 October 1942.

bout figured to realise about $30,000, but the capacity crowd paid $41,240, with the principals each getting 30 per cent of the gate.

"'I gave him a good beating," said Henry afterwards. "I didn't try to knock him out. I just wanted to punish him.'"[244]

From New York, Jack Mahon noted: 'The boys on Jacobs Beach were talking about little Henry Armstrong, the human perpetual motion machine, which slowed down for more than a year but is now working on all cylinders again. Lil Henry licked Fritzie Zivic out in San Francisco the other night. And now he's coming back to the beach.

'The little dynamo should be back here late in December, and he will provide a real Christmas sock for promoter Mike Jacobs, who has just about abandoned all belief in Santa Claus. Mike hopes to stage a third Armstrong–Zivic battle in Madison Square Garden in early January, and if the former three-crown kid wins, that one will put him in against the sensational Ray Robinson, unbeaten Harlem welterweight. "It will be good to see Henry again," said one of the beachcombers. "He was always a fighting champion."'

'Henry quit after his second defeat by Zivic in January 1941. He had some money and said he valued his eyesight more than he did a large bank account. He kept his word but ran into financial difficulties last winter and toyed with the idea of coming back. He had his eyes operated on, the scar tissue removed by a surgeon and then rested until he felt he was ready to make his comeback. He started training last spring and then started on the long road back, won a couple

---

244 *Moline Daily Dispatch*, 27 October 1942.

of fights, lost one, and then resumed a victory string that saw him lick increasingly tougher opponents until he climaxed his campaign with a unanimous win over Zivic Monday night.

'One of the veteran beachcombers, manager Charley Johnston, told the other members on the sands Wednesday, that all this talk of a "comeback" was silly. "Armstrong isn't coming back," said Johnston. "He is back."'[245]

The morning after he licked Zivic in their 'Frisco bout, Henry Armstrong was all over the papers, with headlines jumping off the sports pages: 'RUGGED ARMSTRONG BACK TO FIGHT FOR LIGHTWEIGHT TITLE!' 'ARMSTRONG STAGES GREAT COMEBACK! – FIGHTER IS EYEING LIGHTWEIGHT CROWN!'

Charlie Johnston was right ... ARMSTRONG WAS BACK!

'Armstrong's manager announced today his charge would rest at Hot Springs, Arkansas, for a month before pulling on the gloves again. He said he had 20 offers for fights in his pocket but had signed with nobody, including New York's boxing mogul Mike Jacobs. The little perpetual motion man will begin gunning for the lightweight title, now owned by Sammy Angott, because there is no chance to bag the 147-pound championship. Freddie 'Red' Cochrane, who took the title from Zivic, was now in the navy with the welterweight title probably locked up for the duration. Eight months or so ago, in retirement, Armstrong balanced the scales at 165 pounds. He weighed in at 142½ pounds, four pounds less than Zivic, but both he and his manager, George

---

245 Jack Mahon, *Dubuque Telegraph Herald*, 28 October 1942.

Moore, claim he can make the 135-pound lightweight limit easily.'[246]

United Press item, dated 27 October 1942, stated: 'Lew Jenkins, the one-time lightweight champion from Sweetwater, Texas, joined the United States Coast Guard today. The enlistment, however, will not immediately end the former champ's fistic career. He was placed on the inactive list so that he might meet Henry Armstrong, the Negro ex-welter-weight champion, now on the comeback trail, in Portland, Oregon, 13 November.'[247]

'SETTING IN PORTLAND – CITY OF THE GENTEEL'. William E. Phipps, writing for Associated Press, had good news for the Oregon city. 'Little Henry Armstrong fights Lew Jenkins, late ruler of the lightweights, Friday night – in itself a matter of some importance what with Armstrong really getting places in his comeback. But more important is the fact that the bout is being staged in Portland, better known as a city of homes, roses, cultural pursuits and other genteel activities which even many of the natives will admit are slightly on the mossback side.

'Yes, boxing is thriving here now, mushrooming in a land that let it starve and die before. Oh, Jack Dempsey packed them in here once, but where didn't he do that? Except for such a rare event, Portland, a good baseball and football town, struggled with an occasional card featuring local hotshots.

'But with Portland's shipbuilding and war industries boom came a more rugged and red-blooded type of resident, guys who want to seek the rough stuff. To take advantage of the

---
246 *Galveston Daily News*, Texas, 28 October 1942.
247 *El Paso Herald and Post*, Texas, 28 October 1942.

situation, a group of citizens recently founded the National Boxing Club and named A. J. "Tex" Salkeld as matchmaker. He got off to a profitable start with a bout featuring Manuel Ortiz, high-ranking challenger for the NBA bantam title. That started the revival. The army drafted Salkeld but Joe Waterman took over. Among others, he imported heavyweight Lou Nova for a show. To give you a rough idea how things are going here, Nova's gate was the biggest ever, with the exception of Dempsey's.

'But the ten-rounder between Armstrong and Jenkins is expected to be the biggest plum of all and the take is sure to be very good. All that's worrying Portland's happy fight fans now is – How long can it last?'[248]

'Henry Armstrong, the tireless little boxer from Los Angeles, knocked ex-lightweight champion Lew Jenkins out of his way last night. Henry punched the Sweetwater, Texas boy to the canvas eight times before referee Tom Louttit stopped the one-sided fray and awarded Armstrong a technical knockout in the eighth round. The two former ring rulers drew 4,750 fans and the largest indoor gate in Portland ring history – $16,892.

'Armstrong, forcing the fight with mechanical persistence, bloodied Jenkins's face with a succession of left hooks in the first four rounds, and knocked him down twice – once through the ropes – in the fifth. The same snapping left was good for two more knockdowns in the sixth but the seventh was spectacular. Armstrong put Lew down for nine three times.

---

248 William E Phipps, *Salt Lake Tribune*, 4 December 1942.

'The third time it looked as though the Texan intended to stay down but changed his mind at the last moment, leaped up and into Henry furiously. He gave Armstrong a pretty good going over for the last 30 seconds, but Henry came out in the eighth with the same deadly attack and knocked Lew down for another toll of nine. Lew got up but the referee led him to his corner, bleeding from an eyebrow and cheek.

'Jenkins entered the ring at 143½ pounds, Armstrong at 144.'[249]

Ten days later, promoter Benny Ford brought Armstrong back to the San Francisco Civic Auditorium to face Italian Saverio Turiello. Saverio was sometimes billed as the Milan Panther but he didn't scare Henry. In winning 90 bouts, the Italian had racked up only nine knockouts against the little American's powerful 84 by the short route. Henry had Turiello down in the third round from a left hook, but he was up without a count, only to be floored in the next round with a left to the jaw. Armstrong drove him to the canvas again with lefts and rights, with Turiello taking a nine count this time. He was wobbly on rising and referee Frankie Brown stopped the bout at 1.20 of round four.

'As 1943 slipped on to the calendar, Armstrong wasted no time. Five days into the new year, he celebrated with a ten-round decision over Jimmy McDaniels at the Olympic Auditorium in Los Angeles. McDaniels, who weighed in at 147 to Armstrong's 140¾, was an underdog in the betting, but gave no intimation he realised it as he stood toe-to-toe and slugged it out with Henry for ten blistering rounds. Try as

---

249 *Thomasville Times Enterprise*, Georgia, 5 December 1942.

CHAPTER TWENTY-TWO

he would, Armstrong couldn't put the Irishman on the floor, and, at the finish, left eye closed and face battered, McDaniels still pressed on, flailing away with sweat-sodden gloves on the end of arms that had lost their potency some rounds back.

'The decision of the referee and two judges was unanimous, and ringsiders figured Armstrong won eight rounds to two for Jimmy. Henry not only knew he had been in a fight, he looked it. Henry's best rounds were the seventh and ninth, and in the latter it looked for a moment as if McDaniels was wilting. But the bell saved him from possible disaster, and in the last round Armstrong, dog-tired himself, didn't have enough left to produce a finisher.

'Armstrong immediately started preparations for his next bout, which will be with a surgeon at catch-weights. He had intended to depart almost at once for a Philadelphia scrap with Al Tribuani and a New York date with Beau Jack, but decided to leave his ailing tonsils behind him before braving the frigid clime of the eastern seaboard. The time for the operation hasn't been set, but manager George Moore indicated it would be soon.'[250]

---

250 *Lincoln Star*, Nebraska, 6 January 1943.

Chapter Twenty-Three

THE OPERATION came between Henry's bouts with Jimmy McDaniels and Willie Joyce, and it was reported as perhaps contributing to Joyce's decision win over the former triple title-holder. United Press reporting from Los Angeles: 'A recent tonsillectomy and making the 137½ poundage may have weakened Armstrong and may have taken the sting from his punches, although articles called for the welter limit, 147 pounds. Willie Joyce, a clever and speedy fighter from Gary, Indiana, outboxed Armstrong all the way through ten rounds last night, piling up a terrific margin in points and landing at least three blows for every one he received.

'It was Armstrong's 16th fight in an amazing comeback campaign that has netted him 14 victories and only one other defeat, that one of dubious nature. This beating was so convincing there could have been no doubt at all in the minds of 15,000 spectators, expecting to see the Los Angeles man stop Joyce. From the second round on through the seventh, little Joyce beat a steady tattoo of left jabs on Armstrong's face, and most of them were jammed into Henry's eyes, which have given him so much trouble because of scar tissue.[251]

---

251 *Northern Arkansas Times*, 3 March 1943.

CHAPTER TWENTY-THREE

For United Press Lisle Shoemaker reported: 'The Henry Armstrong express lay derailed today – a siding in the person of Willie Joyce, a dusky wraith-like, snap-punching lightweight who beat "Hurricane Hank" to the punch and rapped out a close ten-round decision last night. Joyce's upset win over Armstrong, who was a 3-1 favourite, was anything but a whistlestop.

'The lithe Gary, Indiana youth, rated No. 2 lightweight in the country behind Beau Jack by the National Boxing Association, had the former triple title-holder missing wildly and swinging ineffectually.

'Although the winning margin was tight, it was decisive and even Henry, suffering his second defeat in last night's 16th comeback attempt, couldn't find fault when Joyce's hand was raised. "I lost the fight all right. I was rusty and missed a lot of punches. Joyce was awfully fast and I just couldn't seem to nail him down. I'd sure like to fight him again – and soon."

'Prospects of a rematch, however, were vague since Armstrong has several commitments coming up soon, the first a ten-round bout with Tippy Larkin in San Francisco this Monday night. Owner of a sizzling jab, Joyce refused to take Armstrong's bait to get in close and punch. He met Henry's rugged bull-like rushes with his stabbing left, slipped over solid rights and then backed away, leaving the former champ flailing in mid-air.

'Armstrong forced the pace but when he did manage to get his direction finder on Joyce, he found the enemy gone before the shell landed. Joyce turned the pace red-hot in the fifth, sixth and seventh rounds, completely taking command with annoying, swift punches that snapped Henry's head back and slithered his mouthpiece to the canvas.'[252]

From Garfield, New Jersey, Tippy Larkin was born Antonio Pilleteri and took the name Tippy from the initials for Tony Pilleteri. He got Larkin from his older brother, who boxed professionally as Bobby Larkin. A good boxer with a sharp punch (40 KOs) they called him the Garfield Gunner. In his last fight three months prior to getting in with Armstrong, Tippy was knocked out in three rounds by Beau Jack at Madison Square Garden in a fight recognised by the New York Commission as for the world lightweight championship.

Larkin's guns were misfiring when he shaped up to Henry Armstrong in the Civic Auditorium at San Francisco on 8 March 1943.

'Using a height and reach advantage, the Jersey boy took the opening round with a number of long lefts and an occasional right. In the second round Larkin dropped his guard for a brief instant and Armstrong flashed in a right that spun Tippy around. A swift left hooked him and he sprawled on the canvas for the full count. His handlers had to drag him to his corner. The round had gone one minute and nine seconds and the 8,000 spectators started for the exits. Thus, Armstrong regained some prestige to atone for the defeat by Willie Joyce at Los Angeles last week. Manager George Moore said that one shouldn't have counted anyway because his boy had not fully recovered from a tonsil operation. As it was, he broke Joyce's jaw.'[253]

---

252 Lisle Shoemaker, *Berkeley Daily Gazette*, California, 3 March 1943.
253 *Evening Star*, Washington DC, 9 March 1943.

CHAPTER TWENTY-THREE

From Philadelphia: 'Sceptical eastern seaboard boxing experts were gathered at Convention Hall last night to write regretful comparisons between the Henry Armstrong of today and the Armstrong that was. But the experts had to toss aside their projected tear-jerking themes and marvel in typewritten black over the "miracle" of the perpetual-motion man after watching the bull-shouldered boxer pound out a ten-round decision over young Al Tribuani of Wilmington, Delaware.

'The experts were forced to admit generally that the Armstrong of today is a better fighter than the semi-blinded gladiator who was stopped by Zivic. The experts had read of Armstrong's 17 comeback fights on the Pacific Coast, but they took those accounts with a grain of aspirin. Hence the miracle of Armstrong last night – a guy who was much more impressive at 30 than he had been at 28. Armstrong was impressive last night, though forced to the full ten rounds by 22-year-old Tribuani, who fought an inspired fight and absorbed unceasing punishment because he simply wouldn't go down.

'Armstrong, making his eastern comeback debut before 12,633 cash customers – the third largest indoor boxing crowd in Philadelphia's history – took command of the fight after the first round, permitting his younger, taller and heavier opponent to fight on even terms in two sessions thereafter. Though the bout was completely lop-sided, it provided an excellent test for Armstrong's questioned ability. The Los Angeles man set a terrific pace from gong to gong and seemed stronger in the closing tenth session than in the opening round.

'Lew Tendler, former lightweight contender, remarked afterwards, "How Armstrong kept up that pace I don't know."

The experts, who had come to make sure he had no chance against lightweight champion Beau Jack at New York on 2 April, wrote instead that Beau Jack will be lucky to last the distance against him.'[254]

'Henry Armstrong proved last night he is the man of 1,000 punches in whipping tough Al Tribuani before a howling crowd who contributed a gross gate of $32,915 at Philadelphia's Convention Hall. By his ever-lasting aggression, Hammerin' Henry threw close to 1,000 punches to gain a unanimous decision. Armstrong gave away nearly eight pounds, weighing 138½ to Tribuani's 146¼. Armstrong will start training Thursday for his 2 April bout with Beau Jack in New York.'[255]

Jack Cuddy, for United Press in New York, wrote: 'Benny Leonard of the US maritime service, an ex-champion who once tried to come back, sat in Stillman's gymnasium watching Henry Armstrong, an ex-champion who is trying to come back. As Armstrong went through his training paces with spar-mate Sammy Daniels, Lt. Leonard said, "I'm going to surprise you with my prediction for Friday night's fight. I pick Armstrong to lick Beau Jack."

'We were properly surprised at Bennah's forecast because the betting odds favour lightweight champion Beau Jack at 11-5. Moreover, Leonard was picking a man of 30 – a guy apparently "over the hill" – to beat a strong, hard-hitting youngster of 22. Benny continued: "Armstrong at 30 is still an unusual athlete physically and one of the smartest boxers I've ever seen. He knows too much for Beau Jack, and he still

---
254 *Fort Madison Evening Democrat*, Iowa, 23 March 1943.
255 *Moline Daily Dispatch*, Illinois, 23 March 1943.

CHAPTER TWENTY-THREE

has the body to put that knowledge into operation. He never was given enough recognition for his cleverness."

'Leonard emphasised that Armstrong is a brilliant "fighter" of the Jack Dempsey type. He said few people ever gave Dempsey credit for his ring brilliance, for his intelligent execution. Most observers appreciated only the Manassa Mauler's dynamic punching. "Armstrong is a bobber and weaver also," Benny said, "but he has a certain jungle rhythm in his attack that I've never seen in anyone else. This rhythm permits him to maintain a terrific pace from gong to gong – the most killing pace, I believe, the ring has known."

'Armstrong taught his style and rhythm to Beau Jack, before the Beau ever had a professional fight. That was when Armstrong was training for his second fight with Zivic – just before he went into retirement. But Beau Jack hasn't had time yet to master the things Armstrong taught him. Perhaps he never will.'[256]

New York was buzzing over the Henry Armstrong–Beau Jack fight, writers calling it the $100,000 fight, the kid and the veteran, teacher and pupil, new champ and old champ.

'The betting boys figure the jumping Jack a five to nine shot to take care of the fighting machine who taught Beau more than one-and-one about the business of busting beaks,' wrote Sid Feder for Associated Press. 'But the price-makers aren't nearly as sure now as they were two weeks ago, because they've shaved the odds all the way down from five to 17. This corner likes Armstrong, simply because Henry is the original buzzsaw and the Jumping Jack is just a good imitation. After

---

256 Jack Cuddy, *The Hammond Times*, Indiana, 30 March 1943.

a layoff for the better part of a year, Li'l Perpetual Motion has been skyrocketing up comeback causeway the last few months, winning 16 of 18 starts, 11 of them by putting the other guy to sleep. He may not be the fearful flailer of a few years back, when he ran up some 46 straight triumphs, but he's still the same kind of always-advancing warrior who's in the other fellow's lap all evening. What's more, while he has slowed up some, he appears to have added some dynamite to his right hand, because it explodes all over the place when he pulls the trigger now.'[257]

'Mike Jacobs is getting $11.50 for ringside pews, and the advance sale points to the first $100,000 gate indoors since Sgt Joe Louis toed the mark,' Harry Grayson wrote. 'Jack's New York edition of the lightweight championship is not at stake. New York considers 15 rounds the titular distance and this one is listed for ten. Armstrong is required to come in at more than 135 pounds. He scaled 138½ in Philadelphia the other night, and probably could do the class limit without undue difficulty. Jack will weigh about 137.

'Although Jack twice shaded Zivic, a tough customer, Armstrong will show him a lot of things he never saw in the way of head, shoulders, elbows and body belts. Armstrong always got away with a lot of stuff, and there is no reason to suspect that they'll stop him this late in his career. Jack does more damage with one punch, especially a right-hand uppercut, which could be used to advantage against the charging Armstrong. Beau Jack fashioned his sweeping attack after that of Henry Armstrong, which is a double guarantee

---

257 Sid Feder, *Winona Republican Herald*, Minnesota, 2 April 1943.

CHAPTER TWENTY-THREE

that no one will be bored. Jack should win on youth, condition and wallop.'[258]

Russ Newland had some interesting points in his column from San Francisco: 'Fritzie Zivic, who lost two decisions to Beau Jack and one to Armstrong within five months, states: "Armstrong gave me a tougher fight than Beau Jack. Armstrong will beat Beau Jack." Tippy Larkin, knocked out by Armstrong in two rounds, after earlier knockout by Beau Jack in three rounds, states: "Armstrong throws more punches and hits harder than Beau Jack." Larkin's manager, Angelo Pucci, said before the fight, "Making weight for Beau Jack killed Larkin for that fight – he'll do something no other boxer has done, drop Armstrong for the full count." After the fight: "I thought Larkin would turn the trick, now I wonder who will."

'George Moore, managing Armstrong, asks: "Does it take an act of Congress to convince some of the New York writers that Armstrong is staging a successful comeback? Two decisions have gone against him and we'll take rematches on those quick, especially Willie Joyce in Los Angeles. Joyce got a decision in all questionable. He also got a broken jaw. Armstrong's eyes are as good as ever since the operations."'[259]

Davis J Walsh, writing for INS, said: 'It's a little bewildering, especially to a man whose arteries are beginning to crackle, to leave New York five years ago and return now to find Henry Armstrong still in the middle of the ring at Madison Square Garden, and drawing $100,000, which apparently he will do with Beau Jack on Friday night.

---
258 Harry Grayson, *Defiance Crescent News*, Ohio, 3 March 1943.
259 Russ Newland, *Cumberland Evening Times*, Maryland, 11 March 1943.

'It's the same Armstrong, whose last entry in the 1941 Nat Fleischer record book reads as follows: "1941 – Jan. 17 Fritzie Zivic, NYC – KO by 12." They thought that was Henry's epitaph. As a matter of fact he hasn't been in the Garden since. But a lot of guys were around, going into a gush about him as he worked out for three rounds at Stillman's Gym yesterday.

'And there were those who said the 2-1 price against Armstrong would recede to 6-5. And Benny Leonard, who ought to know lightweights, was saying this: "Armstrong would have been a first-class lightweight in Gans's day, or mine ... He was a great fighter. Maybe he still is. He doesn't seem much different to me."

'Not much, no. Only the overhang of bulbous tissue around the eyes, making him always look as though he was wearing a headguard. And a teetering effect about the legs as he moves into the attack, and the feeling that nobody who is chasing 32 and has been fighting 11 years can be quite the same, just because of the fact that those things are so. Still he beat Zivic among others in winning 16 out of 18 fights in the comeback, and as long as all he has to beat are the Beau Jacks of this comical profession, it might very well be that he'll come all the way.'[260]

'Beau Jack is the lad with the thankless job of showing he is thankless,' wrote Whitney Martin for Associated Press. 'He meets Henry Armstrong, the man whom he used as a pattern in cutting out his career, and whose friendly advice aided him along the way ... Fighters are peculiar critters. They can shut off sentiment like it was flowing from a spigot.

---

260 Davis J Walsh, *Connellsville Daily Courier*, Pennsylvania, 1 April 1943.

CHAPTER TWENTY-THREE

The average gent wouldn't jump on his best friend and start beating him up if you paid him. Prize-fighters will do it in a minute if you pay them. We are assuming that Beau Jack runs true to form and that he can forget the man he is fighting is Henry Armstrong.

'If he can't, he is beaten before he starts. He's beaten because tucked away in a corner of his mind, if not battling all around in his head, will be the nagging idea: "This is the great Henry Armstrong. This is my friend. This is the man who taught me my best tricks, whose very style I am copying. He's too good for me." Beau Jack may not be able to forget that the Armstrong of today is not the Armstrong of other years.

'He isn't the same Armstrong but we still think there is too much of him for Beau Jack. We've seen them both fight, and just have the idea that Henry will be able to keep moving in faster and longer than his younger rival. And we can't get away from the hazy idea that the naïve Beau Jack won't be able to forget he's fighting the old master.'[261]

Strangely enough, the big fight everyone was waiting for almost didn't happen. Beau Jack didn't want to fight Henry Armstrong. Beau and Henry were more than mere acquaintances. They were friends. Beau lived with Henry in late 1940, while Armstrong prepared for his upcoming fight against Fritzie Zivic. Henry trained and helped Beau develop some of his early boxing skills, while Jack served as his sparring partner. They both had kept in touch ever since. At first Beau was reluctant to fight Armstrong. 'Henry is my friend,' he said.

---

[261] Whitney Martin, *Beckley Post Herald,* West Virginia, 1 April 1943.

Chick Wergeles, Beau's New York manager, was not keen on the idea either. He worried that Armstrong might get hurt because he was getting older and his eyes were not as sharp as they once were. Speaking on behalf of Beau and himself, Chick said, 'Well you've seen Beau fight and they don't come much tougher. And I don't know who it would affect most – me or my fighter – if anything happened to Armstrong.' Only after Armstrong received a thorough physical examination by the New York State Athletic Commission, did Wergeles agree to the fight. Henry, himself, convinced Beau to commit to the match.

'"When Henry learned I was against the fight," explained Beau, "he sent me a long telegram stating that fighting was a business. As such, we were two businessmen trying to make the most money from the best possible matches … it was our duty to give the fans what they want."

'To prepare for their upcoming bout, Beau, as well as Henry, checked into Stillman's Gym before a capacity gathering of viewers. Armstrong recalled: "I can't forget the look of … adoration in his eyes when he first saw me … just like my little daughter."'[262]

---

[262] Robert A. Mullins, *Beau Jack*, 2020.

Chapter Twenty-Four

SO THE big fight was on, and promoter Mike Jacobs had a record-breaking crowd fighting over his 19,986 seats. Armstrong and Beau were lucky that April evening, they got the last two seats in the vast arena! And they didn't have to pay to get into the Garden. The other guys and gals had to choke the box office with $146,976 to watch former triple champion Henry Armstrong fight Beau Jack, the lightweight champion as decreed by the New York State Athletic Commission and the New Jersey Boxing Commission. This was a ten-round contest with no titles on the line. The commission recognised only 15-rounds duration for titular affairs.

Armstrong, the 2-1 underdog in the betting, scaled 138 pounds, two and a quarter pounds more than his young opponent. Beau was actually 22 years old the day before his big fight with the 30-year-old Armstrong. Henry was usually lighter than his opponents. Maybe he was still growing. As the big crowd fidgeted in their seats, ring announcer Harry Balogh announced the ring officials appointed by the commission. Judges Bill Healy and George LeCron; referee Billy Cavanaugh.

The demand for press tickets for the fight were about as big as for one of Joe Louis's outdoor showings, but there weren't nearly as many ringside seats. Among the lucky ones were Davis J. Walsh, Joe Williams, Jack Cuddy and Sid Feder. This is how these guys saw the fight:

'His face was gnarled, as though set in the folds and whorls of a pain that has been long and patiently endured,' said Walsh writing for INS. 'His legs were so stiff they might have been stilts, causing him to engage, not in the expected weave, but in a very alarming gesture that can only be described as an unlovely squat. But, old and battered and declassed though Henry Armstrong may have been Friday night, he very nearly succeeded in knocking out Beau Jack, the lightweight champion, in the tenth and final round at Madison Square Garden, while 20,000 bawled hoarsely and in vain. For, in merely nearly succeeding, the old champion failed utterly.

'The decision unanimously and rightly went to Beau Jack, who won most of the rounds, did much of the punching and a great deal of running in a fight that was to prove nothing that everybody hadn't already known. That, as a fighting age, 22 is better than 32. And that as a sporting town, this place is hotter now than it was even in the days of Rickard and his gold rush.

'The paid attendance Friday night and the gross receipts, for a non-title fight between a man who had once, years ago, known a degree of greatness and another who never would. Perhaps it would be more graceful to accept this as a tribute to Armstrong ... And, in the last two rounds at least, Henry made it worth their while.

'He came on then to punch the other guy down on his teetering heels, scoring first in the ninth round when Beau Jack oddly decided to cease being sensible and agile, and again

CHAPTER TWENTY-FOUR

in the tenth when a long-left swing caught the Beau going away and a series of rights to the body landed with the impact of a club, causing Beau Jack's chin to sag ajar with the hurt of it. Just before the bell, he was staggered by a left swing.'[263]

Associated Press had Sid Feder at ringside, writing, 'It is very fortunate for Beau Jack that the number of bicycles for domestic consumption was increased this week, because if the Jumping Jack didn't have his two-wheeler with the reverse motion, he probably wouldn't hold a decision over Henry Armstrong today. The Jumping Jack climbed on his velocipede in Madison Square Garden's ring last night and back-pedalled furiously for ten rounds. And at the end, two judges and the referee gave him the verdict over the Hammer, who chased him so much the thing began to look like a six-day bike race. A crowd of 19,986 made so much noise booing the decision that the rafters were rocking and announcer Harry Balogh couldn't make himself heard to announce the next fight.

'Beau didn't succeed in convincing anyone – except maybe himself, the officials and a few others – that Hammerin' Hank is anywhere near the hollow shell. For Henry was a whole lot of fighter last night. And when he did manage to catch up with the backward bouncing Beau during the proceedings, he pummelled him around the body until Jack was slowed to a mild canter and "looking for a door" at the finish. Associated Press gave Li'l Perpetual Motion five rounds of the ten, voted four for Jack and called one even.

'Henry's legs may be a trifle slower, but he was hotter in the ninth and tenth than he was in the first, as the weary Beau

---

263 Davis J. Walsh, *Cedar Rapids Gazette*, Iowa, 3 April 1943.

probably was the first to admit at the end. It took Armstrong a couple of rounds to catch up, but in the third he staggered the Beau, and in the sixth the crowd booed because Jack all but fled "headlong backward", which incidentally is a good trick even if he couldn't do it.'[264]

INS had Joe Williams in the Garden that night. 'They gave the decision to Jack at the end of ten rounds,' he reported. 'If you looked at the fight in a casual detached manner you'd have to say the decision was all right. The fight, as it was fought, developed several phases.

'No. 1: it was a fight which set a new all-time record for missed punches. But even on this score it is only fair to look for some plausible explanation. As for Armstrong's misses, we'll just say his timing was off. As for Jack's misses, we'll just say he was facing a bobbing and weaving target and was confused.

'The No. 2 phase of the fight was the skill with which both men scored near misses. "Do you mean to tell me them guys aren't pulling their punches?" hissed a cynic sitting near us. These weren't pulled punches. It was defence at its best. Jack would aim at Armstrong's middle and narrowly miss. You could tell by the expression on Jack's face how this departure from sheer perfection distressed him. At the same time you could sense Armstrong's beaming satisfaction, by his great defensive skill he had been able to evade a power punch.

'The No. 3 phase would have to do with Jack's right uppercut. It is the only punch he has taken from the book

---

264 Sid Feder, *Lincoln Star,* Nebraska, 3 April 1943.

CHAPTER TWENTY-FOUR

and more or less mastered. Against Armstrong, habitually a crowder, it figured to be his bingo punch, but Armstrong complicated matters by fighting at long range in many instances. There was only one round, the ninth, when Armstrong fought his kind of fight; when he leaned on the other guy's chest and went to work with both hands to the body and the head. This was the round that Jack's uppercut should have been very much in evidence. He threw only one and it missed from here to China.'[265]

'Last night's defeat was, in its way, another glorious victory for Henry Armstrong,' wrote Jack Cuddy for United Press. 'The "three blind mice", who officiated at the ten-round non-title bout between Hurricane Hank and lightweight champion Beau Jack, awarded young Jack a unanimous decision.

'But their verdict touched off an explosion of booing among the sell-out crowd of 19,986 cash customers that shook Madison Square Garden's girders, which was followed by a grand ovation for the officially vanquished Armstrong. These manifestations in the house that Rickard built virtually clinched a title fight for Armstrong with young Beau Jack this summer. Such an outdoor meeting doubtless would draw more than a half-million dollars.

'More than 5,000 fans were turned away from this brawl in which 30-year-old Armstrong battled his former pupil, 22-year-old Beau Jack. Armstrong of Los Angeles took a licking in the early rounds of this climax fight on his comeback trail. But Hammering Henry rallied so magnificently in the closing sessions that it seemed the 19th fight of his comeback

---
[265] Joe Williams, *Syracuse Herald Journal*, 3 April 1943.

string would result in victory. However, the unanimous decision was against the little perpetual motion man.

'Before the bout, some observers questioned Armstrong's sight. Afterwards those sceptics questioned the sight of the officials. Judge Bill Healy voted eight rounds for Jack and only two Armstrong: Judge George LeCron decided seven rounds for Jack, two for Armstrong and one even. Referee Billy Cavanaugh gave five to Jack, three to Armstrong and registered two even. The United Press scoring rated the bout even – four, four and two, but if we had to make a decision, we would have thrown the fight to Armstrong because of his aggressiveness.

'Armstrong won the third, fifth, eighth and ninth rounds. He came in with his rhythmic bob and weave, trying to get within range of Beau's fast-moving head. In most of the sessions young Jack back-pedalled to keep away from close-quarters with the experienced bulldogger. There were no knockdowns, but Beau was rubber-legged and on the verge of a kayo in the sixth round in which Henry had him staggering.'[266]

'"The man I didn't want to box at all was my idol, Henry Armstrong," Beau was saying after the fight. "But when he said, 'Beau, our friendship ceases when we go in the ring,' I told my manager I'll take the fight then. The greatest fighter that ever lived as far as I'm concerned. He's a fine man. It's hard enough to win one title and this man got three. In your mind it comes to you: *What must I do?* I was lucky enough to beat him, but if I had to go back over to fight him again, good

---

[266] Jack Cuddy, *Ogden Standard Examiner*, Utah, 3 April 1943.

CHAPTER TWENTY-FOUR

as I love to fight, I don't think that I'd want to do it. I don't think I'd want to go back over it again.'"[267]

"'I know in my heart that I gave Beau Jack everything I had, and I feel sure he was all out to flatten me, if he could," Henry said in the dressing room as the press crowded in. "And I want to tell my friends in St Louis that if I ever won a fight in my life it was that one with Beau Jack." As only friends can do, Armstrong complimented Beau, while at the same time discrediting his punching power. "He's a good boy, tremendously improved since I last saw him, before my retirement, and he's strictly a top-notcher," said Henry. "Frankly, I expected him to be a harder puncher. He didn't hurt me one bit."

'For their efforts, each fighter received $24,158.17. As usual, after a close contest, there was the talk of a rematch. Henry wanted a chance to redeem himself against Jack, but Beau didn't seem disposed to fighting Armstrong again.'[268]

'Fight folks, fans and "experts" alike, still argued today over the decision awarded Beau Jack over Henry Armstrong, so promoter Mike Jacobs started the ball rolling for a return match between the two in one of the local ball parks in June. The bout would be at 15 rounds instead of the ten heats of last night, in which Jack "ran" to victory by back-pedalling furiously through the first eight rounds and hanging on, weary and worn, as Hammerin' Hank came roaring down the stretch.'[269]

---

267 Gerald Suster, *Lightning Strikes*, 1994.
268 Robert A. Mullins, *Beau Jack*, 2020.
269 *Avalanche Journal*, Texas, 4 April 1943.

New York, 5 April 1943 – 'JACOBS ALL SET FOR REMATCH OF JACK–ARMSTRONG' – so ran the headline on Davis J. Walsh's column. 'Mike Jacobs named the first week in June for the return Henry Armstrong–Beau Jack fight in one of the ball parks: if and provided anybody is able to find Beau Jack by that time. He was running the other night in the ring at Madison Square Garden – and apparently he's still running, this time away from an estimated gate of $250,000.

'Anyhow, Uncle Mike was unable to announce that he's made any progress with the Beau Jack people over the weekend with respect to interesting them in a further meeting with the elderly and spavined Armstrong, who lost a unanimous decision in ten rounds the other night and apparently won everybody's heart. "If they won't take Armstrong," Uncle Mike announced, "then I'll put on an Armstrong–Sammy Angott fight for 12 rounds."

'Angott's the young man who mysteriously resigned the world's lightweight championship recently, claiming his hands had degenerated into something resembling a couple of dust-cloths. Not many weeks later, he withdrew from retirement and went into the Garden to slather Willie Pep, the featherweight champion.'[270]

'Angott's retirement was the biggest mystery of the 1942 boxing year,' wrote Jack Cuddy. 'The *New York Daily News* attempted to explain this retirement as having been forced by a New Jersey mob. We doubt this is so. Angott and his manager, Charley Jones, have denied vehemently that Sammy's

---

270 Davis J. Walsh, *Cedar Rapids Gazette*, Iowa, 5 April 1943.

CHAPTER TWENTY-FOUR

retirement was forced – that they gave up the crown rather than "do business". They explained that Sammy had outgrown the 135-pound limit, and that he was suffering from bad hands. Anyway, the New York Commission and the National Boxing Association came in fast with an elimination tournament to decide a new champion … But we are confident that Sammy Angott could whip any of the contenders in the elimination.

'Hence we send this message to Angott and to Charley Jones, two of our warmest friends. "Forget the retirement. Come back and defend the title. The percentage is all in your favour. But whether you win or lose, you'll dispel one of the blackest clouds that ever hovered over the lightweight division."'[271]

'Citizens of Washington, Pennsylvania, have taken great pride in two things: Washington and Jefferson University and Sammy Angott, one-time lightweight champion. During his ring career, few outsiders concurred in this idolatry of the home-town pride, generally looked upon as too unorthodox a scrapper for the public taste.

'His style notwithstanding, Angott was one of the toughest men of his time. He was one of the rare ones against whom Sugar Ray Robinson was forced to go all out on two occasions. Neither time was the incomparable boxer-puncher able to coast against this awkward, pressing foe who gave him a rough argument in two close matches in 1941 and 1942. Few recall that Angott was the man who halted Willie Pep's phenomenal streak of 62 straight victories in Madison Square Garden on 19 March 1943.

---
271 Jack Cuddy, *Racine Journal Times*, Wisconsin, 3 December 1942.

267

'Along the way to winning the lightweight championship, he was called upon to dispose of dangerous Lew Jenkins and capable Bob Montgomery. His victories over those alone stamped him as a fighter of sufficient merit to warrant the pride in him shown by his old home town.'[272]

In putting 132 fights in the book, Sammy won 97 and was stopped only once. Among the fighters Angott defeated were Ike Williams, Johnny Bratton, Baby Arizmendi, Freddie Miller, Allie Stolz, Petey Sarron, Kid Azteca, Lenny Mancini and Aldo Spoldi.

Sammy couldn't beat Henry Armstrong.

Harry Grayson, *NEA* sports editor, thought Sammy could do the trick, writing, 'Sammy Angott finally bumps into someone as rough as himself in tackling Henry Armstrong at Madison Square Garden on Friday night. This pair scarcely could do more damage in more ways were they equipped with knives. To protect them against each other, they really should be ordered to wear gloves on their elbows, shoulders and heads. Because he is a couple of years younger and has been subjected to less wear and tear, I expect Angott to take the decision in ten rounds after showing Armstrong more hammers, scissors and locks than there are in a hardware store. Mike Jacobs has again jacked up the top tariff to $11.50 and scarcely can miss another $100,000.

'Angott came back three months ago to make one of his best fights ... repeatedly fastening holds on the highly regarded Willie Pep and throwing him for falls. Johnny Jones, a rather capable 150-pound sparring partner, tells

---

272 Ted Carroll, *The Ring*, November 1962.

me he never boxed anybody as strong as the Washington, Pa. Italian. Angott does not appear interested in the title he vacated and which is now held by Bob Montgomery, whom he beat three times.'[273]

'They called Angott "The Clutch" because of the way he tied opponents into knots, holding them helpless as he banged away to head and body. Bob Montgomery, who lost three of three bouts to Sammy, called him "The Octopus". Even Sugar Ray Robinson, who won two close decisions over The Clutch, commented, "That guy must have six arms."'[274]

United Press writer Jack Cuddy noted the betting: 'Angott is favoured at 13-10 to win the ten-round bout. Late support for Slammin' Sam shifted the odds from their original 7-5 favouring Armstrong. Angott, bull-shouldered Italian from Washington, Pa., is favoured because he is two years younger than his more famous 30-year-old opponent, who is expected to be worn down by Angott's blistering pace and wrestling tactics.'[275]

'Promoter Mike Jacobs had a reasonable crowd for his Garden main event, 13,364 fans paying $55,502. It was an Armstrong crowd and he didn't let them down, taking a unanimous decision over Angott. The 30-year-old Los Angeles man won this hard fight from 28-year-old Angott because of the shrewd explosions of the dynamite still packed in the perpetual-motion man's aging body. Hammering Henry took command of the fight in the fifth round when his smashing hooks to the head staggered

---

273 Harry Grayson, *Daily Globe*, Ironwood, Michigan, 10 June 1943.
274 *The Ring*, September 1992, 12 June 1943.
275 Jack Cuddy, *Dubuque Telegraph Herald*.

Angott and deprived him of his usual "zing" for the rest of the fight.

'The crowd found no fault with the decision of referee Eddie Joseph and Judges Bill Healy and Jim Gearns. The fans were convinced that Hammerin' Henry had won by a definite, though small, margin over his rugged "cutey" opponent, who was so inherently tough that he rallied to win the tenth round.

'During Friday night's bruising battle, Armstrong suffered such severe gashes of the lower lip that he may be forced to postpone his return engagement with Willie Joyce at Los Angeles on 26 June. Meanwhile, Angott's right eye was almost closed when he climbed down from the ring. The United Press gave Armstrong five rounds, Angott three and called two even. There was one knockdown in the bout. In the ninth round Armstrong landed one of his leaping left jabs flush on Angott's chin. At the time Angott was fast-stepping in Armstrong's corner, which was slippery. As the left jab landed on Angott's face, his right foot slipped out and he went to one knee. Referee Joseph stepped in to help him up, apparently rating the descent as a slip instead of a knockdown. But it was a knockdown – definitely.'[276]

Sid Feder, reporting from New York, wrote: 'The gashed mouth Henry Armstrong was handed in winning through to a ten-round decision over swarthy Sammy Angott has put Hammerin' Hank on the shelf for two months. Before dropping in on promoter Mike Jacobs to pick up his pay cheque of about $15,200 for Friday night's work, Henry kept a date with Dr Alexander Schiff, his physician here in New

---

276 *Madison Wisconsin State Journal*, 12 June 1943.

CHAPTER TWENTY-FOUR

York. The doctor had to cut away considerable scar tissue from inside the buzz-saw's lower lip and put nine stitches in the wound.

'Through his bandaged mouth, Henry then explained that his fights in Hollywood with Willie Joyce and in Portland, Oregon, with Jimmy Garrison would have to be set back until he was able to work again. A scheduled scrap between Armstrong and lightweight champ (New York version) Bob Montgomery had to be taken off the slate, at least temporarily. Armstrong and his manager, George Moore, will head back to California and home next Friday, but expect to head for Pa Knickerbocker's village again in August.

'At that time, the one-time triple title-holder, probably, will meet either Montgomery, Beau Jack, or maybe Ray (Sugar) Robinson, the so-called uncrowned welterweight champion, provided Ray, now an Army corporal, is available.'[277]

Lawton Carver was in the Garden for INS, writing: 'Angott insisted that Armstrong never did hurt him in the slightest; however, he was nailed with one punch that seemed close to being of sufficient authority to floor him. This was a right hand to the body in the eighth round. It doubled Angott up temporarily and caused him to go on the run just when he seemed on the verge of starting a rally. At that point the bout was fairly even, but that punch decided everything. Angott lost the eighth round, then the ninth and the tenth, apparently never completely recovering from a really good wallop from the old man.

---

277 Sid Feder, *Butte Montana Standard*, 13 June 1943.

'He is an amazing old character, no longer the untiring ceaseless puncher on spring legs that he used to be but still capable of winning as he did last night. This gives him 20 wins in 23 comeback starts and puts him in line to regain one of those three titles he held simultaneously in his heyday.'[278]

---

[278] Lawton Carver, *Lowell Sun* Mass, 12 June 1943.

Chapter Twenty-Five

ON 3 December 1942, United Press correspondent Jack Cuddy wrote from New York: 'That Armstrong–Robinson announcement which early today galloped over the wires out of Portland, Oregon, doubtless will be greeted with mingled gratification and apprehension by Eastern boxing fans. The announcement said that Henry Armstrong will climax his surprising comeback campaign by fighting Ray "Sugar" Robinson, Harlem's unbeaten sensation, in New York on 29 January for the "duration" welterweight title. Armstrong's manager, George Moore, disclosed plans for the match.

'The Zivic victory apparently convinced promoter Mike Jacobs that Armstrong's comeback was the "McCoy" so he began negotiations to bring Henry back to New York. The little Los Angeles fighter would fit perfectly into the welterweight picture. Champion Freddie Cochrane is in the navy, his title frozen for the duration. An interim champion was needed. Ray Robinson, slender young man from Harlem, who now has clicked off 134 straight victories amateur and professional, was the outstanding contender since Cleveland's Jackie Wilson was in the army.

'Armstrong will have plenty of trouble with young Robinson on 29 January. It will be a dangerous fight for

Henry, who celebrates his 30th birthday on 12 December and whose brows are balconied with punch gristle and whose mouth is fragile with scar tissue. Never in his career has Armstrong tackled an opponent of Robinson's apparent calibre ... Robinson, who combines the speed of a puma with the kick of a mule, is a menace to a man with battered eyes like Henry's.

'It would be one of the ring's great stories if Armstrong, with his bulling, constant-hooking style, could end Robinson's winning streak. But the seasoned boxing men who sit at the ringside for this fight will be more concerned with the threat to Henry's eyes than the possibility of an Armstrong victory.'[279]

Dan Parker, sports editor of the *New York Daily Mirror*, headed his column '20th CENTURY CLUB RATES HERO MEDALS'. 'Those new fighting units of Uncle Sam which have been case-hardened in the heat of battle in North Africa and later in Sicily, aren't the only Americans who are displaying unusual courage these days. When medals are being awarded for well-developed cardiac muscles, the Twentieth Century Sporting club should not be overlooked.

'Two citations are in order for Gen. Mike Jacobs and his valiant band for the following instances of outstanding heroism:

1. For matching Ray Robinson, best welterweight around today, with Henry Armstrong, a highly respected ring veteran who should have remained in retirement when he quit the ring over two years ago, all washed up.

---

279 Jack Cuddy, *Huntingdon Daily News*, Pennsylvania, 3 December 1942.

2. For summoning up the courage – or should we call it unmitigated gall – to ask $16.50 for this one-sided match.

'I'll admit that good or even fair matches are scarcer these days than porterhouse steaks. But does that justify the world's foremost boxing club in digging into pugilism's graveyard for its pseudo attractions and then charging prices for them that would be out of line even for high-class matches … the blunt truth, with respect to Henry Armstrong, is that his interests would be served best by asking him to retire while he still has his faculties. Of course those who make money out of Henry will cry out with hypocritical indignation at this suggestion. "You are prosecuting a boy who has always been a credit to boxing." They looked into their hearts, however, that if Robinson is turned loose against Henry the result would be a disgrace to boxing.'[280]

Hugh Fullerton Jr., on the day before the fight, observed: 'Mike Jacobs has been absorbing a few blasts for setting a $16.50 top for tickets for tonight's Hank Armstrong–Ray Robinson fight, but Mike can take it as long as he can take it … but some of the more solvent beachcombers point out that the customers all over the country are demanding ringside seats at any price and won't go for the cheap tickets.'[281]

Writing from Chicago, INS columnist Davis J. Walsh said: 'It wasn't so long ago that Dan Parker was complaining fretfully, as is his wont, about the $11.50 top being charged for Angott and Beau Jack, Mr Parker's outcries becoming so audible that one of the rival managers took alarm. "Aaah,

---
280 Dan Parker, *High Point Enterprise*, North Carolina, 24 August 1943.
281 Hugh Fullerton Jr., *Wisconsin Rapids Daily Tribune*, 27 August 1943.

don't pay no attention to him," said Mike, shortly, "he ain't goin' to buy any tickets.'"[282]

Harry Grayson was another of the press boys to find fault with the New York promoter, writing: 'Ray Robinson shows more sense than Mike Jacobs in not wanting to box Henry Armstrong at Madison Square Garden on 29 January. [The fight was postponed for six months, reason not made public, possibly Corporal Robinson's military duties.]

'Opponents are a might scarce these days, but Sugar Robinson realises that a match with the once great Armstrong would do neither himself nor the business any good. A promoter pairing the shop-worn Armstrong with a boy like Robinson is like the saloon keeper who helped bring on prohibition by peddling drinks to drunks.

'Armstrong, now 30, was the 20-year-old Robinson's idol. Robinson gave that as a reason when he declined the match.

'Then the current handler of Armstrong, George Moore, told a San Francisco sports editor that the acquaintanceship of Armstrong and Robinson was only casual, indicated that the Harlem lad was afraid of the old champion. The old steam-up, of course, and promoter Jacobs and his matchmaker, Nat Rogers, are trying to work on it and Robinson. Anything for a $60,000 gate.

'If Armstrong was unfit two years ago, he certainly is not now capable of meeting Robinson, who easily could be the most formidable welterweight since Mickey Walker. The battered Armstrong is at a stage where he might be

---

282 Davis J Walsh, *Cedar Rapids Gazette*, Iowa, 29 August 1943.

CHAPTER TWENTY-FIVE

permanently injured by a swift and hard hitter. Sugar Robinson doesn't want the match.

'Neither do those with the best interests of boxing at heart. Fighters never know when they have had enough. Someone has to tell them, and Henry Armstrong should be told right now.'[283]

Well, there were two men who didn't agree with the forgoing prognosis, the ex-champ himself and his manager, George Moore. 'Henry Armstrong meets Ray Robinson at Madison Square Garden on Friday night and Henry will win,' Moore told columnist Whitney Martin of Associated Press. 'He thinks Armstrong will win because Robinson never has been up against anything quite like the somewhat retarded buzzsaw, and he may be right, at that. Armstrong is on the stocky, solid side, and Robinson is built along the loose, general lines of a scaffold. If Henry gets in close and starts to knock the joints out of that long frame, Robinson is liable to collapse.

'Armstrong's comeback manager says he figures Henry is about 75 per cent of the fighter he was in his prime. He doesn't throw as many punches but he throws harder, set punches. Not long ago he broke Willie Joyce's jaw a second time, this time on the other side, making it necessary to again wire Willie for sound.

'Joyce put up a real battle the second time,' Moore says. 'He broke his jaw in the fifth round. You could hear it pop all over the place, but it was a smaller ring where he couldn't run so much, and when Henry got him cornered he fought like a cornered lion, regardless of his broken jaw.

---

283 Harry Grayson, *Fort Madison Evening Democrat,* Iowa, 4 January 1943.

277

'At one time Henry carved easier than an overdone turkey, and he practically had spigots over his eyes from which the gore ran. The only cut Henry has suffered in his comeback was a mouth gash inflicted by Sammy Angott. The little guy obviously is not as fast as he once was, but there is something amazing about his endurance, as in his fights with Angott and Beau Jack he was going stronger toward the finish than at the start.'[284]

'The only thing that will keep Henry Armstrong in the ring after the first of the year is a shot at the world lightweight championship,' wrote Sid Feder. 'And it has to be the whole apple pie – not one of those part-time baubles that'll be recognised only in Waycross, Georgia, Forty Fort, Pennsylvania, and a few way stations.

'"All in all," Henry the Hammer explained on Wednesday, "I'd say I'll have a dozen more fights at the most before the end of the year … I'm 32 now," the one-time three division champ points out, "and I've been fighting a dozen years. None of us lasts forever. However, I can round out this year and then call it a career." That doesn't mean the old rocking chair is going to get Henry when he is through fighting. He's planning to build up a stable of fighters and manage them.'[285]

An Associated Press item dated 23 August reported: 'Corporal Ray Robinson, who has a ten-round engagement with veteran Henry Armstrong in Madison Square Garden Friday, is expected here from Fort Meade today to complete his training. It is believed Sgt Joe Louis will accompany him here.' This was one date at the Garden Joe Louis missed.

---
284 Whitney Martin, *Findlay Republican Courier*, Ohio, 25 August 1943.
285 Sid Feder, *Mason City Globe Gazette*, Iowa, 25 August 1943.

CHAPTER TWENTY-FIVE

Columnist Joe Williams had the story in the next day's newspaper: 'One of the War Department's brass hats speaking with valorous swivel-chair authority made it clear to Sgt Joe Louis that he was not to attend the fight in Madison Square Garden last night. "Your presence must not be used to help exploit a purely professional enterprise," the world's champion heavyweight was told in words to this effect. The champion must have thought to himself: "My gosh, how do they figure these things out? Here's Robinson who is a soldier just like me and the government lets him fight to get himself some dough, but they won't even let me see him fight because they fear I might help him get some more dough."

'Cpl Ray Robinson was fighting old Henry Armstrong, the former triple-plated champion, and the word fighting is used advisedly. He won every round of the ten. Nothing happened in any of them. The addicts began to boo in the third round. It was unbelievably bad.

'It wasn't anything like a massacre, as you might expect when everybody agrees almost punch for punch. Armstrong lost, was beaten but he wasn't battered. He bobbed and weaved and snorted and frowned and at widely separated intervals he landed a punch. Honestly, we counted only three he landed … We don't want old Henry to keep on fighting, especially against the likes of Robinson. Nothing is ever going to happen to him. The few times Robinson let loose, he made old Henry look like a rank novice. But it was significant that every time Robinson, using a left jab and a right uppercut exclusively, seemed to hurt old Henry he would clinch. The answer came quickly. Robinson just didn't want to hurt old Henry.'[286]

---

[286] Joe Williams, *El Paso Herald Post*, 28 August 1943.

From United Press from New York on 26 August 1943: 'Ray Robinson, uncrowned king of the welterweight division, was established today as a 2½-1 favourite to defeat Henry Armstrong in their ten-round shot at Madison Square Garden. Both ended their training at Fred Irving's Harlem gymnasium yesterday and seemed to be in excellent shape, although Robinson said that, "Five months of army life have slowed me up a bit and it's a strain to work up my speed." Robinson has had only two bouts since entering the army in March and he said this would be his last fight for the duration. Robinson said he would weigh in at about 145 pounds. Armstrong expects to enter the ring at 139.'[287]

At the midday weigh-in Henry actually scaled 140 pounds, conceding five pounds to the pride of Harlem. Mike Jacobs was not too happy with the figures, given next day as 15,371 who paid a gate of $60,789.31. Maybe that more people read and digested Dan Parker's column in *The Mirror*, shows that, as one sportswriter put it, "It doesn't pay to put the sniff on a crusading columnist."

In the *St Louis Post Dispatch*, Armstrong's hometown newspaper, John Wray had written, almost as a warning to Robinson: 'Never before has he met a man of the experience, strength and indomitable will-to-win of Armstrong.' Still, Wray conceded that Armstrong was facing a 'much younger, faster and more virile opponent in Robinson.'

'When Sugar Ray was asked by Hype Igoe of the *New York Journal – American* if he would be able to hurt Armstrong, who was someone he obviously admired, Robinson's manager,

---

[287] *Ames Daily Tribune*, Iowa, 26 August 1943.

CHAPTER TWENTY-FIVE

George Gainford interrupted, his tone sharp. "You remember his first Golden Gloves final, Hype? You remember how he knocked down that Spider Valentine boy? They were pals for years. Shot marbles together. Did everything together. But that didn't stop Robinson from knocking him down. No room in this business for friendship, Hype." And yet, Henry Armstrong believed, really believed, he could beat Sugar Ray Robinson.'[288]

United Press reported: 'Blurred vision and fear of blindness suffered in earlier fights caused Henry Armstrong's retirement from the ring last night. His action was not inspired by any harm suffered in his "stinkeroo" defeat by Corporal Ray Robinson at Madison Square Garden. It was an unfortunate farewell for Armstrong, but it was doubly unfortunate for young Corporal Robinson, who was either just too timid or "under wraps".

'Robinson back-pedalled to victory, though he won the unanimous decision of the three ring officials and took seven of the ten rounds on the United Press score sheet, which credited two to Armstrong and called one even. If the fight was "arranged" by the two principals, it was poorly arranged. Robinson, only 21, nearly ten years younger than 30-year-old Armstrong, and possessing advantages of punch and speed in addition to five pounds in weight, fled before the ancient "perpetual motion man" during most of the rounds as if old Henry were Joe Louis.

'Armstrong, who looked like a little crouching bulldog against a slender, streamlined puma, tried to make a fight

---

[288] Will Haygood, *Sweet Thunder*, 2009.

of it. But Robinson kept speeding away from him, flicking him with left jabs and then halting to throw uppercuts, most of which missed Hammering Henry. There were no knockdowns. Armstrong suffered a re-opening of an old gash in his lower lip, but it did not bleed much. Only two good punches were landed during the farce. Armstrong rocked Robinson with a left hook to the chin in the fifth and Robinson staggered Henry with a right bolo uppercut in the sixth. After the fifth round, Armstrong ran out of gas. This was unusual, because Homicide Hank, even on the comeback trail, has been a slow starter and a strong finisher.'[289]

'Armstrong chased the Harlem youth from start to finish, but on only two occasions did he get close enough to land some good punches. His heaving tactics from a crouching position made Robinson miss repeatedly, but not enough to reduce his big lead on points. Robinson was content to back-pedal and jab, jab, jab from long range. Only occasionally did he cut loose with the two-fisted savage attack that earned him a terrifying reputation. He seemed to hurt Armstrong on these occasions, but showed a healthy respect for his opponent and never followed up his advantage.

'The crowd, keen for the kill, didn't like Robinson's caution and booed lustily. The skinny Harlem youth asserted afterwards that Armstrong was the "greatest I ever fought. I never could get him in trouble". Armstrong said afterwards he was dazed by Robinson's first left but "after that I got on to it and he didn't bother me. I know it looked bad," referring to the booing from the third round on. "It's my style of fighting.

---

[289] United Press, *Nevada State Journal*, 28 August 1943.

CHAPTER TWENTY-FIVE

If Robinson had come in, instead of staying away, it would have been different. Ray just wouldn't fight. He told me he was going to run. I almost knocked him out in the third round. I said, Ray, this is the Garden and they're booing. I've never been booed in the Garden, so they must be booing you. Why don't you come in and fight?" He said, "To hell with you, Hank. I ain't going to get hit like that no more. If you can catch me, catch me. I'm going to try and win this fight on decision."'[290]

'Again we say farewell to Henry Armstrong as an active fighter. We are gratified that he earned enough money during his comeback campaign of 27 bouts to put him on "Easy Street" and that he apparently evaded the blindness that threatened during every venture into the ring. As he fought on along the comeback trail, the vision of his left eye became blurred. It bothered him so much that he finally went to a Hollywood physician, Dr Simon Jesberg. The doctor told Henry that a scar tissue growth – similar to a cataract – was forming inside his left eyeball. He advised him to quit fighting as soon as possible.

'The blur increased, Armstrong admitted last night, and – although he is signed to fight Slugger White at Los Angeles on 18 September – he will withdraw from that bout and never fight again. He will manage a stable of fighters in the future. And Henry hopes that the $100,000 he earned since the death of manager Eddie Mead can be enjoyed in sunshine, not in darkness.'[291]

Whitney Martin observed: 'Most of the crowd present

---
290 Tead Meir, *High Point Enterprise,* North Carolina, 28 August 1943.
291 Jack Cuddy, *Ogden Standard Examiner,* Utah, 28 August 1943.

had the idea that Ray Robinson was spilling a little of the milk of human kindness in his bout with Henry Armstrong at Madison Square Garden last Friday night. That is, that out of sympathy and respect, he refrained from knocking out the worn and weary warrior. If such was the case, it was history making ditto marks, with Armstrong drawing the interest on a little investment in chivalry on his part. It wasn't too many years before that Armstrong, then at his peak, had met a fading Barney Ross.

'Those who saw that battle, memorable because of the refusal of Ross to quit when hopelessly beaten, carried away the vivid impression that Armstrong eased up in the late rounds out of tribute to his gallant opponent, who was determined to go out as a champion should go out – doing his best and asking no quarter. Those who saw that battle also probably never imagined that someday, a few years away, this same Armstrong would be in a position similar to that of Ross, saved from a knockout by the compassion of a younger and stronger rival.'[292]

In his 'Sports Round-up' column, Hugh Fullerton Jnr. wrote on the Robinson–Armstrong contest: 'We never saw Armstrong at his best, but we'd much prefer to remember him as the little fellow who won three world titles and lost them gamely than as the outworn prize-fighter who shuffled around the ring swaying his head like a sea lion begging for a fish ... With that weaving style, Henry was as hard to hit as the swinging target in a shooting gallery – and Ray Robinson didn't win any marksmanship medals ... The payoff was

---

292 Whitney Martin, *Lethbridge Herald*, Alberta, 31 August 1943.

CHAPTER TWENTY-FIVE

when a disgruntled fan spotted Harry Mendel leaving the Garden and shouted, "We'd rather have your six-day bike races back, Harry!" [Harry Mendel was a tubby New Jersey press agent who in the past had promoted six-day bicycle races in Madison Square Garden and helped promote some of Joe Louis's fights.]'[293] Fight fans were happy to hear Henry's announcement that he was retiring from the ring after his lop-sided defeat by Robinson. Well, not everybody. The news didn't sit very well with promoter Joe Lynch in Los Angeles, and nor with Sam Lampe, manager of Luther 'Slugger' White. 'Armstrong has been matched to meet Slugger White in Los Angeles on 18 September, but it is all off, of course, if he retires.

"'I've run up a lot of expenses and somebody has to make them good," Lynch declared. Lampe was even more emphatic. "I'm going to sue Armstrong," he asserted. "Why shouldn't I? I've turned down match after match for White because George Moore (Armstrong's manager) has been telling me since Henry fought Beau Jack that Armstrong was always going to meet the Slugger."'[294]

Henry would fight White, but it would be 21 fights along the road before he swapped punches with the Slugger.

---
293 Hugh Fullerton, Jnr., *Benton Harbour News Palladium,* Michigan, 28 August 1943.
294 *Cedar Rapids Gazette,* Iowa, 29 August 1943.

Chapter Twenty-Six

'BELIEF IN some boxing circles that Henry Armstrong has twice retired from the ring are untrue, he said. There has been only one comeback attempt, he explained, and this is it. There was a time after he lost to Ray Robinson in New York that he was not so active, he explained, but that was because he needed a long rest.'[295]

That 'long rest' kept the former triple champion out of the ring just over four months, taking him just two weeks into the new year of 1944, before he was packed and ready for the journey to Portland, Oregon, where the posters were already heralding his appearance against the tough Italian Aldo Spoldi for a ten-round main event at the Auditorium.

'Henry Armstrong, the dusky little fighter who has held three world titles in his dozen years in the ring, swaps punches tomorrow night against Aldo Spoldi, a dynamite puncher who might put a crimp in Henry's perennial comeback. Both boys looked impressive in workouts and have a healthy respect for the other.

While Henry racked up a decision over Spoldi in 1937 at Madison Square Garden and later earned a TKO in San

---

295 *Lincoln Star*, Nebraska, 14 January 1944.

CHAPTER TWENTY-SIX

Francisco, he candidly admits that Spoldi is one of the hardest hitters he has met.

'Spoldi needs the bout if he wants a spring match with Sammy Angott, while Henry is anxious to keep his name in the headlines, perhaps regain the lightweight title, although at 31 he could have quit at any time on his laurels. He's an old man in the fight game.'[296]

Portland, Oregon, 15 January 1944 – 'Hammerin' Henry Armstrong today declared himself ready to meet NBA lightweight champion Sammy Angott at New York after taking a big step along the comeback trail last night by knocking out Aldo Spoldi, one of the leading contenders. Armstrong, fully utilising his three-pound weight advantage, sent Spoldi down for the count in the third round with the time-honoured "one-two." A left hook drew Spoldi's guard down and a right cross to the body, carrying his full 141 pounds, sent Spoldi reeling into the ropes and down.

'Armstrong, unmarked despite the furious infighting of the first round and the powerful long-range sniping in the second round, waited for his opponent to get up but Spoldi was unable to raise even one knee from the canvas. After the bout, Armstrong said he was convinced his "old faithful" timing had returned and confidently predicted a victory for himself in his bout with Angott. "I'm still in there hammerin'," he said. Net receipts for last night's infantile benefit gate were $12,603 paid by 4,000 customers.'[297]

Next stop Kansas City for a scheduled 12-round bout with Saverio Turiello of New York. A veteran of 179 fights (90-54-

---
296 *Nevada State Journal*, 14 January 1944.
297 *Ogden Standard Examiner*, Utah, 15 January 1944.

35), Turiello was known as the Milan Panther but his claws no longer drew blood from his victims. He was trying his arm with Armstrong for the third time but was running on empty now.

'Hammerin' Henry Armstrong, romping along the comeback trail, won another knockout victory here last night and a host of well-wishers in his quest for at least one of the three titles he once held.

'The former featherweight-lightweight-welterweight king knocked out Saverio Turiello in the seventh round. But it was not the knockout itself that warmed up many of the ringsiders to Hammerin' Henry's hopes as much as it was the manner in which he did it. Like the perpetual motion of old, he never stopped shooting his triphammer blows, both arms constantly swinging. Three times before the finish, Turiello was down for a nine count. Henry weighed 144 pounds for the bout. Shortly after the contest, his manager, George P Moore, announced they were moving on eastward, that he had signed Armstrong for a ten-round bout with Lew Hanbury in Washington at the Uline Arena on 7 February.'[298]

'Armstrong was too much Hanbury's master during the short time they were in the ring together last night,' wrote George Huber, 'for the local youngster to have much claim for a return go right away, although he claims, and is backed by his board of strategy, headed by Al Weill, that the fight was going almost as planned and that Armstrong was tiring at the time of the sudden and unsatisfactory ending. Hanbury hotly declares he was the victim of a quick count and that he was on his feet and ready to go at nine, but referee Eddie La

---

298 *Salamanca Republican Press*, New York, 26 January 1944.

CHAPTER TWENTY-SIX

Fond definitely tolled out the required ten seconds before Lew was off his knee.

'The record indoor fight crowd of 7,770 appeared dissatisfied at the sudden finish ... So much noise filled the huge plant that it was some time before announcer Jimmy Lake could get in a word as to what actually happened. The end came at one minute ten seconds of the third round. In his dressing room after the fight, Hanbury showed evidence of having taken a beating in the short time he faced the Hammer. His head was swollen, particularly around his left eye. The scene in Armstrong's quarters was much more peaceful. Henry had just finished another easy evening's work for which he collected around $7,000. "I still like the kid's chances and think he may go places yet," said Armstrong, "but I would like to see him lose some of that ego or overconfidence."'[299]

Two weeks later, Henry was back in Kansas City, meeting an old opponent in Jimmy Garrison for the fourth time and beating the Los Angeles welterweight for the fourth time. Maybe Jimmy got the message this time as Armstrong's power punching had Garrison going up and down like a yo-yo before referee Walter Bates got tired of counting and stopped the bout at the 1.58 mark of round five. Henry made light of Jimmy's five-pound advantage in the weights.

Wasting no time, Armstrong moved into Des Moines, Iowa, for a bout with Jackie Byrd, and after one minute 18 seconds of round four the Arkansas Traveller was wishing he had stayed at home. 'A crowd of 3,500 fight enthusiasts watched the former title-holder dispose of Byrd with very

---

299 George Huber, *Evening Star*, Washington DC, 8 February 1944.

little trouble at the Coliseum here Tuesday night. Armstrong landed a dynamite-filled right to the jaw following a series of lefts and rights. Byrd was out cold and it took approximately five minutes before the Arkansas boxer was able to leave the ring.

'Although Armstrong has been fighting for 12 years he still showed remarkable speed and power on Tuesday night. He drove into his opponent like a fullback trying to pick up three yards through right tackle. He put his head down and barrelled in with both hands, swinging short, power-laden punches. Armstrong gave indications that he must be considered a strong challenger for the NBA lightweight title now held by Sammy Angott. This bout was Armstrong's 32nd since he started his comeback. He has lost only four, all by decision. Tuesday night's kayo was his fifth in a row.'[300]

Chasing a bit of winter sunshine, manager George Moore took Henry down to Florida where he picked up a few dollars at Dorsey Park, Miami, knocking out Johnny Jones in five rounds to ruin the New Yorker's vacation. 'Another trip to Washington saw Henry in action at the Uline Arena, where he found stiff opposition from local favourite Frankie Wills. Fighting a defensive bout, Frankie stalled Armstrong's two-handed attack by clinching and jabbing, keeping a left fist in Henry's face most of the night. Armstrong used his right to good advantage and appeared strong at the finish, where he took the unanimous decision after scoring six knockouts.'[301]

---

300 Edgar Wilson, *Waterloo Daily Courier*, Iowa, 1 March 1944.
301 *Fort Madison Evening Democrat*, Iowa, 21 March 1944.

CHAPTER TWENTY-SIX

Associated Press reported from Boston on 25 March: 'Although he fought three times in the short space of ten days, Henry Armstrong today was heading back to his Los Angeles draft board unscarred and unmarked. Armstrong, despite rumours that his vision has been severely damaged, is confident that he can pass his physical test with flying colours. What may have been the great battler's last professional bout for the duration was his easy ten-round conquest of Ralph Zanelli, the rugged Providence, Rhode Island, welterweight, before a 12,941 crowd last night at the Boston Garden.

'Armstrong, who knocked out Zanelli four years ago, the only time the Rhode Islander has been counted out, settled down after a slow start and gave him a terrific beating from the second to the ninth rounds. Since he is 32 and engaged in his second comeback campaign, Hammerin' Henry tired during the last two frames and wound up with six rounds to his credit by the widest of margins. Zanelli's badly battered right eye and nose proved conclusively that the short lefts and rights that Armstrong fires while resting his head out of range on his opponent's shoulders still have plenty of zing. Henry also has retained much of his old-time craftiness, including against Zanelli at least, his favourite tactic of setting his own pace.'[302]

Back home in Los Angeles, Henry walked into a main event at the Olympic Auditorium against John Thomas and hammered his way to a split decision before a 10,000 crowd. 'Referee Abe Roth awarded the bout to the hard-hitting

---
302 *North Adams Transcript*, Mass., 25 March 1944.

Thomas by a narrow margin, but Judges Johnny Indrisano and Charley Randolph balloted in favour of the aggressive former triple-crown holder. After being outboxed by Thomas in the first frame, Armstrong cornered his youthful opponent on the ropes early in the second round and sent him to the canvas for an eight count with two fast lefts to the body and a short right to the jaw. Thomas made a game comeback to take the third, but the relentless jabbing Armstrong sent Thomas to the floor again in the fourth with a stiff left to the jaw.

'Thomas probably fell short of winning with an impressive last-round rally that saw Armstrong reeling from a series of smashing left hooks and jarring rights to the head. The United Press scorecard gave each fighter five rounds but favoured Armstrong on the basis of the two knockdowns.'[303]

A rematch with Ralph Zanelli in Boston came over the 'Massachusetts boxing commission recognising the fact that Freddie (Red) Cochrane's title is in cold storage until the end of his naval service, decreed that the Armstrong–Zanelli melee was between the two outstanding welterweights extant and that the winner therefore should be known as the "duration" champion. It was a near thing for Zanelli though, for the battle was virtually even as the gladiators entered the tenth and final round. But Armstrong's class asserted itself in the finale and he slowed the eager Zanelli down to a walk as he galloped home with the victory.

'Indication of the closeness of the fray was shown in the vote of the officials. Referee Tommy Rawson gave the former triple-crown wearer six rounds while figuring Zanelli for

---

303 *Ogden Standard Examiner,* Utah, 26 April 1944.

CHAPTER TWENTY-SIX

three and the other even. Judges Joe Blumsack and Jimmy McCarron each gave Armstrong five but the former called three for Zanelli and two even while McCarron figured three even and two for Zanelli. The official vote on points gave Armstrong a three to seven-point edge among the three officials, which would indicate that Zanelli, in the most imposing performance of his career, was no part of a pushover.'[304]

'This was a dressing room in Griffith Stadium at Washington DC the night of 22 May 1944 and an 18-year-old kid called Aaron Perry was eating ice-cream as he talked to a sportswriter. "He didn't lick me," the kid said. "I want to fight him again as soon as they can arrange it. Next time I'll know how to handle that overhand right of his."

'This from an Aaron Perry who last night in Griffith Stadium was knocked down six times in the sixth round by Henry Armstrong and lost the fight when Referee Charley Reynolds stopped the action after Hammerin' Hank had floored the local boy with a vicious right to the stomach. Including one trip to the canvas in round four, this was the seventh time Aaron had hit the deck. "I coulda fought him all night if they'd let me. He never hurt me when he knocked me down. The only time he stung me was with that right hand in my stomach, but the rest of the time he was hitting me when I was off balance."

'It is safe to say that few among the 15,241 customers who paid a gross of $60,325 agreed with the 18-year-old local lad. Armstrong had another story to tell. "Of course

---

304 *North Adams Transcript*, Mass., 17 May 1944.

the boy doesn't think he's been licked. He never knew what hit him. He didn't know what he was doing when he got up from those knockdowns." Armstrong smashed the local kid to the canvas once in the fourth round, three times in the fifth, caught him twice again in the sixth with overhand rights and floored him for the final time with a right to the midriff. Referee Reynolds stopped the fight in two minutes 59 seconds of that round.'[305]

'Wealthy Charles Shuster of Los Angeles owns the chain of "Jim Dandy" food markets in southern California,' wrote Jack Cuddy for United Press. 'Although a fight fan for years, he is a newcomer to the boxing business. He bought the contract of Willie Joyce last July. He admired the Gary, Indiana, native for his gameness in two of his three fights with Armstrong. In those particular bouts, Joyce suffered a broken jaw but finished the fight despite the pain. Shuster hired Lou Gross, a well-known Chicago trainer, to handle the fighter for him. Under the Shuster–Gross management, the 25-year-old Joyce has become a prominent contender.'[306]

'Willie Joyce checked the comeback winning streak of Henry Armstrong in a blistering ten-round battle fought in stifling heat in the Chicago Stadium Friday night. The decision of the two judges and referee Norman Garrity was unanimous, but the balloting was close. The verdict was met with mingled boos and cheers. The terrific heat kept the attendance down to 10,387 sweltering shirt-sleeved customers.

'Armstrong forced the battle from the start, firing punches from all angles, but the Gary lightweight kept peppering him

---
305 *Evening Star*, Washington DC, 23 May 1944.
306 Jack Cuddy, *Ogden Standard Examiner*, 1 March 1945.

CHAPTER TWENTY-SIX

with snaky left jabs to the face while in retreat. Armstrong, fighting head-to-head, forced Joyce backwards to escape from his jolting blows delivered at close range. Joyce won the first two rounds decisively by skilful jabbing and with Armstrong's blows falling short or wild. Armstrong, however, came back with the start of the third and won the next four rounds, with the exception of the fifth, which he lost by throwing punches into foul territory. Armstrong fought a relentless tireless battle, chasing Joyce all the way. His punches, however, often fell short or were wild, but he never gave up forcing the issue.'[307]

Jack Cuddy wrote from New York: 'Brown-skinned Henry Armstrong, the poetic pugilist, dreams of the wonderful world of tomorrow in which he will build his young white "miracle fighter" – Keith Nuttall – to ring championships and fabulous wealth, assisted by television. Armstrong enthused about young Nuttall at Stillman's Gym on Monday, just before he stepped into the ring for a workout with Torpedo Reed of Los Angeles, in preparation for Thursday night's dangerous brawl with Al "Bummy" Davis at Madison Square Garden.

'The bull-shouldered veteran in white sweatshirt and blue trunks, who insists that he is only 31 years old, said, "I don't know how long I'll be fighting. I feel swell now, sharp as a razor after plenty of competition. I should lick Davis all right, if I watch his left hook. I can't go on fighting forever. But I want to fight as long as I can store up a war chest with which to back young Nuttall, the most amazing youngster I ever saw. This Nuttall kid is only 13, he's still an amateur, but what he can do with his fists is absolutely unbelievable." Armstrong,

---

307 *Lincoln Nebraska State Journal*, 3 June 1944.

through his Los Angeles attorneys, has a "minor contract" on young Nuttall's services until he is 21 and an option on his services thereafter.'[308]

A few days later, Henry had other things on his mind. He was in the Garden ring with a crowd of 16,084 fans eager to see if he had enough left to take care of young Davis. They called Al Davis 'Bummy', and he had a left hook that would stop a truck. He had won 59 of his 71 bouts and had blasted lightweight champion Bob Montgomery out in 63 seconds!

Associated Press reported: 'Henry Armstrong is still one of the best fighters in the business. The former triple champion demonstrated it last night by flattening Al "Bummy" Davis in less than two rounds. The crowd screamed deafeningly as Hammerin' Hank battered the Brooklyn bad boy to the canvas four times, twice in the first round, before referee Frank Fullam stopped it after 69 seconds of the second stanza. Davis was stretched full length, flat on his face, when Fullam, without bothering to count, waved Armstrong to his corner.

'From the start, Armstrong, a master at infighting, pinned Davis against the ropes. He didn't give Bummy an opportunity to use the left hand punch that kayoed Montgomery. After the first two minutes, Armstrong stepped clear and socked a hard left to the pit of Davis's stomach. Bummy's knees sagged. A crushing left and right crumpled Davis to the floor. He got up at eight, legs shaking, and was knocked through the ropes. He just managed to get back inside the ring as the bell rang. Many thought he had been counted out.

---

308 Jack Cuddy, *Lincoln Nevada State Journal*, 14 June 1944.

CHAPTER TWENTY-SIX

'In the second round Davis went down for a count of four, bounced up and got knocked down again. He started to get up at two, but, exhausted, fell flat on his face as Fullam called a halt.

'"I felt pretty sharp," explained Armstrong later. Both he and Davis weighed 141¾ pounds for the scheduled ten-rounder. Henry was due to fight Nick Latsios in Washington a week after the Davis fight and spoke with promoter Goldie Ahearn, telling him he had a couple of War Bond rally dates to fill but would arrive in Washington shortly. Already strongly entrenched in the capital, Armstrong doubtless will be greeted by an added coterie of fans when he starts workouts at the Liberty AC.'[309]

'Henry Armstrong can continue for the duration of the war to gather in the coin of the realm, if those in charge of his bookings will pick their spots with the same shrewdness displayed so far in more than 90 per cent of Armstrong's battles.' This was the reaction of *Ring* magazine to the brief encounter with Bummy Davis. 'They missed one when they signed Hank with Willie Joyce of Chicago in the Windy City recently, for Joyce emerged the victor and thus spoiled Armstrong's slate.

'But manager Moore wasn't worried over that setback. He went about his booking and signed Hank with a sure-shot target, one Armstrong couldn't miss – Bummy Al Davis – a dumb fighter whose only asset to fame has been a good left hook. "Take that left hook away from him," as Dan Parker of the *Daily Mirror* so aptly put it, "and you've robbed Davis

---

309 *Evening Star*, Washington DC, 16 June 1944.

of all of his fighting qualities. He then isn't even a good preliminary boy."

'Henry Armstrong proved that to the satisfaction of 16,084 persons who paid $58,822 to see the slaughter at Madison Square Garden. He took Davis's left hook away from him, and the "Brownsville Terror" was at the mercy of the former triple title-holder. By keeping in close, right on top of his target and whipping both hands to the body at a rate that was a reminder of Homicide Hank at his best, Bummy didn't get a chance to land more than a couple of punches. Hammering Henry dropped his man four times and at the last, so helpless was the victim, that Referee Fullam dispensed with the count. The time of the knockout was 59 seconds of the second round.'[310]

In his column of 16 June 1944, Harry Grayson addressed the current *Ring* ratings: 'Designating the best he has tackled, Henry Armstrong makes clearer than ever to what extent the grade of glove-men has dropped since the Hammer came out a dozen years ago. Armstrong calls Ray Robinson the finest all-around performer he met, Barney Ross the most polished boxer, Ceferino Garcia the hardest hitter, Lou Ambers the cagiest, Baby Arizmendi the toughest, Fritzie Zivic the foulest.

'Sugar Robinson wasn't around long enough to prove his true worth even had there been someone capable of putting him to the acid test, and the others hardly will be listed among the greats. Only two fighters of the last decade stick out. One is Joe Louis, of course, the other Henry Armstrong.'[311]

Bob McShane, writing for a Montana newspaper: 'Win, lose or draw, Henry Armstrong always has been the fighter

---

310 *Ring*, September 1944.
311 Harry Grayson, *Burlington Daily Times-News*, North Carolina, 16 June 1944.

CHAPTER TWENTY-SIX

for our money. Pound for pound, Henry just about tops the list of all-time great boxers. Look over the list of ring men and find one who has done what he has.

'More than once the experts said Henry was through. That has been the cry for years. Henry again upset the dope recently when he knocked out Aaron Perry, a sensational comer, in Washington DC. Yet Henry insists he always has been a pacifist who avoids arguments and heartily dislikes fighting. How is it, then, that a man who detests fighting can work up so much fury when he steps into the ring? The answer is simple – Henry needs the money. He is fighting for room and board.

'He remembers cheerfully how his likeable ex-manager, the late Eddie Mead, managed to mess up their finances following every big bout. Gene Kessler, a Chicago sportswriter, tells of some of Mead's get-rich-quick ideas. There was the movie, *Keep Punching*, in which Henry was star actor, co-director and financial angel. All Henry got for his bankroll in that venture was a few souvenirs and still-life photos of himself. There was the flash-front chop suey joint in Los Angeles which packed in customers but, strangely, showed no profit. In fact, it kept Henry broke feeding the good citizens of Los Angeles from his fight purses until a sheriff gracefully closed the doors.

'It wasn't love of fighting that brought Henry back to the ring. It was necessity, coupled with the lure of war-fattened bankrolls. And this time he was going to take care of his own finances. The total gate for his match with Perry grossed $60,000 in Washington. Other good-sized gates have given him a comfortable chunk of cash.'[312]

---

312 Bob McShane, *Dillon Examiner*, Montana, 14 June 1944.

They liked Henry Armstrong in Washington DC. Since February 1944, he had boxed twice at the Uline Arena and once at the big Griffith Stadium, and now in June he was back to fight Nick Latsios at the Stadium, ten rounds or less. "'Frankie Wills proved that a big man with a left jab can annoy Armstrong, and I think I can hold him off until I find an opening,' says Latsios. 'He isn't going to find me the wide-open target some of the others have been, and I have enough reach to pester him plenty."

'Nick Latsios will have one factor in his favour when he fights Henry Armstrong at Griffith Stadium next Wednesday night. The local youngster will tower fully five inches over the squat, bull-shouldered Armstrong at 5ft 10in. Nick has agreed to post a forfeit of $1,000 as a guarantee that he will make 147 pounds for the bout. The biggest local boy to get a shot at the veteran, Latsios feels that he will benefit by a proportionate advantage in reach.

'The Bolling Field corporal gave Alexandria fans a treat yesterday when he boxed several rounds with amateurs at the St Mary's Boys' Club. Lew Pavone and Bobby Schwartz, two of his best friends, set a terrific pace throughout the drill and forced Nick to bear down.

'Armstrong is scheduled to pull in here Friday to step through public workouts at the Liberty Club gym over the weekend.'[313]

'"There are two ways to fight Henry Armstrong. Get out of the ring, or if you stay in there, keep away from him." That is the comment of Nick Latsios on the fight he made against the

---
313 *Washington Evening Star DC*, 14 June 1944.

murderous little man from Los Angeles at Griffith Stadium, a battle that ended with Armstrong getting a unanimous nod from Judges J.A. Trigg, Col. Claude Gamble and Referee Charley Reynolds.

'"I wanted to slug it out with him," Nick says. "A couple of times when he hurt me with overhand rights, I'd have given my right arm to go in there and punch, but I fought the way I was told, the only way a guy like me can last ten rounds with that guy."

'Latsios obediently followed for ten rounds the battle plan his wise handler, Naiman Massey, had mapped out for him. He back-pedalled most of the way, with an exasperated Armstrong trying to catch up with him, and only once did Hammerin' Hank manage to tag him. It was in the tenth round when the youngster's bicycle broke down and Henry slapped him with a hard right that spun Nick into the ropes. But for the rest of the exhibition, Armstrong was shadow-boxing with a ghost that was never in the right place at the right time for Hank's purposes.

'The Hammer was talking to himself most of the way, giving comical imitations of Latsios' style, and generally acting like a man on the verge of a nervous breakdown. "That was no fight, it was a track meet," is Armstrong's comment on the evening's proceedings.'[314]

'Henry Armstrong, one of the biggest little men in ring history, vowed again today to continue fighting "as long as I can win and make money out of the game. I like boxing and apparently the fans like me," he said. "I'm going to stay in the

---

314 Bob McLean, *Washington Evening Star DC*, 22 June 1944.

game until they quit paying to see me. When the gate receipts drop, then I'll know it's time to quit."

'Henry decisioned Nick Latsios, an almost unknown Greek–American lad from Alexandria, Virginia, over ten rounds last night. About 8,000 spectators paid to see the bout. In previous appearances here and elsewhere he's attracted far more from the ring faithful.'[315]

The Fourth of July was holiday time across the United States, more so in Los Angeles for local lightweight contender John Thomas. He was getting a crack at veteran Henry Armstrong at the Olympic Auditorium, scene of their first scrap three months previously that saw Armstrong take a sizzling ten-round split decision.

'Although not a stiff puncher, Thomas fought a smart fight to keep Armstrong from inflicting damage, keeping well protected on the defence and circling Armstrong's lunging attack to spin the 32-year-old battler out of position.

'Armstrong started fast in the first round with his shuffling, weaving attack, and fired heavily to Thomas's face, but Thomas used all his speed and tricks in the second round to sweep into command of the fight, never relinquishing it in the following eight rounds. Invariably, Thomas would get in seven or eight crosses and jabs before Armstrong could get close. A few times the eastern fighter managed to corner Thomas on the ropes, and when he did he would rock him with overhand rights and short-arm left hooks. Thomas's left crackled in jabs and hooks and his right sizzled with uppercuts and crosses to completely baffle his opponent

---

315 *Helena Independent Record,* Montana, 22 June 1944.

CHAPTER TWENTY–SIX

during the fight. Armstrong's defeat was partly due to his failing speed. The decision was unanimous. Thomas weighed 139 to Armstrong's 139¾.'[316]

Hollywood, 14 July 1944, United Press reported: 'Perennial Henry Armstrong mixes it up tonight with a rival who fights Armstrong-style, Luther White, the perpetual-swinging slugger from Baltimore, in a ten-round bout slated to draw a packed house of 7,000 fans at Legion Stadium. Hammering Hank will enter the ring a solid favourite to ship the slugger. The two have never met before but White's imitation of the famed Armstrong style has netted him wins against John Thomas, Juan Zurita, NBA lightweight title-holder, and Willie Joyce. The expected gate of $22,000 will be divided with Service Sports Inc., which supplies athletic equipment for US armed forces.'[317]

'ARMSTRONG–WHITE BATTLE TO A DRAW: Henry Armstrong hit harder but Luther (Slugger) White landed more often and so their furious ten-round bout before a sell-out crowd was termed a draw. There were no knockdowns or clinches and there was hardly a let-up in the violent exchange of hooks and uppercuts, with both hands at close range. Referee Abe Roth awarded Hammering Hank eight rounds, Judge Benny Whitman called White the winner by a shade, and Judge Frankie Van called it a draw.

Armstrong spent most of the evening absorbing a bevy of stiff punches to the face from the continuous jabbing youngster, only occasionally landing a telling blow. In the eighth heat Armstrong cornered White on the ropes, but

---
316 *Lincoln Star*, Nebraska, 5 July 1944.
317 *Norwalk Reflector Herald*, Ohio, 15 July 1944.

the slugger fought his way out of the trap to capture the round. The fight ended with White landing all the blows and Armstrong weaving and bobbing around the ring without doing any punching.'[318]

Some nine months before he fought Armstrong, Luther White got his big break – a fight for the world championship. They called Sammy Angott 'Sammy the Clutch' because of his habit of grabbing his opponents. In October of 1943, they called Angott the lightweight champion of the world as recognised by the National Boxing Association, and on 27 October 1943, Sammy gave Luther White a crack at the title. The Slugger had already won a slice of the title as recognised by the State of Maryland. Now he was meeting a world champ.

The fight took place in Hollywood at the ball park, and upwards of 15,000 fans filled the arena, the first lightweight title bout in California since 1914.

Frank Frawley, ringside for AP, reported: 'Sammy Angott is still the lightweight champion and the very last fellow to dispute it today would be Luther (Slugger) White, of Baltimore, who got the boxing lesson of his life last night in 15 rounds. It was one of the most interesting and unusual fights ever held here. As the boys started the fourth round, a generator failure plunged the Hollywood baseball park into darkness. It was an hour and seven minutes before electricians repaired the trouble. The boxers retired to their dressing rooms after waiting for the first half hour.

---

318 *Madison Wisconsin State Journal*, 15 July 1944.

CHAPTER TWENTY-SIX

'Angott was complete master of the situation. He went out in the first round to steal the play from the fast-punching White. He danced away and around the challenger and came back to deliver any number of hard, delayed left and right uppercuts. This tireless smashing had a marked effect on White over a long period of time, and in the 14th and 15th rounds he seemed on the verge of being knocked out. Two judges gave Angott every round while the referee, Benny Whitman, scored 14 rounds for Angott.'[319]

The fourth-round blackout was nothing to Luther White. For the past 12 months, the sight in his right eye had been a blackout for the 26-year-old. Twelve months to the day from the Angott fight, the boxing world was shocked: 'From San Francisco, United Press reported: 'A scheduled ten-round bout Monday night between Willie Joyce and Luther (Slugger) White was cancelled today after a medical examination allegedly disclosed that White has a glass eye.

'Dr A.E. Egerton, physician, asked to make an examination of White by the state athletic commission, reported as follows: "The patient has an artificial right eye. I would not advise that he be allowed to box because a blow over the left eye would be apt to cause a complete retinal detachment of the left eye and result in blindness."

'Benny Ford, disabled American veterans boxing club promoter, said he signed the match "in good faith, but would rather take it on the chin" than allow White to appear in the ring. The strange part of this whole affair is that White was allowed to box at least ten times in southern California.

---

319 Frank Frawley, *Daily Globe* Ironwood, Michigan, 28 October 1943.

305

Either those pre-fight examinations were superficial and inadequate or the results were pigeonholed. The results of White's examination here indicate that the commission in Los Angeles owes the public an explanation.'[320]

Two months after fighting a draw with Henry Armstrong, Luther White fought his last professional bout, taking a decision over Vince Dell'Orto in Baltimore where his hometown crowd roared its protest at the decision.

---

320 *Ogden Standard Examiner,* Utah, 28 October 1944.

Chapter Twenty-Seven

SLEEK CHICAGO lightweight Willie Joyce was feeling quietly confident that August night in 1944 as he slipped between the ropes at the San Francisco Auditorium and trotted to his corner. He was boxing veteran former champion Henry Armstrong in the ten-round main event, knowing that he had already beaten Henry in two of their three fights. Willie was 27 years old and brought a 52-10-7 record to the ring. Henry Armstrong was 31 years old, a pro since 1931 and posting a 145-20-9 tally against the best in four divisions, but according to the talk around the gyms he was already thinking of a life in pipe and slippers.

At ringside for the *Oakland Tribune*, Alan Ward noted: 'Long and loud were the arguments resulting from Referee Frankie Brown's decision favouring Henry Armstrong over Willie Joyce last night at the San Francisco Auditorium, but this writer agreed with the mediator's verdict.

'If Armstrong was hampered by an almost useless right hand, obviously injured before he stepped into the ring, he was benefitted by a pint-sized, squared-circle of only 16 feet. The small ring reduced Joyce's natural speed and permitted the flat-footed plugging Armstrong to pin his adversary in convenient corners on many occasions. Joyce depended largely on a flicking left hand and short slashing punches in close quarters, Armstrong alternated a left-hand attack between head and body. Both missed punches, but Joyce missed the most.

'Off to a casual start, the Transbay fight, which played to an audience of $30,000, quickly set a fast tempo and it wound up at a high pitch of combat – and excitement.

'Armstrong, for all his fistic age and degree of wear and tear, performed in exactly that manner. Come to think of it, Armstrong knows no other style. The ninth was Armstrong's by a wide margin and a pro-Armstrong house in that frame started yelling hysterically for a knockout. The caterwauling was well intentioned but misplaced. At no time was Joyce in immediate danger of being cooled.

'The tenth was Joyce's. He walked into Armstrong, forgot all about his tactics and threw blows from all angles. Hank caught more than he pitched in that final frame. The additional eight rounds were distributed by the fans according to their preference of ring style – to Joyce if they cottoned to boxing, but to Armstrong if they desired the more rugged style of milling.'[321]

Having squared his account with Willie Joyce, coming out even after four bouts – two wins and two losses – Henry moved on take up with Aldo Spoldi. Manager George Moore booked the fight for 16 September 1944, doing Henry a favour since the bout would be held in St Louis, Henry's old home town, at the Kiel Auditorium. A lot of his old fans made up the audience of 6,000, paying a gate of $12,046.

---

321 Alan Ward, *Oakland Tribune*, 22 August 1944.

CHAPTER TWENTY-SEVEN

Henry took $4,800 for his night's work, which didn't take too long.

'Armstrong displayed his old-time weaving and perpetual punching to kayo the New York-based Italian at 2.43 of round two with a fast left jab to the chin. The veteran fighter, who has beaten Spoldi three times previously, used his left almost exclusively.'[322]

In their four-fight series, starting in 1937, Armstrong had taken a decision in ten rounds, and improved with stoppages in the seventh, third and second rounds. He always reckoned Spoldi was a hard fighter. Lightweight great Benny Leonard had a theory about Italian fighters, which he explained to New York columnist Robert Edgren: 'I've found the Italians the hardest to knock out. They can fight all the time and not tire. Their vitality is astonishing. Fellows like Johnny Dundee [born in Sicily as Giuseppe Carrora] are tireless and can stand an immense amount of work without going stale. That's because their ancestors for a thousand years back have been workers and have lived on plain food and little of it. A loaf of bread was a feast to those birds.'[323] Benny beat Dundee in five of their eight bouts.

Armstrong had tough fights with fellows like Spoldi, Saverio Turiello, Al Tribuani and Ralph Zanelli, fighting them several times through his professional career, as he did with guys like Jimmy Garrison, Willie Joyce, Fritzie Zivic, Kid Moro, Perfecto Lopez, Baby Arizmendi and Mike Belloise.

Maybe club fighter Johnny Taylor had the right perspective on fighting Henry Armstrong. Taylor was Henry's comeback

---
322 *Fort Madison Evening Democrat*, Iowa, 16 September 1944.
323 John Jarrett, *The Great Benny Leonard*, 2021.

opponent when he returned to the ring in June of 1942, 16 months after being stopped by Zivic for the last of his world titles.

'I was there that night,' promoter Don Chargin remembers. 'I was a kid, I didn't know much then. But I was amazed. Armstrong was on a downward slide, but he still had an aura about him and he was still perpetual motion. All the way from his dressing room, up the aisle into the ring, he was throwing punches. While he was waiting to be introduced, he was throwing punches. Then the bell rang and he kept throwing punches. He knocked Taylor out in the fourth round. Taylor was a substitute for Cecilio Losada. Three months later they fought again and Armstrong knocked him out in three rounds.

'Years later, I asked Taylor: "You took such a beating the first time; why did you fight him again?" And Taylor told me, "It was an honour being beaten by him."'[324]

'Mike and Steve Belloise were perhaps the finest brother combination in boxing history. They captured a combined 201 bouts, a record for brothers, according to Angelo Prospero who ran the Veteran Boxers Beat column in *Ring* magazine. In the June 1990 issue, Angelo was recalling the Bronx brothers who fought their way to world fame. Both were born in New York City. Mike, the older of the two, was born on 18 February 1911, and had his initial fight as a featherweight in 1932, when he defeated Eddie Vaccia in four rounds. He was undefeated in his first 28 bouts, but lost his first title endeavour when Baby Arizmendi outpointed him over 15

---

324 Thomas Hauser, *And The New…*, 2012.

CHAPTER TWENTY-SEVEN

rounds in 1934. Sixteen bouts later, he became the 126-pound champion by kayoing Everett Rightmire in Chicago in 14 rounds. In 1936, *Ring* selected him as the cleverest boxer of the year.

'Mike defended his title once, beating Dave Crowley, but a year later, on 10 August 1937, he was stripped of the title for not defending it. In 1938 he was defeated by Joey Archibald. Starting in 1939, Mike toured the country, taking on all the top fighters in the featherweight division, including Henry Armstrong, Lew Jenkins and Petey Scalzo. He retired on 3 March 1942 after losing to Chester Rico, but returned six months later. By 1944 he was just an opponent. He lost six of his last eight bouts. Mike had 132 fights, winning 91, losing 29, and drawing 12 times. He rated Armstrong as the best he ever faced.'[325]

They fought three times between 1936 and 1944, Henry winning all three.

'It was Mike, then a champion, whose inability to say "No" to any of the myriad of requests to appear at smokers, that eventually led to brother Steve winding up a pugilist. Strangely enough, Mike, unlike most boxers, rather enjoyed performing at smokers; quite often he would find himself shy of a partner, and finally talked the kid brother into filling the breach one evening. Although not even an amateur, Steve gave the featherweight champion such opposition the first time the pair boxed, Mike got panicky, figured he must be slipping or sick and couldn't rest until he got Steve in there again with him. This time spindly Stephen was even

---

325 Angelo Prospero, *Ring*, February 1990.

tougher, and the realisation dawned on Mike that Steve had something.'[326]

Steve Belloise had enough of something to become a serious contender for the middleweight title, although he never became a champion like his brother. 'He met the best in the world, including Sugar Ray Robinson, Tami Mauriello and Ken Overlin. A spectacular puncher with power in either hand, Steve won 34 of his first 36 fights and gained a crack at Overlin's title. Many observers thought Belloise won the fight, especially after he scored a late-round knockdown. But he lost the decision, as well as the return match. He won 95 of 110 bouts scoring 59 kayos. He rated Robinson the best fighter he ever faced.'

Writing in his 1957 autobiography: 'Armstrong said he had money now. But there was a new idea, about taxes. He had to pay out a lot of it in income tax. The Second World War was on, and the war cost everybody money. Henry grumbled a little at giving Uncle Sam so much of his earnings, but he gave it. Who didn't? Nineteen fights in 1944. Henry won 16 of them. It looked good. Actually it wasn't. By now, Henry knew that "his number was up". The old speed was gone. He just couldn't make the big time, any more. He could fight the second-raters, but the boys near the top were too much for him. He did get some satisfaction from knocking out Mike Belloise in Portland, Oregon, but he knew Mike had had it too.'[327]

AP reported from Portland on 4 November: 'Henry Armstrong, little perpetual motion, knocked out Mike

---
326 Ted Carroll, *Ring*, August 1940.
327 Henry Armstrong, *Gloves, Glory and God*, 1957.

CHAPTER TWENTY-SEVEN

Belloise of New York City here tonight in the fourth round of their scheduled ten-round main event. The Los Angeles fighter, after taking the first three rounds with little trouble, ended the battle with a smashing left hook to Mike's chin. The fight was over just 20 seconds after the fourth-round bell. The net gate was $6,497, part of which goes to the Shrine Hospital for Crippled Children. Armstrong weighed 140, Belloise 138.'[328]

New Year's Day 1945 and Henry was looking at three fight dates already booked on his calendar: Oakland Auditorium for Chester Slider on 17 January, then 6 February with Genaro Rojo in the Olympic Auditorium in Los Angeles, then back in Oakland for a rematch with Slider on 14 February.

United Press reported from the Oakland ringside on 18 January: 'Hammerin' Henry Armstrong fought Chester Slider of Fresno, California, to an upset draw decision Wednesday night.

'A 3-1 favourite in the betting, Armstrong, who weighed in at 140½ to Slider's 146, fell behind in the fifth round before his opponent's heavier weight. Hank was obliged to abandon the famous Armstrong crouch and the two fighters slugged toe to toe in the middle rounds.'[329]

Associated Press saw the fight differently, giving Armstrong two rounds and Slider, a relatively unknown fighter, eight. But Referee Jimmy Evans called it even. The fans thought that Slider should have had the decision. Armstrong was out of condition, slow on his feet and off in his timing. Slider landed most of the punches throughout the

---
328 *Arizona Independent Republican*, 5 November 1944.
329 *Lincoln Evening Journal*, Nebraska, 18 January 1945.

fight, though Armstrong rallied in the third and fifth rounds, landing some sound blows on his young opponent's body and jaw. The ex-champ appeared tired in the last three rounds.[330]

The former triple title-holder went back to the gym and looked fitter, which was just as well as the local was looking to get Armstrong's name on his resume.

'Henry Armstrong battled for ten strenuous rounds last night and finally came out with a unanimous decision over Genaro Rojo. A capacity crowd of 10,000 was on hand at the Olympic Auditorium. The Mexican boy circled and jabbed and kept the veteran Hammerin' Hank at bay until the eighth round when Armstrong let loose with something of his old style, punching his opponent all over the ring with short, solid hooks to the head.

'Up to that point Armstrong had avoided many of Rojo's dangerous right crosses and right uppercuts by bobbing and weaving tactics. In the tenth round Henry caught the tiring Rojo with a left hook to the jaw that sent him rocking and reeling to the corner. This was the closest thing to a knockdown. But Rojo came back and traded punches in a torrid exchange that had the customers on their feet at the final bell. All three officials tabbed the fight for Armstrong.'[331]

Alan Ward, sports writer for the *Oakland Tribune*, received a letter from his friend Harry Fine giving him a brief sketch of his fighter Chester Slider. Harry was one of the best publicity grabbers in the business, and one of the most erudite of fight managers. Harry wrote: 'Chester Slider, the boy who dreamed

---
330 *Brownsville Herald*, Texas, 18 January 1945.
331 *Helena Montana Independent*, 7 February, 1945.

CHAPTER TWENTY-SEVEN

and hoped to step into the shoes of Henry Armstrong when Henry retires, is fast getting his boyhood wish fulfilled. Chester still idolises Armstrong and hopes someday to become nearly as great a fighter as was Henry. Slider has most of the other qualifications of Armstrong. He is a clean-living kid, has a beautiful wife, Rula, and two babies – a boy, Chester Jr., and a girl, Barbara Jean. Truly a respectable boy and a credit to the boxing game. Incidentally, 22-year-old Chester Slider has served 12 months in the army and was honourably discharged about eight months ago.'

On 14 February, Chester Slider stepped into the ring at the Oakland Auditorium ready to go ten rounds or less with his idol, Henry Armstrong. UP reported: 'Chester Slider, 147-pounds Fresno boxer, pounded out a close ten-round decision over "Hammering" Henry Armstrong, fading former triple champion, here Wednesday night before a crowd of 9,000. The decision was roundly booed, but somewhat evened a dubious draw decision given Armstrong in a previous match. Armstrong had a chance to tuck the fight away in the third round when he knocked Slider down with a series of left uppercuts to the head. Slider apparently injured his right ankle in the fall, and after taking a seven count came up limping. It was Armstrong's final fight before leaving 27 February for an overseas USO tour in the European theatre. The crowd paid $21,000 for the card.'[332]

Alan Ward had a more comprehensive accounting of Armstrong's last fight in the *Oakland Tribune*, writing, 'All the ingredients of a good screen play – drama, combat,

---

[332] *Salt Lake Tribune*, Utah, 16 February 1945.

mystery and comedy – were embodied in a local fight show last night at the Auditorium. The drama was provided by Chester Slider of Oakland, when he fought eight of the ten rounds with a broken right ankle against a former three-time champion of the world. The mystery was injected on two occasions – when referee Billy Burke gave Slider a decision he didn't deserve and later had his scorecard "snatched by a fan as he left the ring".

'The combat element was donated by Armstrong and Slider, who engaged in a sensational scrap with not a single clinch registered in the ten rounds. The comedy was contributed in a post-fight session when Burke vaguely tried to explain the existence of two substitute scorecards, the alleged snatch of the original from his burly person and his reasons for some weird scorings on the second duplicate. Come to think of it, the hilarity was confined almost entirely to his newspaper listeners. The humour of the occasion wasn't shared by the irate manager of Armstrong, George Moore, nor by promoter Ray Carlen and matchmaker Jimmy Murray. Even a $21,000 audience sympathetic to a courageous Slider, whose leg injury was obvious at the end of the third round, roared its disapproval of Burke's weird reasoning.

'The intensity of the battle in the ring was matched with a verbal growl in the promoter's office afterward with manager Moore taking the aggressive. Moore, in the ring, declared Burke's decision "was the rawest he'd ever seen". Moore flatly declared he would demand formally of the State Athletic Commission, Burke be suspended. Burke's explanation he had been robbed of his scorecard en route to his dressing room drew derisive chortles from Moore, who challenged Billy's right to make up a second and then a third card from memory in his dressing room.'³³³

Next morning, the rumour factory worked at war-time production speed on the story of 'Three-Card Billy Burke'.

Hal Wood, for United Press, wrote: 'Referee Billy Burke today charged with a "deliberate steal" in awarding a decision to Chet Slider, 147-pounds, in his fight with Henry Armstrong, 141, the former champion. The accusation was hurled by George Moore, Armstrong's manager, who asserted he would take the case to the California Boxing Commission. If he fails to get action there, Moore said he will go direct to Governor Earl Warren.

'The rumpus was the result of Burke's awarding a close fight to Slider. Using the California points system, the UP scoresheet showed 56 points to Armstrong, 54 for the young Fresno battler, but on the round system it ended with three rounds to each fighter with four being even. Moore's major protest was that Burke came out of the ring to tell state inspectors that his scorecard had either been lost or stolen. He told officials that his card showed Slider won by five points but he couldn't recall the rounds and became confused under questioning by state inspectors.'³³⁴

In Oakland on 15 February: 'The referee's licence of Billy Burke, third man in the ring when Chester Slider decisioned Henry Armstrong Wednesday night, was suspended today by members of the California State Athletic Commission. The suspension was meted out because of Burke's failure to turn in a scorecard after the fight, which he awarded to Slider.

---
333 Alan Ward, *Oakland Tribune*, California, 15 February 1945.
334 Hal Wood, *Yuma Sun*, Arizona, 16 February 1945.

Sportswriters at the ringside were agreed that the bout was close but almost unanimously felt that Armstrong should have won. The United Press scoresheet had Armstrong winning by two points; Beecher Kellog of the *San Francisco News* had Henry by five points. Clyde Giraldo, *San Francisco Chronicle*, gave seven rounds to the former champion; Alan Ward, *Oakland Tribune*, thought Armstrong won; so did Eddie Muller of the *San Francisco Examiner*.'[335]

Russ Newland covered the west coast sports scene for Associated Press. From San Francisco, on 22 January 1945, he wrote: 'There is something so pathetic about a former boxing champion who is travelling down the sunset side of his career in a fighting fadeout. This thought flashed through our mind as we watched Henry Armstrong battling his heart out against a younger, heavier and stronger opponent in Oakland the other night. The referee called it a draw; actually Armstrong was beaten. He knew it and so did some 10,000 fans who jammed the Oakland Auditorium with the largest crowd and the biggest gate in the ring history of the place.

'Obviously and admittedly, the squatty, pleasant mittman is not the Hammerin' Hank of old. He still will whip a lot of young men, however. Armstrong is not through as a fighter. He is a former champion, still fighting, and his name still is box office magic. Armstrong has been fighting since 1931, professionally since 1932, and steadily except for the eight months' layoff in 1941 when he retired and underwent an operation to remove scar tissue from over his eyes. He stumbled into what many thought was fistic oblivion after a

---

335 *Delphos Daily Herald*, Ohio, 17 February 1945.

CHAPTER TWENTY-SEVEN

12-round knockout and terrific beating at the hands of Fritzie Zivic, 17 January 1941. Zivic had boxed the welter-weight crown off his head a few months before.

'But Armstrong beat Father Time to the punch, and less than two years later trimmed Zivic in ten rounds. Too bad Zivic had lost the welterweight title by then. We saw Armstrong in some of his earliest fights. He weighed around 124, give or take a pound, and was a fireball. The Armstrong of the other night, in action after a layoff, shuffled wearily to his corner and plopped onto his stool in the closing rounds. Father Time always wins in the end.'[336]

Newland's words triggered a reaction from promoter Joe Waterman that surprised the writer. In his column on 2 February, Newland wrote: 'This is so frank it is amazing and we direct its attention particularly to the boxing trade. It isn't news anymore when a man bites a dog but it is news in my book when a fight promoter gives full credit to a fighter for making him an outstanding promoter.

'Joe Waterman, Portland promoter, has been associated with boxing some 40 years, a nomad of the game who helped build it in Manila, Los Angeles, Denver and many other cities. This is what he writes: "Read your article regarding Henry Armstrong, wherein you wrote this former triple champion rated boxing's 21-gun salute. This should be appreciated by all of us Armstrong rooters…

'"Here is what I propose: That all of us matchmakers and boxing promoters who have been made 'great' whenever Henry fought for us, get together and give him a sort of testimonial

---

336 Russ Newland, *Washington Evening Star*, Washington DC, 22 January 1945.

banquet before he leaves for his overseas boxing tour or before he permanently retires from the ring.

"'Most of us matchmakers on the coast and some in the east have been made 'great' matchmakers the day after Armstrong fought for us. Joe Waterman was the greatest-ever when Armstrong drew $18,000 and $16,000 with Lew Jenkins and Jimmy Garrison respectively ... Henry has drawn an average of about $23,000 every time he fought in the Olympic in Los Angeles for Baby McCoy. Charley McDonald's record for the Hollywood Legion stadium was that open-air show with Armstrong–Garcia, $68,000. The same goes for Bennie Ford, whose Armstrong–Zivic and Armstrong–Joyce fights drew $41,000 and $33,000 in San Francisco. Jimmy Murray of Oakland, who really is about the best of us all, knows the Armstrong pull there. So I say, let us get together. Murray, Ford, McDonald, McCoy, and Waterman, and give Henry a banquet as a testimonial to one of the greatest boxers who ever crushed resin in a ring. A testimonial to the fighter who makes 'great' matchmakers of guys like Waterman and the rest.'"[337]

It was the night after the fight before, the fight Henry Armstrong knew was his last, he knew he was through and almost everyone agreed with him.

Writer Thomas Hauser said it best in his book *And The New...*: 'It's difficult to take a fighter out of one era and know with certainty how he would have performed in another. But the prevailing view is that Armstrong would have been a champion in any era. He's remembered today primarily because he held the featherweight, lightweight and welterweight titles

---

337 Russ Newland, *Reno Evening Gazette*, 2 February 1945.

CHAPTER TWENTY-SEVEN

simultaneously. Putting that accomplishment in a larger perspective, the most credible accounting of his fights lists him as having 149 wins (including 101 knockouts) against 21 losses and ten draws. In the 46 months prior to his losing the welterweight title to Fritzie Zivic, Armstrong's record was 59-1-1. During his reign as champion, he won 21 title fights. He was knocked out only twice in his career … There was a time when he could beat any fighter in the world from 126 to 147 pounds. And that was during the "golden age" of boxing when there were a lot of very good fighters.'[338]

This was the fighter 100 boxing traders gathered to honour at the Hotel Leamington in Oakland, California, on a Thursday night in February 1945. 'City and county officials, business and professional men of Oakland, newspaper writers of this city and San Francisco, assembled at the strictly invitational dinner for Armstrong, first proposed by Joe Waterman and arranged by the local boxing group. Waterman, boxing promoter in Portland, Oregon, and for years a great friend of Armstrong's, came from the Northwest just to be present at Henry's dinner. It was Joe, of the battered face and the fluent voice, who almost stole the show from Armstrong in a talk punctured with this utterance: "Actually we're not here to honour Armstrong the great fighter, Armstrong the three-time champion of the world, but Henry Armstrong the man, the great American."

'Henry has been the guest of honour at dinners, attracting far more persons than were present at the gathering last evening. More eloquent praise has been heaped on his sturdy

---

338 Thomas Hauser, *And The New…*, 2012.

shoulders. But this Oakland salute touched the heart of the great boxer, who before the end of the month will leave on a USO tour to European battle fronts, as it never has been touched before. "I don't belong to Oakland," Henry said in his talk, "yet Oakland friends have honoured me. I've won no title, but I've been greeted like a champion. It's mighty swell. I'll never forget it. I've had banquets, I've been handed bouquets – but, honestly, none has been quite as nice as this." Each speaker praised the honoured guest not only as one of the greatest ring men of all time, but as a fellow in whom the principles of sportsmanship, of hard but square combat was instilled.

'Before the evening programme had ended, Sheriff Gleason had presented Armstrong with a gold badge and named him an honorary deputy sheriff; a parchment and leather scroll bearing the names of all men present had been given to him, and the Oakland boxing coterie – Jimmy Murray, Ray Carlen, Tommy Simpson and Frank Tabor – made him a gift of a set of luggage.

"'I'll be back in Oakland," Henry said as he bade goodbye to his well-wishers. "But not until I return from one of the battle fronts. Whether I fight here again or whether I just drop in to say hello isn't important. But I'll be back.'" [339]

United Press staff correspondent Hal Wood was ringside at the dinner, writing: 'Boxers, managers, promoters, matchmakers, sportswriters and just plain John Q. Fan turned out here last night for the testimonial dinner honouring Henry Armstrong; the former triple fight champion who leaves 27

---

339 Alan Ward, *Oakland Tribune*, California, 16 February 1945.

CHAPTER TWENTY-SEVEN

February for an overseas tour with the USO. Hammerin' Hank, on the last leg of one of the greatest ring careers in all boxing's history, stole the show – as usual. He had the platform for a 15-minute talk in which he gave his recipe for success as follows: "Shooting for a star, if you give it your all, you'll get there." That Henry "gave his all" was well attested to by those present ... manager George Moore termed Armstrong "one of the finest fighters of all time", and Oakland promoter Ray Carlen, who saw Henry win all three of his crowns and drop two titles, said that "Armstrong will go down in history as one of the all-time greats of the fight game."

'However, with all this praise, the general theme of the testimonial was to the fact that "the champ" was, first of all, a man; after that, a darn fine piece of fightin' machinery. While Henry was all in earnest, Alan Ward, *Oakland Tribune* sportswriter and master of ceremonies, pointed out that he doubted if Hank lived up to his intentions the night he fought Irish Johnny Taylor, the handsome Oakland pugilist, whom he kayoed in practically nothing flat, after meting out a short-lived, but savage, beating. To this statement, Mr Taylor, who was present, added a loud: "Amen!"'[340]

---

340 Hal Wood, *Nevada State Journal*, 18 February 1945.

Chapter Twenty-Eight

SINCE UNCLE Mike Jacobs had no more work for Henry Armstrong, Uncle Sam had plenty of vacancies. The army needed men to entertain the troops overseas – and who could be better for that than the three-time champ? Every man in the world knew Henry Armstrong. He could do a great job of it. He put on an army uniform and went out with Kenny Washington, the famed UCLA football star, Bill Yancey of basketball fame, and Joe Lilliard, the New York cop and former drop-kicking football star from Oregon State. It was called 'The Henry Armstrong Sport Unit No. 500.' Of course it didn't pay much. Henry didn't expect it to. This was his patriotic 'bit' for his country.

'They toured a few Army camps in the States while they were waiting to be shipped across the water. Henry met a lot of old friends. He met a lot of fight managers who would ask him to drop around at the gym to watch some new boy they had; they would drop a bill in Henry's hand, just by way of gratitude, before he left the gym. Sometimes it was ten dollars; more than once it was a poor little one-dollar bill. The managers tried to be nice about it. They said they knew Henry was a little short of cash. They were right, he was. Good old Mike Jacobs asked him to drop in at the Garden – and put

CHAPTER TWENTY-EIGHT

a cheque for $500 in his hand, just for old time's sake. Mike said it might help Henry put a kayo on Hitler's jaw. And he told Henry to drop in again, sometime.'[341]

New York, 8 May 1945, the Sports Roundup by Hugh Fullerton Jnr read: 'Arthur Donovan, the fight referee, was explaining his theories on judging fights to the members of the New York Boxing Writers' Association, who have been somewhat confused by Commissioner Eddie Eagan's efforts to find a more satisfactory system ... The referee summed it all up in one question that no one could answer: "So what system are you going to have outside of what has remained from all those systems that didn't hold up? If they'd been any good, they would have held up."

'About that time, a late arrival, Henry Armstrong, was called upon for a few words before his departure for an overseas USO tour along with Kenny Washington and other noted Negro athletes ... "I wandered in here in the middle of a discussion on scoring," Hank remarked. "I've had some bad decisions against me, like that one against Chester Slider out in Oakland where I beat him every round, broke his leg and still lost the decision. I've often wondered how those things were scored." ... That broke up the meeting.'[342]

In February 1945, American sports pages carried the news 'BOOK COMPLETED BY EX-CHAMPION'. Associated Press writer Frank Frawley penned the review from Los Angeles, writing: 'Henry Armstrong has just finished the story of his life in a book depicting his struggle for three world

---
341 Henry Armstrong, *Gloves, Glory and God*, 1957.
342 Hugh Fullerton Jnr., *Burlington Daily Times News,* North Carolina, 8 March 1945.

championships, but he left unanswered the question put by many sports chroniclers here in his hometown. Why is Armstrong still fighting, three years after he lost his last title? Fritzie Zivic stopped him in the 12th round in New York City on 17 January 1941. He said he was through with fighting. He knew what happened to fighters once they began going downhill.

'But the war took many of the top-notchers from the game and Henry saw a chance to make some money, and he started a highly successful comeback – successful at least from the financial standpoint. Armstrong says he has earned a million dollars in the 15 years he has been in boxing, but since the war he has made more money than during the years he was a champion.

'For a long time Henry spent money about as fast as he made it. In recent years, Fistiana's "perpetual motion man" considered himself "property poor" and said he was fighting so he could pay his taxes. California boxing commissioners once barred him on the grounds that further damage to his ring-scarred eyes might cause him to become blind. But he's fighting again in his native state; lost his last one, in fact, to Chester Slider in Oakland.

'Hank is due in New York soon and from there he will head for the European war theatre with an entertainment group that may include several outstanding Negro athletes. Henry won't get paid but he's glad he's got the chance to box for the GIs. They'll like him. He always has been worth the admission price. It always was a real fight when Henry was in the ring.'[343]

---

343 Frank Frawley, *Monroe Morning World*, Louisiana, 24 February 1945.

CHAPTER TWENTY-EIGHT

A month later, a report from New York noted Henry's arrival in the China–Burma war theatre with 'a special Negro sports unit sponsored by USO camp shows. Armstrong is accompanied by Kenny Washington and Joe Lilliard, All-America football stars, Bill Yancey, the baseball and basketball expert, and Dan Burley, sportswriter and managing editor of the *Amsterdam News*.'[344] (Founded in 1909, the *Amsterdam News* is a weekly Black-owned newspaper serving New York City.)

Ten days later, Armstrong and his unit were in Casablanca, Morocco, where they spent 14 days entertaining the troops. Henry was fascinated when they reached Cairo. Like any awestruck tourist, he visited the old temples, thinking of the people who had worshipped there, wondering … The magnificent sight of the Pyramids and the giant Sphinx again had the ex-champ thinking that maybe Joseph and Mary and their Babe had stood in the same spot out there on the desert sands. In Egypt, Henry thought a lot about God, the Voice came clearer in the desert. Travelling to India, the sight of the beggars in the streets of Karachi distressed him terribly. 'They were so poor, so hopeless … God didn't mean anybody to live like *that*. Henry knew he could give them money, give them food, they needed more, their bodies were alive, but their hearts were dead.

Visiting Calcutta, 'he was stunned, not only by the beggars, but by the little children dying in the streets, Untouchables sleeping in the gutters, on the sidewalks, you had to step over them when you walked down the street. They were a

---
344 *Cleveland Call and Post*, 21 April 1945.

multitude of the living dead – and Henry Armstrong forgot all about prize-fighting, all about money, all about Henry Armstrong, as he looked at their terrible faces and their dull, glowing helpless eyes, and he knew that somebody had to do something for them and about them, for God. God never meant them to be like this ...

'The horror of it, the longing to do something about it, was still upon him when he got the cablegram from home saying that his father had passed away. Now, he said, his heart cried out for – *mercy!* This was more than he could take. He was in a daze. The whips of God hurt more than any blows he had ever taken in the ring. The army was merciful; the army said, "Go home, immediately." They cancelled several weeks of the itinerary ahead and brought him back. The final blow fell when he reached California and found that his father had been buried. He was not even to see him again.'[345]

'The war was over. Mead was gone, Jolson was gone, Jacobs was sick and would soon be gone. Henry returned to Los Angeles, bought a yellow convertible and tried to move fast. But he was really standing still while the world had moved on. His marriage was broken. His old friend Harry had left him. Henry was alone. He tried managing fighters – Cecil Hudson, Keith Nuttall, Roy Miller, Levi Southall, Billy Reed, Cleo Shans, Smuggy Hersey – but none of them got anywhere.'[346]

On a Monday night in December 1945, United Press reported: 'Cecil Hudson, brawny young boxer from Los Angeles, left-handed a thorough trouncing to Sgt Fritzie

---

345 Henry Armstrong, *Gloves, Glory and God*, 1957.
346 Bill Libby, *Boxing Illustrated Wrestling News*, January 1964.

CHAPTER TWENTY-EIGHT

Zivic, 32-year-old ex-welterweight champion at Madison Square Garden … Zivic, suffering his ninth defeat in his last ten starts, landed hardly a solid punch, much to the disappointment of 7,481 fans. Hudson, a protégé of Henry Armstrong, was the 3-1 favourite. The former champ taught him well enough to lick his old nemesis. Zivic, in his 17th Garden main event, his 16th year as a professional, said, "I wasn't sharp tonight because I'm still in the army." It was Hudson's best fight, and his first main event in the Garden.'[347]

Hudson was probably Henry's best fighter, meeting guys like Jake LaMotta, Sugar Ray Robinson and Rocky Graziano for a 118-bout career between 1939–62. Lightweight Adolph Pruitt was a St Louis protégé of Armstrong's, a good puncher with 32 kayos in 46 winning bouts. 'They all *looked* good,' Henry would say, 'but in the end they all lost money – Henry's money!'

'In 1956, long after his marriage had gone sick – it died in official divorce – Armstrong went to court to seek his community property share of their $50,000 estate. The newspapers reported he was seeking alimony. "I just wanted what was mine," he said sadly. "I had little enough left." After his return to St Louis, he met his high school sweetheart, Velma, again and they married. They have been living there, in her large house with one of her five children, a married daughter, the daughter's husband and their three children. Henry has also been able to spend some time with his sister and his daughter and grandchildren.

---

347 *Waterloo Daily Courier,* Iowa, 11 December 1945.

'I have annuities which pay me about $4,000 a year,' he explains, 'and property which brings me about $2,000 a year. And my wife has some money.'[348]

In St Louis, Henry agreed to train light-heavyweight Jesse Bowdry for manager Eddie Yawitz. The round-faced slugger had won 23 of his 34 fights by knockout, but shown a reluctance to train and Yawitz had farmed him out to a meat packer and refused to book him any fights.

'Bowdry returned contrite, and Yawitz hired fistic immortal Henry Armstrong as trainer. Armstrong changed Bowdry's mental attitude and taught him his two-fisted, close-in attack. Bowdry used it in the fight that got him a shot at the NBA light-heavyweight title, an upset decision over fourth-ranked Willie Pastrano in Willie's home town, Miami Beach.'[349]

Armstrong had Bowdry in tip-top condition for the vacant NBA title, but the smart money had Harold Johnson a 3-1 favourite when they clashed in the Convention Hall at Miami Beach in February 1961.

'Johnson was the artist, Bowdry the tenacious bulldog making himself a difficult target. The first few rounds were uneventful. Late in the sixth round, Bowdry landed a couple of good punches and suddenly became too brave. He drove in again and was clipped by a left hook. He started to throw another punch but suddenly fell apart in a delayed action fall.

'He took a count of nine. With two seconds to go in the eighth a right and left combination dumped him in a jack-

---
348 *Boxing Illustrated-Wrestling News*, January 1964.
349 *Norwalk Reflector Herald*, Ohio, 7 February 1961.

CHAPTER TWENTY-EIGHT

knife pose. He was resting on the back of his neck when the gong sounded.

'Johnson was a whirring pinwheel of action as the ninth opened. He threw punches from everywhere with a solid left to the midsection the clincher. Bowdry went down for the final time and would have been a sitting duck when he arose had not the referee intervened.'[350]

It was in one of the closing rounds when Henry and Yawitz had an argument in Bowdry's corner and Armstrong stormed from the ring. In the next round, Bowdry was knocked out. So Henry didn't get his champion.

When his career was done, Armstrong would observe: 'When you're champ, you have to keep going to stay on top. You have only a few years to make your money. After that, you're just another has-been. When you're through, you're through. When you're old, you don't get young again … After Armstrong's boxing days were over, life came at him with the same merciless pounding that he'd dealt out to others in the ring.'[351]

'Early in 1949, he was driving – allegedly drunk – when stopped by police, who did not recognise him. "If you put me in jail, I'll put a curse on you and you'll die within three hours," the ex-champ challenged. But they threw him in the tank anyway. A judge fined, lectured, then released him. Henry shuffled in bewildered sorrow to another gin mill to get drunk again.

'Later that night, he raced his car through the darkness along the beach area, as though he wanted to crash. But, he

---
350 *Dubuque Telegraph Herald*, Iowa, 8 February 1961.
351 Thomas Hauser, *And The New…*, 2012.

says, he felt a hand on his shoulder, restraining him from self-destruction. He says he felt the hand strike his face. He pulled the car to a stop ... ready to fight. But he was alone. As he recalls, "I said, 'You win, God, I give up.' Right then and there, on that dark road, I knew I was heading in the right direction for which I was fated. I knew religion was the only way for me." He began to study for the ministry and was eventually ordained at the Morning Star Baptist Church in Los Angeles.

'He explains, "Although I had been brought up a Baptist, I do not consider myself a member of any organised religion. I am a Christian, an evangelist, who spreads the good work wherever and whenever I can. I had a big home in California, with a $5,000 bar that I converted into a pulpit, and where I practised preaching. I didn't have, and don't have my own church. But I have preached at many ... wherever they'll have me. I have found, because of my name, that people will listen to me. Particularly Negroes, but people of all races, too. And youngsters. They could never have seen me fight, but they have heard of me ... or their fathers have told them about me. So they listen and I hope I can do them some good ... show them how to avoid the mistakes I made."'[352]

'I became friendly with Henry late in his life,' recalled Don Chargin, the late Hall of Fame promoter and matchmaker. 'He'd given up drinking by then. He was very likeable, very talkative, constantly quoting from the Bible. He talked a lot about how his drinking days and carousing days were behind him, that he hadn't been a very good husband or father when

---

352 Bill Libby, *Boxing Illustrated Wrestling News,* January 1964.

he was young, but that he was a much better person and much happier now that he had found the Lord. I think he was sincere. He seemed to have peace of mind.'

Trainer Don Turner was also very impressed with the ex-champion. 'They brought him to Cincinnati to work with Aaron Pryor for a couple of days. Pryor fought like Armstrong used to fight, and his management team thought that maybe Pryor could learn something from him. It was the sort of thing where you go over to someone you admire and introduce yourself. We talked in the gym for about 15 minutes, small talk. And it was wonderful. He was a very nice humble man.'[353]

'Henry Armstrong got involved in politics and drinking, then religion and the fight against drinking. In October 1954, Armstrong spoke to the Temple Baptist Church about his drinking. Four years earlier he had been ordained by his father-in-law, W.L. Strauther, at the Morning Star Baptist Church. In 1959, after 25 years of marriage, Armstrong was divorced by Willa Mae Armstrong, who said she no longer felt loved. The couple had one daughter, Lanetta.

'Henry left Los Angeles in 1967 and moved back to St Louis, where he took a job as assistant director of the Herbert Hoover Boys' Club. He also became a minister at the Mount Olive Baptist Church. He married again and had two children, Henrietta and Edna, with his second wife, Velma. Friends of Armstrong thought he was doing well until Velma died.

'The former Gussie Henry, who said she married Armstrong ten years ago, took him out of St Louis and brought him back to Los Angeles. But Armstrong's friends

---

353 Thomas Hauser, *And The New…*, 2012.

said he would have been much better off if he had stayed in St Louis. "We tried not to let him leave here," said James Reddick, who has known Armstrong for fifty years. "I know he was getting up in age, getting senile and forgetful, but he should have stayed."

"'Armstrong's financial plight is widely known in boxing circles," said veteran trainer Ray Arcel. "Whether it was bad investments, the divorce, the drinking or whatever, Armstrong had run out of money by the mid-1960s."

'Gussie, Armstrong's third wife, said their only income is the monthly Social Security cheque of $800. "I don't have any money and he don't have any money," she said. "He had a lot taken from him. You think people are honest, but they aren't." She refused to let Henry be taken to a nursing home because she thinks she will lose the Social Security money. "What can I do?" she asks. "I need something to live on."'[354]

'It was the humid evening of 28 August 1938 in New York City. It was the night little Henry Armstrong, a handsome, wide-shouldered fighter who had hammered his way out of a tar paper shack in Columbus, Mississippi, with two fists that never stopped moving, won his third world boxing championship by beating Lou Ambers in one of the most dramatic fights of the past quarter century. The victory made Armstrong the first, and last, simultaneous triple title-holder in boxing history.

'In the streets outside the Garden, the remnants of the crowd of 20,000 milled about happily. Most of the gay throng were delirious with joy over the fact that "our

---

354 Thomas Bonk, *Los Angeles Times*, 14 and 24 August 1988.

CHAPTER TWENTY-EIGHT

Hennery" had helped lift his people still another notch up the ladder of physical and social success. Most of them had followed Armstrong's career from the beginning of his first phenomenal outbreak into the big time. They talked about it now as though they had been with him all the way. Few knew about the early years of hardship and heartbreak, the misery of prejudice or the endless hitch-hiking from one tank town to another – all of the pitfalls and frustrations of a determined Negro on the road to greatness. For Henry Armstrong, this "helluva night" was the climax of an unparalleled career which began in 1931 when he fought around St Louis under the name of Melody Jackson.'[355]

'Finished with the prize ring, Armstrong … seemed headed for oblivion. "When there was no place else to turn I found almighty God," Henry said in his book. He plunged into his new work with the same gusto that made him a triple champion. He worked feverishly to save men's souls and spent his last cent for an elaborate set of plans for a Boys' Town to be modelled after the famous Father Flannagan's home at Omaha. That was his dream, The Henry Armstrong Home for Wayward Boys to be located in the lush San Fernando Valley where Henry would teach young denizens about God and maybe, if there was time, about leaning into a left hook.

'Seeing him today makes you gape in awe. You know what he's been through and you wonder how he ever managed to live through it. You don't pity him because you know that at last he's found the most valuable asset on earth – peace.

---

355 Edward Brennan, *Boxing Illustrated Wrestling News*, October 1961.

'One day a reporter was interviewing the Reverend Armstrong in Los Angeles: "Henry," this reporter asked, "who was the better fighter, Henry Armstrong or Melody Jackson? Henry grinned and remained silent for a few moments. Then he said slowly, "That's a surprising name to mention, I haven't heard it in years. I really don't know. But I would think that if Melody Jackson had an Eddie Mead to look after him, he'd have done all right. When I look back to the days you're talking about I like to think that Melody was pretty good for his age. Yes, Mr Mead would have made Melody Jackson a success."'[356]

---

356 Stanley Weston, *Boxing and Wrestling*, November 1956.

Chapter Twenty-Nine

'WHEN THEY wheeled him into hospital for the last time,' wrote long-time boxing writer Bob Mee, 'Henry Armstrong couldn't see too well; he was a little senile; the effects of pneumonia, anaemia and other less specific ailments, not to mention his complete disinterest in food and drink, had shrunk his body to a pitiful seven stone. And he was as near broke as makes no difference.

'Luckily, most of us are judged, not by the manner of our death, but by the quality of our life. But it was a matter of barely expressible poignancy that Armstrong, one of the greatest fighters the world has ever seen, died in circumstances such as these.

'He died 23 October 1988, aged 75. "He's resting and all his miseries are gone," his widow Gussie told a *Los Angeles Times* reporter. "I did all I could for him and so did everybody else."

'Ike Williams, the lightweight champion of the 1940s, was at the Armstrong home paying his respects when the *LA Times* man arrived. "Centuries from now, they will talk about how he held three world titles at one time," said Williams. "That's when championships meant something.

Today it's nothing. They've ruined boxing. But oh my ... Henry! He was something terrific."'[357]

Veteran trainer Ray Arcel was saddened to hear of Armstrong's death. 'He was an outstanding performer and a decent human being,' he said. 'I don't know if there will ever be anyone like him again. Will there ever be another Joe Louis? Will there ever be another Jack Dempsey? Will there ever be another Henry Armstrong? These fellows were a credit to boxing. Honest decent people. Henry will be missed. He was a unique individual, one of the greatest fighters I ever saw. He fought three minutes every round. I saw him in most of his championship fights. He could be classed with the greatest fighters of all time. If you ever wanted to see a fighter, then you would look at him because this was the kind of a guy you would say was a great fighter. The word *great* is misused a lot when it is used to describe many boxers, but Henry Armstrong *was* great.'[358]

'Sugar Ray Robinson told me that Henry Armstrong was an all-time great,' Don Elbaum recalls. 'Rocky Marciano told me that Henry Armstrong was an all-time great, Willie Pep told me that Henry Armstrong was an all-time great. That tells me all I need to know.'[359]

Boxing historian Bert Randolph Sugar wrote, 'Henry Armstrong was a physical loan shark, a fighter who adopted General Clausewitz's theory that the winning general is the one who can impose his will upon the enemy. One hundred and forty-nine times Armstrong imposed his will on his

---

[357] Bob Mee, *Boxing News*. London, 25 November 1988.
[358] *Los Angeles Times*, 24 November 1988.
[359] Thomas Hauser, *And The New...*, 2012.

opponents, suffocating them in his swarming style, firing off his punches and then running over them, much like a runaway locomotive. By 1937, betting on Armstrong was like getting money from home without writing. He fought an incredible 27 times that year and won all but one by kayo.

'No one who ever saw this fighter known as "Hammerin' Hank!" or "Homicide Hank" or "Hurricane Hank," will ever forget him: a non-stop punching machine, his style more rhythmic than headlong, his matchstick legs akimbo, his arms crossed in front of his face, racing the clock with each punch, and each punch punctuated by a grunt. His likes will never be seen again. The feats of Henry Armstrong are a benchmark against which all future generations will be measured.'[360]

'Benny Leonard, one of the cleverest fighters in the history of the ring, said of Armstrong that he maintained the most killing pace of any fighter the ring has known ... How many fighters in the history of the world have held three ring titles at one time? The world knows the answer to that – one fighter. Henry Armstrong.'[361]

'Armstrong began his fighting career in the nauseating Battles Royal which were still being shamefully conducted in St Louis as late as 1929. Then he travelled anywhere, looking for fights in Montana, Nevada, Oregon and California, ready to fight anybody for a few bucks. It seemed as if times hadn't changed since the early days of the near-starving Joe Gans.

'There was one important difference, though. Gans had been a master of boxing. Armstrong was an incredible fighter, willingly taking one to land five and never stopping his frontal

---

360 Bert Randolph Sugar, *Boxing's Greatest Fighters*, 2006.
361 Jim Day, *Bakersfield Californian*, 5 April 1943.

assault, his fast and furious barrage of leather. His body was physically exceptional. "A freak of a generation," one doctor subsequently declared in a medical report.

"'He is so perfect a human dynamo that he is scarcely a fair opponent for any normal man near his weight. He must have an oversized heart, not to the point of pathological enlargement, but above normal. His pulse beat of 59 compared with the normal 72 makes him capable of astonishing endurance.'"[362]

Sports columnist and author Grantland Rice questioned Armstrong after he had been bouncing around during a workout and still not taking an extra breath: "'Two or three specialists asked me the same thing," Armstrong said. "At first they couldn't figure it out. Later on, they made a complete examination of my physical make-up and finally decided it was the size of my heart. They told me that weighing around one hundred thirty pounds, I happen to have a heart that should belong in a one hundred ninety pound body. I don't know much about these things, but I suppose it is like having a big motor in a small car."

'Even doughty veterans like Hype Igoe and Joe Woodman admitted, "Armstrong doesn't belong with the fighters of today. He was for the old era, when forty-round fights were the rule rather than the exception."'[363]

When he died in October 1988, W.J. Weatherby wrote: 'He was in the class of Muhammad Ali, Sugar Ray Robinson and Jack Johnson, and had the kind of personal independence that made him reject the limitations of racial segregation outside the ring. He was to be seen with white women friends

---

362 Gerald Suster, *Lightning Strikes*, 1994.
363 Stanley Weston, *The Ring*, November 1956.

CHAPTER TWENTY-NINE

on his arm like his hero Jack Johnson, at a time when that could get a black man killed in the United States. "I live my life," he once told a bully in New York. "You don't live it for me." He promptly knocked out the bully and walked on with his lady.

'Most of his fights ended in quick knockouts: he had a powerful punch with each hand and could knock out, with one blow, an opponent 20 pounds heavier. "As a kid," he once told me, "I built up my punching power by jabbing at tree trunks. None of my opponents was ever as tough to hit as an oak tree." Asked recently about such fighters as Mike Tyson, Marvelous Marvin Hagler and Sugar Ray Leonard, he grinned and said, "Jack Johnson and I could have taken on the lot." It was said without arrogance: he was simply assessing what he thought was a basic difference between fighters who came up the hard way – and there was no harder way that to be a black boxer in segregation times – and the men who are part of today's multi-million dollar show business scene.'[364]

Author Budd Schulberg, in his 2006 book *Ringside*, paid homage to Henry Armstrong, writing, 'I have only to shut my eyes and put my mind into rewind to watch again the nonpareil Henry Armstrong in with one of my all-time favourites, the inscrutable Baby Arizmendi … I see them still, in perpetual motion, and I knew back then I was in the presence of the greatest fighter I had ever seen … What I'm trying to say is, when you see an Armstrong, you spot the genius right away.'

---

364 W.J. Weatherby, *The Guardian*, 25 October 1988.

After Armstrong completed his famous triple title victory by taking the lightweight championship from Lou Ambers, adding it to the welterweight and featherweight titles he already held, Damon Runyon wrote: 'Henry Armstrong, the brown-skinned fighting fury from Los Angeles ... completed the total extinction of the Caucasian race from the pugilistic world championship map.'[365] Of eight recognised titles, Joe Louis held the heavyweight title, John Henry Lewis held the light-heavyweight title, Sixto Escobar of Puerto Rico held the bantamweight title, and Henry Armstrong held the three titles from featherweight to welterweight. There was no recognised flyweight champion, and the white Al Hostak held the middleweight title.

In June 1965 Red Smith, then columnist for the *New York Herald Tribune*, wrote: 'The Reverend Henry Armstrong, preacher and fight manager, is the only ordained minister in human history to have held the featherweight, lightweight and welterweight championships of the world at the same time, a circumstance that introduced the word "simultaneously" into the vocabulary of the fight mob. He also advanced medical knowledge by teaching the fight mob that all God's chillum got a sacroiliac joint. Because ticket sales were slow for his welterweight title bout with Ceferino Garcia in 1938, Henry helpfully arranged a postponement by having a training "accident". Pencils and notepaper poised, the press assembled to hear the examining osteopath's report on a lame back.

'"He has a slipped sacroiliac articulation," the doctor said. Not a pencil moved.'

---

365 Damon Runyon, *Syracuse Sports Journal*, 18 August 1938.

CHAPTER TWENTY-NINE

On the big screen Henry starred in a 1939 drama titled *Keep Punching* and he made a cameo appearance in a 1946 production of *Joe Palooka, Champ*.

Henry Armstrong defeated 16 world champions and made a big impression on famed Detroit trainer and manager Emanuel Steward: 'I look at films of the old time fighters a lot. Henry Armstrong is the first boxer I ever saw who was like a machine. It wasn't combinations as much as it was punches coming all the time. Nobody could throw that many punches, but he did. He had incredible stamina and was absolutely non-stop. He was a perpetual-motion punching machine. When the bell rang, he got in your face and started throwing punches from every angle. He was like a machine gun. It wasn't bang! It was bang-bang-bang-bang-bang-bang! Nothing stopped him. He just kept coming and coming and punching like a windmill in a hurricane.'

That was Henry Armstrong, boxing's super champion.

Boxing's Super Champ

- Henry Armstrong was the only fighter to win and hold three world boxing championships simultaneously, at a time when there were only eight weight classes.
- In his career he defeated 16 world champions.
- Boxing historian Bert Randolph Sugar ranked Armstrong the second greatest fighter of all time.
- In 1954 he became a charter member of the Boxing Hall of Fame, inducted in its opening year along with Joe Louis and Jack Dempsey. In 1990 his name was added posthumously to the International Boxing Hall of Fame.
- He was ranked second in *The Ring* magazine's 2002 list of the 80 best fighters in the last 80 years.
- Armstrong fought 27 fights in 1937 and won all of them, 26 by knockout.
- He won the featherweight title by knocking out Petey Sarron, jumped two divisions to beat Barney Ross for the welterweight title, then dropped to lightweight and beat Lou Ambers for the title – three world championships within nine months.
- He fought 12 title fights in 1939 and won 11 of them.
- During his reign as champion he won 21 title fights.
- All-time lightweight champion Benny Leonard said of Armstrong that he maintained the most killing pace of any fighter the ring has known.

Bibliography

Armstrong, Henry, *Gloves, Glory and God* (London; Peter Davies 1957).
Bromberg, Lester, *Boxing's Unforgettable Fights* (New York; The Ronald Press 1962).
Fleischer, Nat, *Homicide Hank Vol.II* (New York; The Ring O'Brien Press 1938).
Gallimore, Andrew, *Baby Face Goes To Hollywood* (Dublin; O'Brien Press 2009).
Hauser, Thomas, *And The New ...* (Fayetteville; University of Arkansas Press 2012).
Haygood, Wil, *Sweet Thunder; The Life and Times of Sugar Ray Robinson (*New York; Alfred A. Knopf 2009).
Heinz W. C. & Ward, Nathan, *The Book of Boxing* (Kingston, New York; Total Sports Illustrated 1999).
Jarrett, J., *Dynamite Gloves* (London; Robson Books 2001).
Mullins, Robert A., *Beau Jack* (Jefferson, Nth. Carolina; McFarland & Co. 2020).
New York Times, *The Complete Book of Boxing* (New York; Arno Press Inc. 1980).
Odd, Gilbert, *Ring Battles of the Century* (London; Nicholson & Watson 1948).
Pantalone, Gene, *From Boxing Ring to Battlefield* (Lanham, Maryland; Rowman & Littlefield 2018).
Roberts, J. B. & Skutt, A. G., *The Boxing Register* (Ithaca, New York; McBooks Press 2011).
Ross, Barney & Martin Abramson, *No Man Stands Alone* (London; Stanley Paul & Co 1959).
Schulberg, Budd, *The Harder They Fall* (London; The Bodley Head 1948).
Sugar, Bert Randolph, *Boxing's Greatest Fighters* (Guilford, Conn.; The Lyons Press 2006).
Suster, Gerald, *Lightning Strikes* (London; Robson Books 1994).

Magazines
Boxing Illustrated
Boxing News
Boxing & Wrestling
The Ring
Sports Illustrated
Time

Websites
BoxRec.com
Newspaperarchives.com

Newspapers

Amarillo Daily News
Aniston Star
Arizona Independent Republic
Billings Gazette
Bluefield Daily Telegraph
Burlington Times
Charleston Gazette
Chester Times
Daily Globe
El Paso Herald Post
Elyria Chronicle Telegram
Evening Independent
Finlay Morning Republican
Galveston Daily News
Idaho State Journal
Indiana Evening Gazette
Iowa City Press-Citizen
Joplin News Herald
Kingston Daily Freeman
Lima News
Lowell Sun
Manitoba Free Press
Mansfield News
Montana Standard
Nevada State Journal
New Castle News
New York Journal
New York Times
Oakland Tribune
Ogden Standard Examiner
Portsmouth Daily Times
Salt Lake Tribune
Sandusky Register
Sheboygan Press
Syracuse Herald
Twin Falls Daily News
Waterloo Evening Courier
Winnipeg Free Press

Acknowledgements

To Jane Camillin and her wonderful team at Pitch Publishing – Duncan Olner, Graham Hales, Dean Rockett and Alex Daly, for putting this thing together. To the helpful staff at NewspaperArchives.com, and to BoxRec. Invaluable.

I must make special mention of my daughter Glenda and my son-in-law John for their contribution to my labour of love.

To my sons Derek and Jeff and daughter Diane.

Mike Hills, a voice in the Colorado wilderness.

Thank you all!

John Jarrett, 12 May 2023

Index

Abad, Davey 32-34, 112,113
Adams, Caswell 191
Ahearn, Goldie 297
Alaska 20
Alexander, Pete 142,190
Ali, Muhammad 340
Amateur Athletic Union 10
Ambers, Lou (Herkimer Hurricane) 5, 6, 57-60, 68-80, 83-85, 89-92, 105, 107-131, 136,137,171,173,174, 184, 201, 236, 298, 334, 342, 344
Amsterdam News 327
Anfield Football Ground, Liverpool 99
Angelmann, Valentin 35
Apple Myers Bowl, North Braddock, Pennsylvania 13
Apostoli, Fred 144, 146, 233
Arana, Ventura 27
Arcel, Ray 209, 334, 338
Archibald, Joey 88, 89, 311
Arizmendi, Alberto 'Baby' 20, 24-32,34, 37-41, 45, 91, 92, 97, 268, 298, 309, 310, 341
Armstrong, America (Iroquois Indian) mother 7
Armstrong, Harry trainer 11, 12, 15, 52, 97, 105, 154
Armstrong, Lanetta baby daughter 32, 97, 103, 333
Armstrong, Velma 329, 333
Associated Press 44,88, 93, 104, 108, 120, 125, 132, 133, 153, 198, 205, 239, 253, 256, 261, 277, 278, 291, 296, 313, 318
Attell, Abe 81, 82
Atchison, Lewis F. 182, 183
Azteca, Kid 141, 268
Baer, Buddy 227

Baer, Max 199, 227
Bagley, Frank (Doc) 52
Bakersfield, California 22, 339
Balogh, Harry 75, 187, 259, 261
Bang, Ed 77, 135
Baptist Minister 6, 7
Bates, Walter 289
Battles Royal 339
Bass, Benny 15, 112
Battalino, Battling 64
Beauhuld, Billy 48, 57-59
Belloise, Mike 25, 28, 38, 42-47, 49, 77, 88, 89, 309, 310, 312, 313
Belloise, Steve 310, 312
Best, Johnny 99-101
Biers, Joe 109
Bill, Black 35
Bimstein, Whitey 78, 128
Birch, Jimmy 11
Black, Alton 33
Blaettler, Ivan 36
Blake, George Vincent 38, 91, 134, 158-160, 162, 164-169
Bland, Tommy 185
Bloom, Jack 135
Blumsack, Joe 293
Borden, Eddie 165
Boston Garden 169, 170, 291
Bowdry, Jesse 330, 331
Bowen, Ray 181, 182
Braddock, Jim 92, 93
Bratton, Johnny 268
Brennan, Edward 73, 83, 84, 335
Brewer, A. L. Reverend 25
Britton, Jack 82
Bromberg, Lester 69, 70, 75, 173, 345
Brown Derby restaurant Los Angeles 166

Brown, Frankie 234, 246, 307
Brown, Jackie 35
Brown, Lydia T. 170
Buck, Al 217, 218
Budweiser 61
Burke, Billy 316, 317
Burke, Jackie 226 - 230
Burley, Dan 327
Burns, Sammy 15
Butte, Montana 37, 196, 271
Byrd, Jackie 289, 290
Cairo 327
Calcutta, India 327
California 167, 168 174, 180, 186, 189, 192, 193, 195, 213, 219, 220, 222, 224, 225, 231-233, 250, 271, 294, 304, 305, 313, 317, 321, 328, 332, 339
California State Athletic Commission 20, 37, 144, 147, 155, 158, 317
Canzoneri, Tony 63, 64, 68, 119, 214
Caplin, Hymie 172, 175
Capone, Al 64
Carlen, Ray 316, 322, 323
Carmel New York State 108, 115
Carnera, Primo 214, 227
Carnival of Champions, New York City 49, 69, 142
Carpentier, Georges 100
Carroll, Ted 60, 61, 80 , 83, 84, 216, 217, 268, 312
Carney, Luke 186, 187, 200, 216
Carter, Frank 227
Carver, Lawton 111, 112, 200, 205, 271, 272
Carver, Dr. W.L. 151
Casablanca, Morocco 327

Casanova, Baby Rodolfo 32
Caucasian race 342
Cavanaugh, Billy 73-75, 95, 06, 144, 259, 264
Celio, Margaret Miss 111
Central Avenue, Los Angeles 16, 38, 149
Cerdan, Marcel 106
Chargin, Don 310, 332
Chatman, Henrietta (fraternal grandmother) 8
Chavez, Tony 20, 93
Chestnut Arena, Reno 33
Chevalier, Maurice 106
Chicago Ghetto 64
China-Burma war theatre 327
Chocolate, Kid 25, 28, 41, 48, 49
Christmas Fund show, Cleveland, Ohio 90, 204
Civic Auditorium, Oakland, California 230
Civic Auditorium, San Francisco 226, 233, 239, 241, 246, 250
Clacton-by-the-Sea, England 100
Clark, Tommy 134
Clausewitz, General 338
Cleveland Arena 90
Cochrane, Freddie 'Red' 228, 238, 239, 243, 273, 292
Cohn, Art 42, 118, 167, 235
Coliseum, Des Moines, Iowa 289, 290
Colton, California 16
Columbus, Mississippi 7, 66, 334
Conde, Joe 27
Conn, Billy 152, 179, 193, 198-200, 215
Convention Hall, Miami Beach 330
Convention Hall, Philadelphia 251, 252
Corbett, Young 141, 157, 158
Corvo, Tully 32
Cosmos Hotel, Mexico City 26
Coulon, Johnny's Gym, Chicago 15
Covadonga Sports Association 27
Covelli, Frankie 33
Cox, Tom 17, 18
Crowley, Dave 311
'Crow Jim' 147
Cuddy, Jack 77, 78, 143, 151, 152, 184, 189, 194, 195, 252, 253, 260, 263, 264, 266, 267, 269,
273, 274, 283, 294-296
Cunningham, Glenn 190
Currence, 'Stubby' 228
Dado, Speedy 15
D'Ambrosio, Luigi (Lou Ambers) 119
D'Ambrosio, Tony 68
'Dame Fortune' 27
Daniels, Sammy 252,
Dano, Pablo 141
Dano, Speedy 141
Davis, Al 'Bummy' 295-298
Dawson, James P. 75, 79, 80, 123
Day, Davey 94, 95, 97
De Foe, Johnny 37
Dell'Orto, Vince 306
Dempsey, Jack 9, 20, 145, 152, 190, 196, 199, 230, 244, 245, 253, 338, 344
Derks, J. C. 98, 99
Diamond, Lou 186
Diaz, Mark 33
Dixon, George 65, 74, 81, 82
Donovan, Arthur 28, 47, 54, 55, 57-59, 86, 116, 121-125, 127, 131, 143, 176, 178, 187, 207-210, 212, 325
Dorsey Park, Miami, Florida 290
Douglas, James P. 211, 212
Doyle, Jack 159
Driscoll, Jem 81, 82
Duffy, Jimmy 167
Dunbar Hotel, Los Angeles 16
Dunbar, Lee 231
Dundee, Chris 186
Dundee, Johnny 82, 309
D. Walker Wear, New York State Athletic Commission 137
Dyckman Oval, Manhattan 28
Eagan, Eddie New York Boxing Comissioner 325
Eagle Thomas 16
Egerton, Dr. A. E. 305
Elbaum, Don 338
El Toreo de Cuatro Caminos, Mexico City 30
Epsom salts bath 56
Erwin, Jim 54, 232, 233
Escobar, Sixto 342
Espinosa, Gene 23
Evans, Jimmy 313
Exposition Hall, Portland, Maine 172
Father Flannagan Boys Town, Omaha 335
Fauntleroy, Lord 124
Feder, Sid 125, 126, 176 185, 186, 198, 199, 201, 202, 253, 254, 260-262, 270, 271, 278
Feldman, Lew 71, 93, 93, 138
Ferguson, Harry 94, 95, 127, 142, 177, 178, 206
Fernandez, Ignnacio 141
Ferrer, Juan Bautista Zurita (Juan Zurita) 237
Fine, Harry 314
Firpo, Luis Angel 190
Fitten, Jimmy 237
Fleischer, Nat 16, 17, 27, 50, 51, 55, 60 , 64, 65, 70, 74, 75, 80, 121, 130, 177, 216, 256, 345
Fontaine, Richie 36, 37, 133, 134
Foran, Ginger 77
Forbes Field, Pittsburgh 193
Ford, Benny 234, 241, 246, 305, 320
Foster, Eddie 'Mississippi' 10, 12
Foster, Charlie 'Pop' 158
Frawley, Frank 304, 305, 325, 326
Frye, Clayton 159, 223
Fullam, Frankie 296, 298
Fullerton Jnr. Hugh 120, 275, 284, 285, 325
Fullum, Frank 122
Furr, Phil 181, 182, 196, 204
Gainford, George 281
Gamble, Claude Col. 301
Gans, Joe 21, 45, 65, 74, 207, 256, 339
Garcia, Ceferino 6, 84-87, 89, 90, 138, 142-146, 148-158, 160, 169, 173, 233, 298, 320, 342
Garcia, Evangeline 144
Garden, Madison Square 50, 58, 60, 69, 70, 76, 85, 100, 142, 144, 152, 185, 190, 199, 208, 242, 250, 266, 268, 276-278, 284, 286
Garden, Madison Square Bowl 5, 69
Garrison, Jimmy 134, 136, 137, 271, 289, 309, 320
Garrity, Norman 294
Gearns, Jim 270
Ghnouly, Joe 137, 138
Gibbons, Tom 152
Giesler, Jerry, Chairman California Commission 158, 167

INDEX

Gillespie, Clarence 81
Gilmore, Freddie 22
Gilmore Stadium, Los Angeles 155, 160
Giraldo, Clyde 318
Glaser, Joe 220
Gleason, Sheriff 322
Godfrey, George 230
Goldman, Charlie 78, 128
Goldman, Herb 40
Golden Gloves 64, 214, 281
Graham, Dillon 108, 109, 153, 154
Graziano, Rocky 329
Grayson, Harry 109, 110, 138, 139, 172, 173, 185, 254, 255, 268, 269, 276, 277, 298
Greb, Harry 52, 68, 108, 152
Greenfield, Al 21
Greenwood Lake, New York 172
Grier, John P. 190
Griffith Stadium, Washington DC 181, 182, 293, 300, 301
Gross, Lou 294
Grossinger's, Catskills, New York 174
Guenther, Jack 148
Guiterrez, Luis 49
Hagler, Marvelous Marvin 341
Hamas, Steve 199
Hanbury, Lew 288, 289
Harringay Arena, London 99
Harris, Roy 173
Hartley, Pete 54
Hauser, Thomas 18, 210, 220, 221, 331, 333, 338
Haynes, Leroy 17
Heany, John E. 130
Heeney, Tom 169
Henry, Gussie 333, 334, 337
Hess, Rex 42, 43, 91, 221
Herbert Hoover Boys Club 333
Hersey, Smuggy 328
Hickey Park, Milville, Pittsburgh 15, 218
Hollywood Post, American Legion 138, 146, 147
Hollywood Legion Stadium 141, 159, 320
Hostak, Al 136, 146, 168, 342
Hot Springs, Arkansas 196, 201, 243
Huber, George 288, 289
Hudson, Cecil 328, 329
Hurley, Jack 110, 111
'Ice Tong Punch' 20

Igoe, Hype 58, 280, 340
Independent Packing Company St. Louis, Missouri 8
Indrisano, Johnny 292
Ingram, Bob 232, 233
International News Service 200
Irving's Harlem Gymnasium 280
Iovino, Al 13, 14
Jacobs Beach 80, 186, 194 Jacobs, Mike 49, 53, 69, 70, 76, 90, 142, 147, 172, 176, 179, 183, 199, 200, 203, 204, 214, 254, 259, 265, 266, 268-270, 274-276, 280, 324
Jack, Beau (Sidney Walker) 249, 250, 252-261, 263, 265, 266, 271, 275, 278, 285
Jackson, Emma Lou, sister-in-law 12, 218
Jackson, Henry Snr. (Indian, Irish, Negro stock) 7
Jackson, Henry Jnr (Henry Armstrong) 4, 7, 8, 10-14, 17, 48, 115
Jackson, Melody (Henry Armstrong) 10, 13-15, 17, 335, 336
Jackson, Ollus 7
Jadick, Johnny 185
Jeffries, Jim 33
Jenkins, Katie 174, 175
Jenkins, Lew 170-180, 183, 199, 200, 206, 214, 239, 244-246, 168, 311, 320
Jesberg, Dr. Simon 283
'Jim Dandy' food markets, California 294
John Affleck Park, Ogden, Utah 227
Johnson, Harold 330, 331
Johnson, Jack 33, 92, 218, 340, 341
Johnson, Roy 12
Johnston, Charley 243
Johnston, James J. 81, 83, 186, 206
Jolson, Al 5, 40, 42-45, 52, 127, 152, 221, 328
Jones, Charlie 266, 267
Jones, Johnny 268, 290
Jones, Tiger 233
Joseph, Eddie 270
Joyce, Peggy Hopkins 52
Joyce, Willie 248-250, 255, 270, 271, 277, 294, 295, 297, 303, 305, 307-309, 320

Junior, Paul 169-173
Karachi, India 327
Keck, Harry 13, 14
Keeler, Ruby 40
Keep Punching film 343
Kellog, Beecher 318
Kelly, Tony 82
Kennedy, Jack 92, 158
Kessler, Gene 299
Kiel Auditorium, St. Louis 308
King Cotton 8
Kilrain, Jake 99
'L' Street Arena, Sacramento 32
LaBarba, Fidel 159, 165
Labranch, Tony 90
La Fond, Eddie 288
Lake, Jimmy 289
Lampe, Sam 285
La Motta, Jake 329
Langford, Sam 230
Lardner, John 45, 117-119, 195, 196, 239
Larkin, Bobby 250
Larkin, Tippy (Antonio Pilleteri) 249, 250, 255
Latka, George 221
Latsios, Nick 297, 300-302
Lawless, Bucky 13
Lazzeri, Tony 190
Leamington Hotel, Oakland, California 321
Leavitt, Leo 34, 36
Le Cron, George 75, 86, 259, 264
Lee, Glen 85, 145
Lello, Pete 183
Lemos, Richie 221
Lenny, Harry 82
Leonard, Benny 71, 137, 186, 207, 252, 253, 256, 309, 339, 344
Lesnevich, Gus 152
Levinsky, Battling 82
Lewis, John Henry 342
Lewis, Lee 220
Liberty AC, Washington 297
Liberty Club Gym 300
Liebling, A. J. 118
Lilliard, Joe 324, 327
Long Island City, New York 5, 60, 62, 229
Lopez, Perfecto 21-24, 309
Los Angeles 6, 16-18, 20, 22, 27, 31-33, 36-38, 41-43, 46, 48, 49, 71, 85, 91, 102, 112, 131, 133, 134, 138, 146-149, 151, 155, 157, 159, 166, 170, 178,

349

199, 215, 221, 226, 230, 237, 246, 248, 250, 255, 263, 269, 273, 283, 285, 289, 291, 294-296, 299, 301, 302, 306, 313, 319, 320, 328, 332-334, 336, 338, 342
Losada, Cecilio 310
Loscalzo, Joseph Robert (Midget Wolgast) 35
Louttit, Tom 245
Louis, Joe 20, 51, 53, 57, 70, 97, 107, 113, 149, 193, 198-200, 254, 259, 278, 279, 281, 285, 298, 338, 342, 344
Lozada, Cecilio 231
Lynch, Joe 43, 56, 84, 187, 222, 285
MacDonald, Charlie, Hollywood Post, American Legion 147
Mahan, Leo 13
Mahon, Jack 144, 242, 243
Madison Square Garden Corporation 100
Main Street Gym, Los Angeles 17-20, 138, 149
Maloney, Jim 169
Mancini, Lenny 268
Man o' War 190
Manfredo, Al 90, 91, 132
Manhattan 17, 28, 72, 173
Manuel, Baby 22
Martin, Johnny 169, 170, 172
Martin, Whitney 126, 127, 256, 257, 277, 279, 283, 284
Marston, Lester 34
Maryland State Boxing Commission 183
Massey, Naiman 301
Matthews Harry 'Kid' 159
McAuliffe, Jack 81, 207
McCarney, Billy 80, 81
McCarron, Jimmy 293
McCoy, Babe 273, 320
McDaniels, Jimmy 246-248
McGovern, Terry 80-82, 109
McLemore, Henry 46, 62, 63, 65, 115, 116, 124, 151, 156, 165-167, 180
McLarnin, Jimmy 63, 64, 157, 158, 214, 230
McPartland, 'Kid' Billy 86
McShane, Bob 298
Mauriello, Tami 312
Mee, Bob 337, 338
Mead, Eddie 40, 42, 44, 51, 56, 69, 84, 85, 88, 91, 97, 100,

101, 106, 110,118, 121, 127, 129, 131, 137, 150, 152, 157, 159, 164, 171, 173, 175, 176, 180, 205, 209, 212, 217, 220-222, 283, 299, 336
Meade, Fort 278
Meany, Tom 122
Mendel, Harry 285
Mexico City 26, 30, 34, 38, 39, 237
Middleton, Drew 85, 88, 89, 98, 103, 104
Midnight Mission, Los Angeles 16
Miller, Freddie 22, 27, 28, 31, 34, 52, 89, 268
Miller, Harvey National Boxing Association 132
Miller, Heime 181
Miller, Ray 64, 214
Miller, Roy 328
Missouri Pacific Railroad 9
Monroe, Marty 75, 187
Montague, John 110
Montana, Small 141
Montanez, Pedro 69, 119, 138-140, 171
Montgomery, Bob 268, 269, 271, 296
Moore, George 222, 223, 227, 229, 233, 237-239, 244, 247, 250, 255, 271, 273, 276, 277, 285, 288, 290, 297, 308, 316, 317, 323
Moran, Owen 82
Morgan, 'Dumb' Dan 82, 153
Morning Star Baptist Church, Los Angeles 25, 332, 333
Moro, Kid 21-23, 309
Muller, Eddie 318
Mullins, Moon 48
Municipal Auditorium, Denver 134, 225
Municipal Auditorium, Oakland, California 36
Murray, Jimmy 223, 316, 320, 322
Nagler, Barney 8, 43, 53, 74, 128, 129
Nash 1927 automobile 12
National Boxing Association 27, 38, 40, 43, 89, 132, 182, 237, 249, 267, 304, 344
National Sporting Club, London 99
National Stadium, Mexico City 26, 27

Neil, Edward J. memorial trophy 198
Nestell, Bob 159
Newland, Russ 255, 318-320
New Jersey Boxing Commission 259
New Year's Day 28, 313
New York Boxing Commission 25, 44, 179
New York Boxing Writers Association 198, 325
New York City 9, 20, 48, 107, 310, 313, 326
New York Hippodrome 50
New York State Athletic Commission 47, 83, 89, 145, 187, 258, 259
Nichols, Joseph C. 55, 187, 188
Nineteenth Street Arena, Bakersfield, California 23
Ninth Ward, Lawrenceville, 184
Nova, Lou 245
Nuttall, Keith 295, 296, 328
Oceanside, California 174
Odd, Gilbert E. Editor *Boxing News* London 102, 105, 106
Ogden Arsenal 227
Olympic Auditorium, Los Angeles 21, 43, 91, 134, 141, 221, 237, 291, 302, 313, 314
Olympics Antwerp 1920 184
Oregon State 244, 271, 273, 286, 287, 312, 321, 324, 339
Orfilla, Ernest, American Legion 147
Ortiz, Manuel 20, 233, 245
Oslo 159
Overlin, Ken 164, 186, 233, 312
Pace, Georgie 35
Pacho, Bobby 92, 93, 134, 135, 141, 185
Pack, Lorenzo 171
Paderewski 107
Palmore, Baby 23
'Palooka, Joe, Champ' 343
Panama 20
Panton Street, London 101
Paris, France 35, 105, 106
Parker, Dan 274, 275, 280, 297
Parnassus, George 141, 143, 148, 159, 164, 231
Pastor Bob 81, 152, 159, 179
Pastrano, Willie 330
Patterson, Floyd 173
Pavone, Lew 300

INDEX

Pedersen, 'Big Boy' 214
Pep, Willie 35, 266-268, 338
Perry, Aaron 293, 299
Petre, Ben 226, 267
Petrolle, Billy 63, 64
Phelan, Gen. John J. 52, 60, 176, 179
Philippines 20, 144, 145
Phipps, William E. 244, 245
Pismo Beach, California 22
Pittman, Las Vegas 231, 232
Polo Grounds, New York City 9, 70, 172, 178, 179
Pompton Lakes, New Jersey 71, 107, 109, 112, 115
Porters and Waiters club, Ogden 227
Post, Emily 124
Potter, John 187
Prospero, Angelo 310, 311
Pruitt, Adolph 329
Pryor, Aaron 333
Pucci, Angelo 255
Purificato, Rev. Gustave 68, 76
Pyramids 327
Quaid, Paddy 17
SS *Queen Mary* 97, 98
Quezon, Manuel, President Philippines 145
Raft, George 5, 42, 43, 48, 52, 220, 221
Ramirez, Rodolfo 230, 231
Randolph, Charley 292
Rangel, Sheik 224
Rawson, Tommy 292
Ray, Johnny 186
Reddick, James 334
Redman, Don 220
Reed, Billy 328
Reed, 'Torpedo' 295
Reynolds, Charley 293, 294, 301
Rice, Grantland 65, 107, 108, 112-115, 152, 156, 340
Rickard, Tex 49, 260, 263
Rico, Chester 311
Rightmire, Everett 311
Ringside Gym, Los Angeles 17
Riverview Park 132
Rizal Memorial Sports Complex, Manila 145
'Roaring Twenties' 222
Roberts, Fred 235
Robinson, Pat 190, 197, 198
Robinson, Sugar Ray 242, 267, 269, 271, 273-286, 298, 312,
329, 338, 340
Rocha, Tony 28
Rodak, Leo 77, 89, 233, 234
Roderick, Ernie 94, 96-106, 109, 119
Rogers, Nat 197, 276
Rojo, Genaro 313, 314
Roman Circus 84
Ross, Barney 15, 58, 59, 61-66, 69, 74, 79, 94, 95, 110, 220, 284, 298, 344
Ross, Wirt (One Shot) 18, 34, 41
Roth, Abe 44, 158, 291, 303
Rupppert's Brewery, New York City 198
Ruth, Babe 190
Sacramento 22, 32, 225, 226
Salas, Joe 159
Salica, Lou 233
Salkeld, A. J. (Tex) 245
Salvation Army gym, Pittsburgh 13
San Bernardino Valley 84
Sanchez, Joe 23 San Francisco 34, 141, 232-234, 239-242, 246, 249, 250, 255, 276, 307, 318, 320, 321
San Jose Auditorium, California 223
Sanstol, Pete 159
Santa Anita $100,000 Handicap 151
Sargasso Sea 34
Sarron, Petey 5, 38, 40, 43, 44, 48, 50-56, 74, 77, 268, 344
Savold, Lee 152
Sayre, Francis B. 145
Scalzo, Petey 311
Scarpati, Tony 108
Scherr, Stanley, Maryland Commission 183
Schiff, Dr. Alexander New York Commission 73, 83, 84, 195, 208, 212-214, 219, 222, 270
Schmeling, Max 58
Schulberg, Budd novelist, screenwriter 341
Schwartz, Bobby 300
Scott, Harry 132
Scott, Howard 133
Scripps Howard Newspapers 63
Service Sports Inc. 109, 303
Shandy, Willa Mae 25
Shank, Reuben 225, 238
Shans, Cleo 328
Shea, Eddie 15
Shields, Don California Boxing Commission 230
Shields, Fred H. 170
Shields, Owen F. 170
Shoemaker, Lisle 249
Shrine Hospital for Crippled Children, Portland, Oregon 313
Shuster, Charles 294
Siki, Battling 98
Simpson, Tommy 230
Singer, Al 9, 41, 48, 214
Singer, Jack 41
Slider, Barbara Jean 315
Slider, Chester 313-317, 325, 326
Slider, Chester Jnr. 315
Slider, Chet 317
Slider, Rula 315
Sloan 'Haystack' 20
Small's Paradise, Harlem night club 66
Smiley, William 229
Smith, Walter Wellesley (Red) 215, 342
Smith, Wilfred 100, 105, 115
Snead, Sam 200
Social Security 334,
Sommers, Freddie 221
Sphinx Egypt 327
Spoldi, Aldo 45, 46, 226, 240, 268, 286, 287, 308, 309
Steele, Freddie 141
Steward, Emanuel 343
Stillman's Gym, New York City 19, 57, 80, 81, 128, 175, 252, 256, 258, 295
Stillman, Lou 151
Stolz, Allie 268
Stone's Chop House, Panton Street, London 100
St. Nicholas Arena, New York City 88
St. Louis Coliseum, Missouri 10
St. Mary's Boys' Club, Alexandria, Virginia 300
Strauther, Walter L. Reverend 25, 333
Sugar, Bert Randolph 218, 338, 339, 344
Sweetwater, Texas 171, 244, 245
Sylvester, John 230, 235
Tabor, Frank 322
Tagologs, Filipino tribe 148
Talbot, Gayle 57, 58, 71, 142, 200, 205, 206, 208, 209

351

Tampico Kid 91
Tarleton, Edna 99
Tarleton, Nel 99
Taub, Sam 190
Taylor, 'Irish' Johnny 171, 223, 225, 232, 309, 310, 323
Temple Baptist Church 333
Tendler, Lew 71, 186, 251
The Henry Armstrong Home for Wayward Boys 335
The Henry Armstrong Sport Unit No. 500 324
'The Thin Man' 173
Thomas, Jimmy 13
Thomas, John 291, 292, 302, 303
Toussaint L'Overture Grammar School, St.Louis Missouri 8
Tribuani, Al 247, 251, 252, 309
Trigg, J. A. 301
Trujillo, Eddie 21
Tunney, Gene 11, 52, 150, 152
Turiello, Saverio (Milan Panther) 246, 287, 288, 309
Turner's Arena, Washington 204
Turner, Don 333
Turner, Earl 235
Twentieth Century Sporting Club 51, 274
Tyson, Mike 341
Uline Arena, Washington DC 288, 290, 300
United Press 26, 28, 62, 77, 102, 115, 127, 145, 146, 166, 170, 210, 232, 241, 244, 248, 249, 252, 264, 269, 270, 273, 280, 281 303, 305, 313, 318, 322, 328
United States Coast Guard 244
United States Olympic Team 18
Universal Hat Shop St. Louis Missouri 10
U.S Patent Office 142
Vaccia, Eddie 310
Valentine, Spider 381
Van, Frankie 303
Variety Club, Washington 204

Vashon High School, St. Louis, Missouri 8
Ventura Athletic Club, California 23, 27, 33
Venturi, Enrico 59
Vernon Arena, California 159
Vigil, Toby 159
Villa, Pancho 141, 144
Villaflor, Johnny 143
Walcott, Joe 45, 65, 74
Walker, Dr. New York Commission 59, 210
Walker, Eddie 97
Walker, Mickey 276
Walsh, Davis J. 255, 256, 260, 261, 266, 275
Wallace, Frankie 91
Wallish, George 199
War Department 279
Ward, Alan 34, 36, 192, 193, 223-225, 232, 234, 241, 307, 314, 315, 317, 318, 322, 323
Warden, Al 238
Warren, Gov. Earl 317
Washington and Jefferson University 267
Waterman, Joe 43, 44, 245, 319, 321
Washington, Kenny 325, 327
Weatherby, W. J. 340, 341
Weill, Al 5, 59, 60, 69, 70, 76-78, 108, 117, 118, 121, 174
Welles, Orson 142
Wergeles, Chick 258
West Coast 15, 64, 141, 147, 156, 220, 318
White, Larry 158
White, Luther (Slugger) 72, 283, 285, 303-306
Whitman, Benny 303, 305
Willard, Jess 92
Williams, Bert 98
Williams, Ike 237, 268, 337
Williams, Joe 63-65, 87, 139, 140, 207, 208, 260, 262, 263, 279

Wills, Frankie 290, 300
Wills, Harry 230
Wilson, Edgar 290
Wilson, Jackie 13, 77, 273
Wilson, Jimmy 200
Witz Abie 13
Wolgast, AD 81, 230
Wolgast, Bobby 35
Wolgast, Midget (Joseph Robert Loscalzo) 35
Woods, Chuck 185
Wood, Hal 232, 317, 322, 323
Woodman, Joe 340
Wood, Wilbur 175
Wray, John 280
Wright, Albert (Chalky) 71, 97
Wrigley Field, Los Angeles 37, 38, 40, 138, 146, 147, 157
Yancey, Bill 324, 327
Yankee Stadium, New York City 49, 70, 107, 109, 114, 120, 121, 124
Yarosz, Teddy 13
Yawitz, Eddie 330, 331
Ybarra, Joe 225, 226
YMCA Pine Street, St. Louis Missouri 10
Zale, Tony 168
Zanelli, Ralph 'Rough House' 170, 171, 291-293, 309
Zivic, Eddie 187, 188
Zivic, Fritzie (Ferdinand Henry John Zivcich) 6, 119, 183-186, 189-191, 193-212, 214-219, 238-243, 251, 253-257, 273, 298, 309, 310, 319-321, 326, 329
Zivic, Jack 184
Zivic, Mary Kepele 183
Zivic, Pete 184, 186
Zurita, Juan 237-239, 303